Dates with Destiny

1898   The novel *Futility* is published by Morgan Robertson, telling of how the *Titan*, the largest ship ever built, sank in the North Atlantic after hitting an iceberg, killing thousands. Fourteen years later, the *Titanic* would suffer the same fate.

1899   Thomas Ismay, founder of the British shipping company, White Star Line, dies, leaving the direction of the company to his son, J. Bruce Ismay.

1900   The Marconi International Marine Communications Company is formed and begins providing steamships with wireless telegraph equipment.

1902   White Star Line is bought by International Mercantile Marine, a trust run by American tycoon J.P. Morgan.

1907   White Star starts designing the three sister ships, *Olympic*, *Titanic*, and *Britannic*, hoping to attract customers with unprecedented size and luxury.

1909   The *Titanic* is under construction at the Harland and Wolff Shipyard in Belfast, Ireland.

May 31, 1911   The *Titanic* is launched prior to being outfitted at the Thompson Graving Dock.

April 10, 1912   The *Titanic* embarks on her maiden voyage from Southampton, England, bound for Cherbourg, France; Queenstown, Ireland; and New York.

April 14, 1912, 11:40 p.m.   The Titanic *hits an iceberg in the North Atlantic approximately 400 miles from Newfoundland. At 2:20 that morning, the ship sinks as some 1,500 passengers and crew are lost. Just over 700 are saved in lifeboats.*

April 15, 1912   Many U.S. newspapers mistakenly report that all *Titanic* passengers are safe.

April 18, 1912   The *Carpathia* arrives in New York with the *Titanic* survivors.

April 19, 1912   The U.S. Senate opens an inquiry into the disaster that concludes on May 24.

May 2, 1912   The British Board of Trade opens an inquiry into the disaster that concludes on July 3.

alpha
books

Dates with Destiny (continued)

May 6, 1912   A seance is held in England at which the spirit of a deceased *Titanic* passenger, W.T. Stead, is said to have appeared and communicated with his daughter, Estelle, who was present, for over 40 minutes.

May 18, 1912   Thousands turn out for the funeral of *Titanic* bandleader Wallace Hartley in Lancashire, England.

May 1912   The 10-minute screen melodrama *Saved from the Titanic*, starring *Titanic* survivor Dorothy Gibson, opens in American theaters.

1912   The song "De Titanic" is written and performed by blues singer Huddie "Leadbelly" Ledbetter.

1914   The International Ice Patrol, later to become part of the U.S. Coast guard, is created in response to the *Titanic* disaster.

1943   The Nazi propaganda film *Titanic* is produced, featuring a fictional German ship's officer who behaves heroically.

1953   The Hollywood film *Titanic* is released, starring Clifton Webb and Barbara Stanwyck.

1955   Walter Lord's non-fiction best-seller *A Night to Remember* is published. The film based on the book was released in 1958.

1960   The Broadway musical *The Unsinkable Molly Brown* is staged, based on the life of one of the *Titanic's* passengers. The show became a film starring Debbie Reynolds in 1964.

1976   Clive Cussler's best-selling spy thriller, *Raise the Titanic*, is published. A film based on the book came out in 1980.

September 1, 1985   A French-American search expedition led by Dr. Robert Ballard discovers the wreck of the *Titanic*.

1987   The first of many salvage expeditions is launched and the first of thousands of artifacts are recovered from the wreck.

1991   Danielle Steel's *Titanic* romance novel, *No Greater Love*, is published.

1992   Stephen Low's IMAX film, *Titanica*, documenting the wreck, is released.

1997   The Broadway musical *Titanic* opens at the Lunt-Fontaine theater, where it set box office records.

1997   James Cameron's film *Titanic* is released, to become the biggest international box office success of all time.

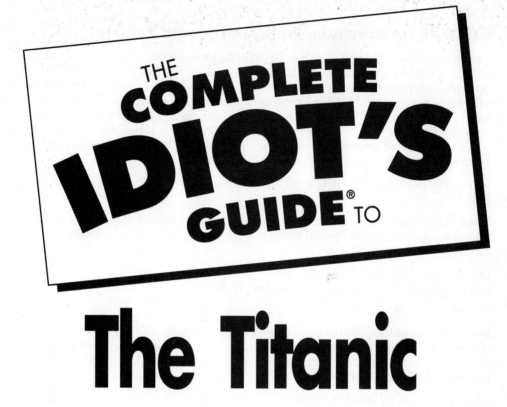

THE COMPLETE IDIOT'S GUIDE® TO

The Titanic

by Jay Stevenson

alpha
books

A Division of Macmillan General Reference
A Simon & Schuster Macmillan Company
1633 Broadway, New York, NY 10019-6785

Macmillan Publishing books may be purchased for business or sales promotional use. For information please write: Special Markets Department, Macmillan Publishing USA, 1633 Broadway, New York, NY 10019.

International Standard Book Number: 0-02862712-1
Library of Congress Catalog Card Number: 98-85968

00 99 98   8 7 6 5 4 3 2 1

Interpretation of the printing code: the rightmost number of the first series of numbers is the year of the book's printing; the rightmost number of the second series of numbers is the number of the book's printing. For example, a printing code of 98-1 shows that the first printing occurred in 1998.

Printed in the United States of America

Note: This publication contains the opinions and ideas of its author. It is intended to provide helpful and informative material on the subject matter covered. It is sold with the understanding that the author and publisher are not engaged in rendering professional services in the book. If the reader requires personal assistance or advice, a competent professional should be consulted.

Alpha Development Team

Publisher
Kathy Nebenhaus

Editorial Director
Gary M. Krebs

Managing Editor
Bob Shuman

Marketing Brand Manager
Felice Primeau

Senior Editor
Nancy Mikhail

Development Editors
Phil Kitchel
Jennifer Perillo
Amy Zavatto

Editorial Assistant
Maureen Horn

Production Team

Production Editor
Christina Van Camp

Cover Designer
Mike Freeland

Photo Editor
Go Fish Images, Inc.

Illustrator
Jody P. Schaeffer

Designer
Nathan Clement

Indexer
Chris Barrick

Layout
Angela Calvert

Contents at a Glance

Contents

Part 5: Hard to Fathom   203

19 Salvage Schemes   205

20 High Tech Meets Low Wreck   215

Foreword

"How did they build *Titanic*?" a crewman sings as the Broadway musical *Titanic* begins. "Forty-six thousand tons of steel, eleven stories high, she's a great palace floating, quiet as a lullaby."

The crown jewel of Britain's White Star Line, she was the largest, strongest, finest and grandest ocean liner ever to sail the seas. Quite literally, the largest moving object in the world!

Eighty-five years after the supposedly unsinkable ship hit an iceberg on her maiden voyage and went to the bottom of the Atlantic, her story is still being told: a tremendous success onstage, a film breaking all box-office records, a dozen or more books on the world's best-seller lists.

It was one of the great events that shaped our century. The ship carried the dreams of a new era, one that had complete faith that steam and steel and coal could create something stronger than nature. They were wrong.

Then there are the people. Their stories endlessly fascinate because they were forced to respond to the extreme pressure of a cataclysmic event. There are stories of cowardly behavior and chaos, but also of extraordinary sacrifice and heroism.

On that fateful maiden voyage, the *Titanic* carried 1,314 passengers in first, second, and third class, plus a crew and service staff of 914. She set sail from Southampton, England, on April 10, 1912. After stops in Cherbourg, France, and Queenstown (now Cobh), Ireland, she headed west, across the North Atlantic, for New York.

She never arrived.

Those are the bare bones of the story. What this book contains, like all of the volumes in this wonderful series, is a concise, straightforward, well-organized, fact-filled narrative that tells you all you want to know about this astonishing event.

You think you already know everything about it? How wrong you are! And what a fascinating journey lies ahead.

—Peter Stone, Tony Award-winning author of the Broadway musical *Titanic*

Taking the Plunge

Walk into any bookstore and you'll see at least one shelf full of books dedicated to this century's most memorable maritime disaster: the tragic loss of the *Titanic* and over 1,500 passengers and crew on her maiden voyage. With the release and phenomenal popularity of James Cameron's film *Titanic*, the public has rediscovered a fascination with the history of the ship and her passengers—a fascination that has faded and returned time and again since the night of April 14, 1912.

The idea propelling *The Complete Idiot's Guide to the Titanic* is to give you a good handle on every angle of the story of *Titanic*. Most other *Titanic* books focus on just one or two aspects of the ship, its history, its discovery, and its place in this century's history. Here, we've tried to put everything together.

The expression "it takes all kinds" really applies to *Titanic* buffs. They come in all different stripes. Some like old ships, others are into lifestyles of the rich and famous in 1912, others are into the controversies, and still others go in for deep-sea exploration and salvage. And this is only the tip of the iceberg, so to speak!

You may already know what you're looking for in *Titanic* lore. If that's the case, you should find it here. On the other hand, you may be curious to find out just what there is to know about the big ship and the big waves it has caused. In either case, a description of the parts of this book can help you chart your own course:

Part 1, "All Aboard!" begins with an overview of *Titanic* history and then deals with the people on the ship. We break the passengers down by class (that's how they did things back then!) and then talk about the ship's officers and the rest of the crew. The ship has been called a "floating city" and this first part gives you a tour of the neighborhoods.

Part 2, "Liner Notes," is for the ship buffs. It talks about steam ships and the shipping industry, describing the passenger-shipping business as it was run in 1912. It also deals with the building of the *Titanic* itself. Finally, there's a chapter on other famous shipwrecks.

Part 3, "Cruisin' for a Bruisin'," tells the true story that has engrossed millions since the day it occurred. Here is a detailed account of the voyage, the ice warnings, the collision with the iceberg, loading the lifeboats, the famous rescue, and the aftermath of the disaster.

Part 4, "Lowering the Boom," covers investigations into the disaster, including newspaper coverage and official inquiries in the U.S. and England. Here you can read about the major controversies stemming from the incident and the laws that were passed to prevent future catastrophes at sea.

Part 5, "Hard to Fathom," brings the *Titanic* story into more recent times, describing the search for the wreck, its discovery, and exploration and salvage expeditions. This part includes explanations of the undersea technology used and what we've learned from exploring the wreck.

Part 6, "Titanimania," talks about how people have applied the *Titanic* disaster to their lives. This part explores the myths and mysteries that have sprung up, and deals with the many books, poems, songs, shows, and movies based on the big sinking.

In addition, we've included some features for easy reference. Right at the beginning, there's a chronology of *Titanic*-related events. At the back of the book are six appendices: a glossary of *Titanic* terms, a list of ships and submarines that have figured into the history of the *Titanic*, an annotated list of key people involved with the shipwreck, a passenger list, the *Titanic*'s cargo manifest, and a list of materials for further reading and viewing.

These features don't mean we expect you to take a pointy-headed approach to the *Titanic*. We'd prefer to think of you keeping a copy of this book next to your bathtub rather than gathering dust on your bookshelf. That way you can just browse through and see what you find. To encourage browsing, we've included some features that stand out on the page containing facts and trivia, definitions, and quotations of interest. Here's what they look like:

Lifesavers
As bad as the *Titanic* disaster was, many good things have come out of it. This feature highlights the uplifting elements of the story.

Blow Me Down!
These are surprising facts and ideas, including the many bizarre and ironic circumstances and coincidences that the *Titanic* has become famous for.

Catch the Drift
This feature provides definitions of nautical terms and other specialized words that get used in the main body of this book.

SOS
Here are encapsulated problems that have beset the ship and efforts to deal with the disaster. Also included are myths and fallacies to be aware of as you learn about *Titanic*.

Ahoy There!

Here are first-hand accounts of those who were actually involved in the events under discussion, so you can get the story straight from the horse's mouth.

Acknowledgements

Many thanks to our helpers in Austria: to Christian Bachler for so generously sharing his *Titanic* knowledge, to Lisa Zimmermann for her translations, and to young Madlin Zimmermann for her research assistance. And thanks especially to Nancy Stevenson, the perfect emissary.

Part 1
All Aboard!

Among the most fascinating things about the Titanic disaster are the ways the people involved reacted. Thousands of people took part in the events surrounding the big sinking, and each one has a different story to tell—although, unfortunately, many of these stories were lost with those who lived them. Even so, plenty of amazing stories survive, revealing sides of all kinds of people you don't usually see. Some of these stories make you proud to be a human being. Others—well, nobody's perfect. Many, of course, are sad. In general though, they can give you a new perspective on being alive.

Full Steam Ahead

In This Chapter

➤ An overview of *Titanic* doings

➤ Wealth, commerce, and technology at the turn of the century

➤ *Titanic* symbolism

➤ Historical significance

➤ Responses to the wreck

Unless you live at the bottom of the sea, you've probably noticed the tremendous amount of interest these days in the *Titanic*, a big ship that hit a big chunk of ice and sank in the North Atlantic over 85 years ago. This event has taken on great importance over the years for a number of reasons—historical, legal, sociological, cultural, economic, scientific, and sentimental. And the subject is a veritable gold mine for trivia buffs! All kinds of people have found all kinds of different fascinating things about the *Titanic*.

The dreams that were built into the ship and the tragedy that it became are easy to relate to for anyone who has ever had high hopes and suffered big disappointments. In our own way, most of us feel somehow as though we've been there—we've experienced the kind of transformation implied by the tale of the *Titanic*. We've all felt like we were steaming along on a starry night over a smooth, untroubled sea, only to be suddenly ripped apart by the cold, hard iceberg of reality. And then that sinking feeling, the sense of loss, and the desire to be saved!

Against the background of this basic, emotionally captivating scenario, the details of the *Titanic* stand out with poignant significance. Little things suddenly mean a lot, having been part of one of the biggest tragedies of the century. Writers, film-makers, scientists, legislators, and historians have been doing a great deal with these details ever since.

Launching a Legend

Even before it became the most famous shipwreck in history, the *Titanic* was big news. Building began in Belfast, Ireland, in 1909 at the Harland and Woolf shipyard, taking more than two years to complete. At the time it was the largest ship ever built. In fact, it was the largest moving thing ever made by human beings.

The biggest ship afloat in 1912.

Mary Evans Picture Library

R.M.S. TITANIC.

The *Titanic* was over 880 feet long and over 46,000 tons. There were about half a million rivets in the flat, bottom portion of the hull alone. Altogether, these weighed about 270 tons. That much weight is hard to imagine, so here's a statistic that may help you grasp how heavy the *Titanic* was: each link of the chain that held the *Titanic*'s anchor weighed about 175 pounds.

Blow Me Down!
The *Titanic* was the length of four city blocks. Ads for the ship depicted it standing on end next to the tallest buildings of the time, and rising above all of them.

A "First" Time for Everything

The *Titanic* was a man-made wonder at a time when a number of amazing "firsts" were happening. For example,

➤ The Wright brothers flew their first airplane in 1903.

➤ The first movie theater was opened in 1895 by the Lumiere brothers, who invented the cinematograph.

➤ The first dirigible (passenger blimp), invented by Ferdinand von Zeppelin, made its first flight in 1901.

➤ The first transatlantic wireless telegraph message was transmitted by Guglielmo Marconi in 1901.

➤ The first vacuum cleaner was invented in 1901 by Herbert Cecil Booth.

These are only some of the modern-tech firsts that took place near the beginning of this century. You might think that, with all of this new stuff being invented, the construction of a huge passenger steamship would get lost in the shuffle. Not so. Lots of people were excited about the *Titanic*.

Bon Voyage

For many, it symbolized the idea of progress—the idea that people were getting somewhere: getting there with style (the *Titanic* was the most luxurious of luxury liners), and getting there fast (steam liners took a fraction of the time that sailing ships took).

In its way, the *Titanic* represented a new spirit that, like the big boat itself, could carry huge numbers of people along with it. In fact, the *Titanic* had room for over 3,500 people, including passengers and crew. This, of course, was one of its most significant features for those who designed the ship. At this point in history, more people than ever before were traveling between Europe and America.

SOS
When reports that the *Titanic* was in trouble reached New York City, White Star Line Vice President P.A.S. Franklin announced, "We place absolute confidence in the *Titanic*. We believe the boat is unsinkable." Unfortunately, by the time he had spoken these words, the ship had already spent the night on the bottom of the sea!

Who wouldn't be tempted by ads like this?
Archive Photos

All of the moving back and forth was part of the spirit of progress. People had business to attend to and new opportunities to explore. Whoever they might be, the *Titanic* had room for them. Lots of plain but clean, comfortable rooms could accommodate immigrant laborers hoping to find work in America, and the most luxurious appointments satisfied the tastes of the aristocrats traveling abroad. The *Titanic* was not just an ocean-going Greyhound bus, it embodied modern society itself, pushing ahead into the future. It's no surprise, then, that the sudden wreck and sinking of this symbol on its first and only voyage created shockwaves that are still rippling almost 90 years later.

The Titanic *is loaded in Southampton, England.*
Brown Brothers

On April 14, 1912, at 11:40 p.m., the *Titanic* scraped its *starboard* side against an iceberg, popping a number of rivets that secured its steel hull. As its *bow* sections filled up with ice-cold sea water, the ship did a nosedive, hiking the *stern* upward until the force of gravity cracked the *Titanic* in half like a multi-million dollar breadstick, sending the largest man-made vehicle of all time to the bottom of the ocean. It was a powerful blow to the spirit of the modern age!

Ahoy There!

There is an impression among a portion of the general public that the provision of Turkish Baths, gymnasiums, and other so-called luxuries involved a sacrifice of some more essential things, the absence of which was responsible for so many lives. But this is quite an erroneous impression. All these things were an additional provision for the comfort and convenience of the passengers, and there is no more reason why they should not be provided on these ships than in a large hotel.

—second-class passenger Lawrence Beesley

Bad news.
Brown Brothers

Titanic Attraction

We're still coming to terms with the significance of this disaster. Certainly worse tragedies have occurred before and since the *Titanic* went down. This particular mishap, however, is especially stirring and fascinating. For millions of people, the *Titanic* is a subject of irresistible curiosity.

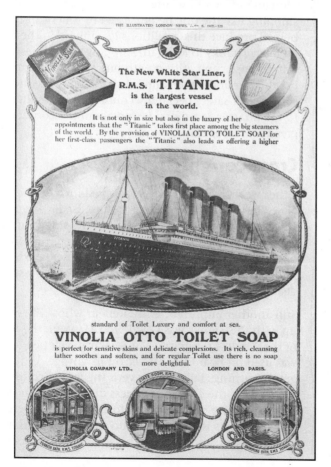

Catch the Drift
Starboard is the right hand side of a ship. **Port** is the left hand side. The **bow** is the front part of the ship. The **stern** is the rear.

All That Glitters

For historians and sociologists, the event provides telling commentary on a unique moment in American and European history. The period is often referred to as "the Gilded Age," after the name of a novel by Mark Twain. The phrase refers to the unprecedented new wealth accumulated by entrepreneurs of the day, but also suggests the superficial, shallow, and selfish values underlying the quest for money and power.

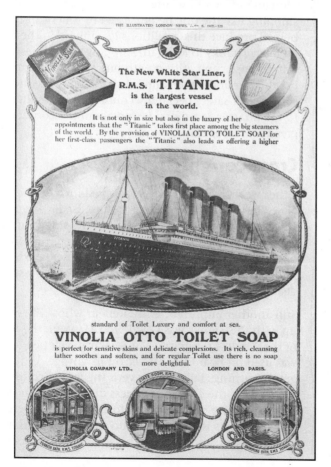

THE ILLUSTRATED LONDON NEWS, ...

The New White Star Liner,
R.M.S. **"TITANIC"**
is the largest vessel
in the world.

It is not only in size but also in the luxury of her appointments that the "Titanic" takes first place among the big steamers of the world. By the provision of VINOLIA OTTO TOILET SOAP for her first-class passengers the "Titanic" also leads as offering a higher

standard of Toilet Luxury and comfort at sea.
VINOLIA OTTO TOILET SOAP
is perfect for sensitive skins and delicate complexions. Its rich, cleansing lather soothes and softens, and for regular Toilet use there is no soap more delightful.
VINOLIA COMPANY LTD.,   LONDON AND PARIS.

The Titanic *supplies recognition for a soap company in this ad from the period.*
Topham/The Image Works

Many of these fabulously wealthy Gilded-Agers played key roles in the Titanic disaster and the events surrounding it. Their stories alone show how various and complicated the many lessons of *Titanic* can be.

Sinking Money into Ships

One of the most notable figures of the Gilded Age was steel magnate and railroad king J.P. Morgan. Since the start of the Civil War in America, railroads played a crucial part in American industry, and Morgan controlled them. It wasn't enough for him to control how people got around on land, however; he wanted to control sea travel as well. So he invested heavily in North Atlantic shipping and bought controlling stock in White Star Line, the company that built, owned, and operated the *Titanic* under the name of the International Mercantile Marine.

Blow Me Down!
Shortly before buying out White Star Line, Morgan bought out the steel empire of Andrew Carnegie to form U.S. Steel. This trust provided raw materials for Morgan's trains and ships.

Morgan's efforts to secure a monopoly in international shipping like the one he possessed in American railroads helped produce the conditions leading up to the *Titanic* tragedy. Thanks to Morgan, shipping companies entered into intense competition with one another, leading them to build faster and larger ships. As speed and size increased, concern for safety became secondary. As a result, many point to the disaster as a moral lesson about the consequences of greed and arrogance.

Cross Currents

Other wealthy Gilded Agers involved include the owner of New York's Macy's department store, Isador Straus, and his wife, Ida. They perished together as the ship went down when she refused to board a lifeboat, preferring to remain on board with her husband. Stories like these have led commentators to celebrate the ability of the *Titanic*'s passengers to deal with tragedy.

Lifesavers
Wireless operators who contacted help for their crippled ships were often hailed as heroes. Most notably, Jack Binns caused a sensation in 1909 when he stayed on board the sinking ship *Republic* to fix wireless equipment damaged in the collision that doomed the vessel and successfully sent out last-minute distress calls. *Titanic* wireless operators Jack Phillips, who went down with the ship, and Harold Bride, who survived despite severe frostbite, were also lauded as heroes.

Still another important entrepreneur whose life was bound up with the *Titanic* was Guglielmo Marconi, the inventor of the wireless telegraph. This newly developed technology was used on board the *Titanic* on its voyage. While telegraph warnings failed to prevent the fateful collision with the iceberg, the *Titanic*'s wireless distress calls succeeded in summoning help for those fortunate passengers and crew members who made it into the lifeboats. Marconi, his invention, and the way this invention was used are important subjects for those interested in the practical lessons to be learned from the disaster. In fact, one of the first S.O.S. signals was sent from the *Titanic*.

Taking New Bearings

One view of the meaning of this disaster is that it stands as dramatic evidence that modern society was unable to control the economic forces driving it. People wanted money, power, splendor, and convenience—all the fruits of industrial technology—but weren't ready to face the risks of producing and maintaining these things. To some extent, the *Titanic* spurred people to reconsider their society as a whole.

Immediately afterwards, the wreck of the *Titanic* provided a kick in the pants for government and business, getting them to rethink their approaches to commerce and industrial development. In the years leading up to the wreck, shipping companies had been vying with one another for customers by building ever bigger, faster, and more luxurious ships. These new, state-of-the-art liners had progressed so far and so fast that existing safety regulations were no longer adequate to keep them safe against disaster.

Investigations into the *Titanic* incident resulted in regulations aimed at better ensuring the safety of ships and their passengers. Beyond this, however, some observers began calling for drastic changes, not only in safety rules, but in the social conditions that enabled a select few to enjoy tremendous power and control at the expense of everyone else. In the eyes of these people, the fate of the *Titanic* reflected more than inadequate safety rules: It was symptomatic of widespread social injustice. The strict Edwardian caste system prevailed aboard the *Titanic* even while the ship was sinking. The stewards were vigilant in keeping steerage passengers below as long as possible so that their "betters" in first class could enter the lifeboats first! An example of this class snobbery is depicted in James Cameron's film *Titanic* as Rose's arrogant fiancé Cal is sure that the accident won't affect "the better people" while her mother wonders if seating in the lifeboats will take place according to class.

General disregard for safety and fairness stemmed in part from attempts on the part of competing shipping companies to make money and control the industry. Workers whose jobs were essential to safety were often badly paid. As a result, they were likely to be negligent in their work. Concern for this issue tied in with broader criticism that the rights of working-class people were often ignored.

SOS

According to rules passed by the British Office of Trade, the *Titanic* had more than the required number of lifeboats, even though it only had enough for half of the passengers.

SOS

An inquiry into the disaster conducted by the British Board of Trade concluded that third-class passengers were not unduly denied access to lifeboats. No surviving third-class passengers, however, were called upon to testify!

There is disturbing evidence that this was the case on the *Titanic*: a higher proportion of third-class passengers perished compared to first-class passengers. Reports by survivors indicate that large numbers of third-class passengers were not warned of the danger as the ship sank, and that many were even denied access to locations on deck where lifeboats were being launched.

Coming Up for Air

SOS
Soon after the wreck of the *Titanic* was rediscovered in 1985 by a team led by Dr. Robert Ballard, Congress attempted to prevent salvaging operations by declaring the wreck an international memorial. Despite this ruling, the French Institute of Oceanography, backed by American and European investors, recovered some 1,800 objects soon afterward. Their right to do this was protected by international law governing salvage operations.

The historical importance of the *Titanic* has begun to resurface—literally—over the past decade and a half with the discovery of the sunken ship itself and the recovery of many artifacts that were on board. This has been undertaken by scientists working in conjunction with government and naval organizations as well as by private adventurers and collectors.

Because the waters in which the *Titanic* sank were so deep—about $2^1/_2$ miles down—even locating the wreck was a tremendous undertaking. Actually getting all the way down required newly developed submarine technology. Bringing the hull to the surface has been tried—without success—and remains a formidable challenge to undersea engineering.

All of this has sparked renewed interest in the ship, providing fresh evidence about how it sank as well as treasures and curiosities that had been lost for most of the century. In addition, these efforts have fueled debates about whether the ship and its contents should be left alone, and who has a right to salvage them.

Cultural Undercurrents

In addition to the significance of the *Titanic* for its own moment in history, the ship and its loss have left a rich cultural legacy. Ever since the big boat went down, people have been learning about it and contributing to the growing body of ideas, information, and artifacts based on the event.

Psychic Waves

While interest in the *Titanic* among scientists and collectors has picked up in recent years, popular interest has remained strong ever since the moment the ship went down. Among the strangest popular responses to the *Titanic* disaster are claims that mysterious psychic and religious circumstances surrounded the wreck.

Memorial illustration commemorating the Titanic.
Popperfoto/Archive Photos

Some of these claims involve psychic warnings received by would-be passengers prior to the event that the disaster was going to take place. Other claims are that the ship embodied, even as it was built, a defiance of Christianity and Catholicism. Most striking of all the evidence that the *Titanic*'s demise was a paranormal event is the short novel, *Futility*, by Morgan Robertson, written years before the disaster, about a huge passenger steamer called the *Titan*, which sank after hitting an iceberg!

Spinning Yarns

Claims that the *Titanic* has mystic significance are hard to believe, but so are some of the sensationalistic reports that have appeared in newspapers and radio accounts down through the years. Media coverage feeding endless curiosity for strange details concerning the *Titanic* has had a tendency to go overboard!

Just about everyone seems to have at least some interest in the disaster and can find a way to relate to the incident. Even groups who were not represented on the *Titanic* have found it to be a stirring symbol of their own situations. Currently, audiences all over the world, including China and Russia, are flocking to see the *Titanic* on screen.

Long before the recent movie was released, rural blacks of the American South have treated the wreck in songs and folk tales. Most notably, singer/songwriter Huddie

Blow Me Down!
Ticket scalpers in Moscow have been getting as much as $25 a ticket from Russians dying to see the James Cameron *Titanic* film.

"Leadbelly" Ledbetter, in his song "De *Titanic*," expresses gratitude that no black people went down with the big liner. Folk stories known as "toasts" have also centered on the ill-fated ship. The basic message underlying many of these is "stay away from rich white people and their luxurious possessions!"

In England, the poet Thomas Hardy has memorialized the wreck of the *Titanic* in "The Convergence of the Twain," a poem recounting the collision between the ship and the iceberg that ripped its hull open. Like the "toasts," Hardy's poem cautions against luxury and pride.

Facing the Music

New meanings for the most famous disaster in the history of shipping continue to emerge in books, movies, TV, and on Broadway. It seems practically everyone has seen the James Cameron film, which is only the latest of a slew of cinematic sinkings of the *Titanic*, beginning with the 1912 hit, *Saved From the Titanic*, a silent film starring Dorothy Gibson, an actress who survived the actual event!

The many facts and stories that have emerged out of the disaster serve as reminders of the uniquely modern problems involved with advanced technology, long-distance travel, and close contact among different nationalities and races and among rich and poor. Perhaps it is because we continue to face these problems that the tragic note struck by the sinking of the *Titanic* has resonated throughout the century. While the ship's grandeur represents the possibilities of 20th-century life, its loss represents the dangers we face.

The Least You Need to Know

➤ Modern technology started to come into its own at the turn of the 20th century.

➤ The *Titanic* is symbolic of what Mark Twain called "the Gilded Age."

➤ Competition for business led to the production of larger, faster, more luxurious steamships.

➤ The *Titanic* disaster led to new regulations for safety and to criticism of shipping business practices.

➤ The wreck of the *Titanic* was discovered in 1985 by a team led by Dr. Robert Ballard.

➤ James Cameron's movie, *Titanic*, is only the latest of a large and growing body of popular work concerned with the ship.

Chapter 2

Sinking Fortunes

In This Chapter

➤ *Titanic* millionaires

➤ New money and the old elite

➤ Unsinkable Molly Brown

➤ The Astors, the Strauses, Ben Guggenheim

➤ The Duff-Gordons, the Wideners

➤ Memorials and endowments

During the "Gilded Age," the gap between rich and poor was obvious. People who were rich were very rich. People who weren't were pretty darn poor. This gap was evident on the *Titanic*, where first-class passengers outnumbered second class; meaning that for people who could afford better than third class, the price of making the trip in high style wasn't too much to pay—at least not in financial terms!

History buffs look back on these days with a mixture of nostalgia for the elegance and luxury available to the lucky few, and concern for the poverty and social injustice faced by just about everyone else. As a result, the many stories of what happened to the *Titanic* millionaires present a very mixed attitude toward those involved. On one hand, we admire them for their style, elegance, and accomplishments. On the other, their success often seems to come at the expense of those less fortunate.

A dramatic illustration of this social injustice is the fact that only 12 percent of adult male third-class passengers survived, compared with 34 percent of the men in first class. Almost all of the women in first class were saved—all but four of 144. In third class, well over half the women were lost—89 of 165. Even so, you can't really blame people for surviving. What's more, many of *Titanic*'s millionaires went down with real class.

Riding High

Most of the millionaires on board the *Titanic*—and there were quite a few—were Americans who had piled up heaps of money in banking, commerce, and industry. Many had spent the winter of 1911–12 vacationing around the Mediterranean. The French Riviera was just becoming a fashionable, high-class resort area with its beautiful beaches and expensive casinos.

With April well under way and the weather warming up, it was time to get back to the states. The *Titanic* went from Southampton, England, to Cherbourg, France, to pick up these people—and their mountains of baggage—before making a final stop at Queenstown, Ireland, and sailing off into history.

Keeping Up with the Astors

Although from a money-making perspective the American millionaires were pretty free-wheeling, in many respects they were extremely concerned with propriety and appearance. Traditionally, the rich people of the world came from old, established, aristocratic families. This old elite set a high tone for behavior that the "new money" people often tried to live up to.

The easiest way for a newly made millionaire to fit in with the old money crowd was to spend money on luxurious, elegant things—like first-class passage on the maiden voyage of the *Titanic*. This was a great way to show off one's newly acquired elegance and mingle with the upper crust.

This social scenario explains the presence of newly rich Margaret "Unsinkable Molly" Brown on board the *Titanic*. She just happened to run into New York millionaire J.J. Astor and his wife while vacationing in Egypt. She altered her traveling plans in order to sail with them back to the states.

Blow Me Down!
A number of factors contributed to the growing number of American millionaires at the turn of the 20th century. Industrialization and trade were generally encouraged by government, with few regulations limiting money-making activities. Plus, no matter how much cash they were raking in, nobody had to pay any income tax!

SOS
Even many who were not millionaires or aristocrats felt the urge to appear to be. One passenger booked a second-class berth under the name "Baron von Drachstedt." On boarding, he found his accommodations unacceptable and changed to a first-class room. When he was questioned at the disaster inquiry in the United States, it turned out he was plain old Alfred Nournay!

Ahoy There!

The pleasure and comfort which all of us enjoyed upon this floating palace, with its extraordinary provisions for such purposes, seemed an ominous feature to many of us, including myself, who felt it almost too good to last without some terrible retribution inflicted by the hand of an angry omnipotence. Our sentiment in this respect was voiced by one of the most able and distinguished of our fellow passengers, Mr. Charles Hays, President of the Canadian Grand Trunk Railroad...“The White Star, the Cunard and the Hamburg-American Lines,” said he, “are now devoting their attention to a struggle for supremacy in obtaining the most luxurious appointments for their ships, but the time will soon come when the greatest and most appalling of all disasters at sea will be the result.”

—first-class passenger Colonel Archibald Gracie

High Society

If you should get transported back in time and find yourself in the *Titanic*'s first-class smoking room or on one of the promenade decks, here are the big names you'll want to know representing the most prominent passengers:

➤ **Colonel John Jacob Astor**   Real-estate mogul reputed to have been worth $100 million; his market bottomed out when he went down along with his Airedale named Kitty.

➤ **Benjamin Guggenheim**   Swiss-American sultan of smelting who became immortalized for spending part of his final hours changing into his formal evening wear, in order to go down like a gentlemen. Guggenheim's valet also decided to go down with him.

➤ **Isidor and Ida Straus**   Elderly owners of Macy's department stores; the story of Ida refusing a seat in a lifeboat to stay with her husband has been lumping up throats for over 85 years.

➤ **Mr. and Mrs. George Widener and son Harry**   Hosts of *Titanic*'s swanky last supper. George and Harry were lost, but she survived and later endowed Harvard's Widener Library in Harry's name.

➤ **Mr. and Mrs. John B. Thayer**   The self-made president of Pennsylvania Railroad. He died, but she and her son went on to provide poignant commentary on the disaster.

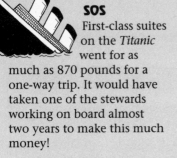

SOS
First-class suites on the *Titanic* went for as much as 870 pounds for a one-way trip. It would have taken one of the stewards working on board almost two years to make this much money!

➤ **Sir Cosmo and Lady Lucile Duff-Gordon** She was a cutting-edge dress designer and he was an English baronet. They signed on board the *Titanic* under the assumed name, "Mr. and Mrs. Morgan."

➤ **"Unsinkable" Molly Brown** Outspoken "new-money" refugee from a Western silver mine. When her estranged husband heard she survived, he said, "She's too mean to sink"!

➤ **Mrs. Charlotte Drake Cardeza** Famous for arriving on board with three baggage crates, four suitcases, and 14 trunks. She later valued her luggage at over $175,000.

Running the World

The richest of them all was Colonel John Jacob Astor, thought to be worth about $100 million at the time. Astor inherited a fortune made by his father in the fur business, and augmented by investments in real estate. Because he inherited his millions, Astor has been depicted as being as lazy as he was rich.

This characterization is unfair, however, since he was a shrewd investor in his own right, as well as an inventor (he invented a brake for bicycles, among other things), a soldier (he saw action in Cuba in 1899–1901 where he was made colonel), and even a novelist (he wrote a sci-fi story about an entrepreneur/inventor who straightens up the tilting axis of the Earth!).

Income-tax records show Astor owned about 700 pieces of property in Manhattan. Many of these were run-down apartment buildings with poor, working-class tenants. Some, however, were in pretty good shape, including New York's most famous hotel, the Waldorf Astoria!

Trophy Wife

Astor was a little past his mid-40s when he boarded the *Titanic*. With him was his second wife, 18-year-old Madeleine Force Astor, to whom he had been married for just seven months. High-toned, proper folks back home were upset by the youth of Astor's bride, as well as by the fact that he married at all after divorcing his previous wife of many years. In fact, priests of the Episcopal Church to which Astor belonged refused to conduct the ceremony. The matter was so serious that the minister who eventually performed the service was heckled into early retirement by the religious community!

The Astors walking their Airedale, Kitty.
Brown Brothers

The circumstances around the wedding started a lot of tongues wagging, so Astor and his very young bride went abroad while things cooled down. They had been on a kind of second honeymoon, traveling in Egypt and France.

Baby Makes Three

The Astors created a big enough stir that they might have wanted to remain abroad even longer. Madeleine, however, was pregnant, and they wanted to have the

SOS
Astor offered several priests and ministers $1,000 to perform a wedding ceremony uniting him to Madeleine Force. Many refused, believing Astor was morally obligated to remain faithful to his first wife.

21

baby back in the states. The *Titanic* must have seemed like the perfect ship for returning home in style.

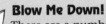

Catch the Drift

A steamship's **funnel** is the counterpart of a smokestack in a factory building. The *Titanic*, like other major ships of the time, had four funnels, but one of them was a dummy, put there in order to make the ship look more symmetrical as well as to appear powerful.

Blow Me Down!

There are a number of legends concerning Astor's behavior on the *Titanic*. One of the best—and most improbable—is that he went to the bar and said "I know I asked for ice, but this is ridiculous!"

SOS

Gossip, fueled by Guggenheim's daughter Peggy, indicates that Guggenheim made the trip with a secret lover—his attractive blonde secretary!

As it turned out, Astor didn't survive the journey. He escorted his pregnant wife to a lifeboat, but failed to get permission from 2nd Officer Herbert Lightoller to stay with her. Lightoller was a stickler for the "women and children first" rule. So Astor promised Madeleine he'd catch a different boat and meet up with her later.

Astor's body was among the first to be identified; he was covered in soot, indicating that he was crushed by one of the ship's *funnels* as it collapsed. Months later, Madeleine had a son and named him John Jacob after his father.

Release the Hounds!

You might think that Astor was just some guy with a lot of money and a fancy hotel. Before he died, however, he performed a selfless act that set him apart from the other passengers: He went to the ship's kennels and let his Airedale, Kitty, out of her cage. While he was at it, he set the other dogs free as well. Witnesses report that dogs could be seen on deck and, later, swimming in the water.

More Swells on the Ocean

Another American millionaire who didn't survive was Benjamin Guggenheim, the Swiss-American mining, smelting, manufacturing, and banking tycoon. Since his day, the Guggenheim name has become widely known thanks in part to the philanthropic efforts of his daughter Peggy (not on board), the art patron who endowed the Guggenheim Museum.

Going in Style

Ben Guggenheim, however, has become well-known among *Titanic* buffs for his actions the night of the collision. When he realized the severity of the collision with the iceberg, he resolved to go down with the ship in his formal evening attire. He did just that, after instructing his steward to tell his wife he died like a gentleman.

Cornering the Market

One of the most inspiring of the many *Titanic* stories concerns Isidor and Ida Straus. Isidor was a German Jew who emigrated to America before the start of the Civil War. During the war, he lived in Georgia and sold war bonds for the Confederate Army. At the close of the war, he surprised his creditors by actually paying them back. This was astonishing, given the defeat and the poverty suffered throughout the South.

After the war, he moved to New York City with no money but with a good reputation for paying his debts. As a result, he was able to borrow enough to start a glassware business with his brother. They arranged with Macy's to use a corner of the store to sell their merchandise in exchange for 10 percent of the profits. By the end of 10 years, they had bought the store!

Blow Me Down!
Isidor Straus served as a U.S. Congressman and was a friend and advisor to Grover Cleveland.

23

Cold Drinks for Two

When their moment of truth came, Isidor and Ida Straus approached the lifeboats together. Ida, however, refused to get in unless Isidor came, too. Other passengers urged the officer in charge to let Isidor into the lifeboat, too, despite the "women and children first" rule. At his age, he would have little hope of surviving.

Lifesavers
Monuments to the Strauses in New York City include a park on Broadway and 107th Street and a plaque above the entrance to Macy's at 135 West 34th Street.

Isidor refused, saying he didn't want special treatment. As he stepped back from the lifeboat, Ida refused her seat, too. Witnesses place them seated together on a deck bench, waiting for the end. They had been married for 40 years.

The Strauses were noted philanthropists. Some 40,000 people attended a memorial service held for them in New York, many of whom had benefited from their generosity. Ida performed her last philanthropic act on board the *Titanic*: She gave her fur coat to her maid, saying, "It will be cold in the lifeboat."

Isidor and Ida Straus.
Mariners' Museum

Fashion Disaster

Most of the wealthy passengers on board the *Titanic* were American entrepreneurs. Fashionable exceptions to this rule were Sir Cosmo and Lady Lucile Duff-Gordon. Before he attained fame in connection with the *Titanic* disaster, Sir Cosmo was known as a baronet and an Olympic fencer, having thrusted and parried for England in 1909. He was also a noted bridge player. Beyond that, he was best known as Lady Lucile's husband.

SOS
The Duff-Gordons signed on aboard the *Titanic* under the assumed name of Morgan and arranged to sleep in separate cabins. To this day, no one has figured out why. Were they *pretending* to be an unmarried couple who were *pretending* to be married? *Trés chic*!

Lady Lucile Duff-Gordon was a successful dress designer with shops in London, Paris, and New York. She and Cosmo were on their way to the states so she could see about business possibilities in Chicago as well. She is credited with two major fashion-business breakthroughs: She is said to have been the first designer to use mannequins in London, and she is also supposed to have been the first to get her models to move around while modeling. (Maybe so she could tell them apart from the mannequins!)

The Titanic's *grand staircase.*
Brown Brothers

Glittering as these achievements are, the couple is best known today for paddling away from the *Titanic* in a lifeboat that was less than half full and paying the crewmen with them not to turn around for survivors in the water. When called upon to testify at a British inquiry in the disaster, Sir Cosmo explained that the crewmen were concerned about their lost belongings and he was merely giving them money to replace them.

Reading Deeply

One of the more prominent families on board the *Titanic* were the Wideners. They are famous for giving a small dinner party for the ship's captain, E.J. Smith, attended by other wealthy families, including the Thayers and the Carters, and by the aide to President Taft, Archibald Butt. Mrs. Widener gave testimony after the sinking that cleared the captain of suspicion that he had been drinking at dinner.

Blow Me Down!
Many patrons who donate money to universities do so on condition that certain pet projects be carried out. Mrs. Widener placed conditions on her generous endowment of Harvard's Widener Library in memory of her son, Harry. One of the conditions she required was that all students learn to swim, believing that Harry might have survived had he learned.

The Wideners had traveled to Europe to shop for clothes for their daughter's upcoming wedding. With them was their son, Harry, age 27, who came along to add to his collection of rare books. His prize acquisition was a rare edition of the essays of Sir Francis Bacon, printed in 1598. At the start of the return voyage, Harry is reported to have put the book in his pocket and said, "If I am shipwrecked, it will go down with me." Unfortunately, he was shipwrecked, and neither he, the book, nor his father, George, survived.

Mrs. George Widener survived, however, and donated a sizable portion of the family funds to Harvard University, which built a library in Harry's name. Here, many of Harry's books found a home. Another important library to benefit from *Titanic* donations was the New York Public, which acquired the large and valuable book collection of Colonel Astor.

Split Decision

The ability to swim was only a limited help to those who did not manage to get into one of the *Titanic*'s lifeboats. Their main problem was not necessarily staying afloat—many of them had cork-filled life jackets—but staying warm in the icy water. One young millionaire who was helped by his swimming ability was 17-year-old Jack Thayer.

Thayer went down with the ship but managed to make his way to an overturned collapsible lifeboat. Another *Titanic* survivor who climbed up on the same boat was ship's Second Officer Herbert Lightoller. From here, Thayer watched the *Titanic* go down.

The Titanic *offered many amenities to its first-class passengers.*
Popperfoto/Archive Photos

Later, he drew a series of illustrations showing what he saw, which were printed in the papers. These pictures showed the *Titanic* breaking in two before sinking to the bottom. For decades, Thayer's take on the way the ship sank was rejected. The standard view was that the wreck sank in one piece. Thayer's pictures were confirmed in 1985, however, when Robert Ballard discovered two sections of the broken hull on the sea floor, almost 2,000 feet apart. (See Chapter 10 for Thayer's sketches of the sinkings.)

Cutting Their Losses

With all the millionaires and near millionaires on board the *Titanic*, you might think insurance companies had a real headache dealing with all the claims for loss of life and property as a result of the wreck. You'd be right. Even though few of the very rich survivors and families of those lost bothered to file claims, insurers of White Star Line were faced with a whopping $16 million in total claims for loss of property alone—a little over twice what the ship itself cost to build.

According to maritime law, however, White Star was required to reimburse claimants for only a small percentage of their losses ($663,000). As a result, despite all of the people and property that went down with the *Titanic*, White Star did not go down with them, but remained in business to sail again.

SOS
When news of the *Titanic* disaster reached New York, flags all up and down Wall Street flew at half mast in honor of the many rich investors on board who had hit bottom.

The Least You Need to Know

➤ Colonel John Jacob Astor was the richest man on board the *Titanic*. He did not survive.

➤ Margaret "Unsinkable Molly" Brown typified the upstart "new money" contingent.

➤ Ben Guggenheim changed into formal evening wear to take the plunge.

➤ Ida Straus chose to remain with hubby Isidor rather than take a seat in one of the lifeboats.

➤ Lady Lucile Duff-Gordon, wife of Sir Cosmo Duff-Gordon, was a noted English dress designer.

➤ Harvard's Widener Library is named for book-loving *Titanic* victim Harry Widener.

Chapter 3

Folks Against Fate

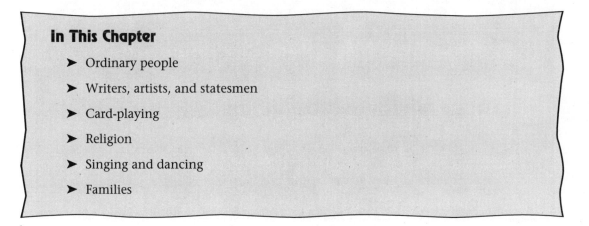

In This Chapter

- ➤ Ordinary people
- ➤ Writers, artists, and statesmen
- ➤ Card-playing
- ➤ Religion
- ➤ Singing and dancing
- ➤ Families

The lives of the famous *Titanic* millionaires and their actions on board are well known. They figured prominently in the public eye before the disaster and their behavior during the disaster was carefully observed and recorded by survivors. Many of them were among the first to know what was going on, so their actions were played out on a stage that had not yet become too chaotic.

As for most of the rest of the passengers, however, their stories went down with them. We can only speculate about how they met their fate. Fortunately, though, a few good accounts of some of the ordinary folks on board have been salvaged. These accounts show these folks at their ordinary best, doing what they ordinarily do—relaxing, singing, dancing, playing games, and talking.

During crunch time, though, things were not quite so ordinary. Accounts of the collision include some strange and soulful stories of how people met their fate—or managed to survive—when the *Titanic* went down.

Cruising and Schmoozing

Not all the important people on board the *Titanic* were millionaires. Many of them wanted to be, however. The *Titanic* voyage provided an enterprising few with an opportunity to hobnob like never before.

Titanic *passengers conversing on deck.*
Illustrated London News/Archive Photos

Tipping to the Top

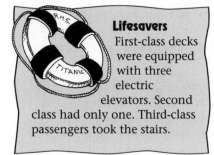

Lifesavers
First-class decks were equipped with three electric elevators. Second class had only one. Third-class passengers took the stairs.

One second-class passenger, Mrs. Henry B. Cassebeer, was smart enough to realize that many first-class rooms were left empty. By slipping a few pounds into the hands of the right steward, she arranged to move into one of the finest rooms on the ship for the price of her second-class room, plus the tip. This move up in the world also gave her access to all the first-class amenities, including the Turkish baths, the swankiest saloons and dining rooms, and the company of people who were incredibly rich, as well as famous writers, artists, politicians, and so on.

Notable Floaters

Here's a list of some of the most notable non-millionaires aboard the *Titanic*.

➤ **Jacques Futrelle**   French mystery writer whose work has been compared to that of Arthur Conan Doyle, the inventor of Sherlock Holmes. Futrelle had just turned 37 when he went down with the *Titanic*.

➤ **Francis (Frank) Millet**   American artist living in England. In his younger days he was a war correspondent in the Spanish-American War and the Russian-Turkish War.

➤ **Major Archibald Butt**   Military aide to President Taft and erstwhile news reporter and diplomat. He attended the dinner for Captain Smith hosted by the Wideners the night of the wreck.

➤ **Samuel Ward Stanton**   Illustrator and editor of marine publications. He had been on a trip to Spain to gather inspiration for a mural he was designing for an American ship.

➤ **Henry Harris**   Theater producer who had a number of plays showing in New York at the time of the disaster. He was returning from England where he had just found another play he planned to produce.

➤ **Helen Churchill Candee**   Progressive American author of *How Women May Earn a Living* and other books. She gave fellow passenger Edward Kent a miniature photo of her mother as the ship sank. The picture was found later together with Kent's body and returned to Candee, who survived.

➤ **William T. Stead**   Influential editor of *Review of Reviews* during the early days of British political journalism who, later in his life, developed a fascination for psychic phenomena and spiritualism. His novel, *From the Old World to the New*, has been cited as evidence that Stead anticipated his own fate through psychic means.

These movers and shakers of their generation weren't millionaires, but they were successful, well-known people who signed on board the *Titanic* as first-class passengers. Historians imagine them as centers of the circles of conversation that formed in the wood-paneled first-class smoking room after dinner. Their talk focused on politics, current affairs, history, and the arts.

Style and Gracie

A notable participant in some of these bull sessions was Colonel Archibald Gracie. Gracie survived the wreck and wrote one of the first book-length accounts of the disaster, *The Truth About the Titanic*. Gracie's book indicates that he was proud of his ability to schmooze with the rich and famous. He had previously written an account of one of the battles of the Civil War, which he persuaded millionaire Isidor Straus to take a look at. Straus lived in Georgia during the war and told Gracie he read the book "with great interest."

Living room on board the Titanic.
Illustrated London News/Archive Photos

Colonel Gracie was a consummate turn-of-the-century gentleman, active in gathering up female passengers and helping them into the lifeboats as the ship went down. He loaned Second Officer Lightoller his pocket knife for cutting the ropes holding down one of the collapsible boats. As that part of the ship became submerged, Gracie jumped and swam for his life.

He reports being afraid of getting scalded to death in water that was heated by the ship's boilers. He made it, however, to the overturned collapsible boat on which Lightoller, Jack Thayer, and some others were also saved. Before he jumped, he was dismayed, in looking back, to see a large group of women clustered together on the deck near the stern. He had mistakenly believed almost all the women had made it into lifeboats.

Luck of the Draw

While Gracie's account of the disaster helped flesh out the picture of many of the first-class passengers' last moments on the *Titanic*, another survivor, Lawrence Beesley, a science teacher from London, wrote a book on his experience as a second-class passenger. Beesley called his book *The Loss of SS Titanic: Its Story and Its Lessons*.

Beesley describes going up on deck and into the second-class smoking room after noticing the vibration of the ship caused by its brush with the iceberg. Here he found some card-players engrossed in their game. They mentioned noticing the berg as the ship scraped past it, then going back to their game, not realizing how serious their situation was.

Hitting the Deck

Card-playing was a favorite pastime aboard the *Titanic*. Among the passengers were a number of professional gamblers who took the voyage for the purpose of relieving some of the wealthier passengers of their excess money. Among the card sharps believed to have been on board were George "Boy" Bradley, Harry "Kid" Homer, and Jay Yates. Whether or not they won any money on the voyage, their luck had run out!

In fact, the name *Titanic* became synonymous with bad luck in gambling circles. During the years following the wreck, one hard-luck card player was given the nick-name "Titanic" Thompson for his tendency to lose large sums of money.

SOS
As a witness in the American inquiry into the disaster, Gracie expressed annoyance that the collapsible boats were so hard to get to. They were stowed on the roof of the officers quarters and tied with ropes. They had to be cut loose and then lowered to the deck on makeshift ramps made of oars. By the time they were ready to go, it was too late to load them properly.

Lifesavers
Beesley was standing on deck above a boat that was being lowered into the water when a crewman told him he had better jump. So he leapt into the boat and survived.

Blow Me Down!
Some passengers chose to spend their final moments playing cards. Believing that things were hopeless, they helped themselves to liquor from the bar and played their last hands until the tables they played on had tilted too much with the sinking ship to hold their cards.

Ahoy There!

After dinner, Mr. Carter invited all who wished to the saloon, and with the assistance at the piano of a gentlemen…he started some hundred passengers singing hymns. They were asked to choose whichever hymn they wished, and with so many to choose, it was impossible for him to do more than have the greatest favorites sung…It was curious to see how many chose hymns dealing with dangers at sea. I noticed the hushed tone with which all sang the hymn, "For those in peril on the sea."

—passenger Lawrence Beesley

Keeping the Faith

While on board, Beesley made friends with the Reverend Ernest Carter and his wife Lilian. Together they discussed the quality of education in England and whether there were enough good ministers being trained for the clergy. Carter asked Beesley the favor of reserving the dining room that evening for a hymn singing he was planning to lead.

The singing was attended by about 100 people. Hymns were chosen informally as participants called out requests. Among the favorites they sang was "Eternal Father, Strong to Save," a hymn with the refrain, "O hear us when we cry to thee for those in peril on the sea." This was Sunday evening. The singing ended around 10:00, about an hour and 40 minutes before the ship hit the iceberg.

A religious service of a different kind took place some two and a half hours later as the *Titanic* was sinking. A Catholic priest, Father Thomas Byles, led hundreds—both Protestants and Catholics—in anguished prayer on deck. Many were reportedly saying the rosary as they were engulfed by water.

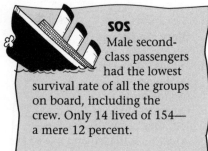

SOS
Male second-class passengers had the lowest survival rate of all the groups on board, including the crew. Only 14 lived of 154—a mere 12 percent.

Shutting the Door

Beesley was among those who noticed it was especially difficult for second- and third-class passengers to get to the lifeboats on the first-class deck. He reports that two women from second class asked an officer to open the locked gate that would let them through, and were told that second class had its own lifeboats on its own deck. This was not true: There was no separate second-class deck with lifeboats.

The Cheap Seats

The *Titanic* had 337 first-class passengers, 271 in second class, and 712 in *steerage*, or third class. First-class was largely made up of wealthy Americans returning home after vacationing in Europe. Second class consisted mostly of middle-class English people visiting friends and family in the States. Third class included people from all over the world who were emigrating to America in search of jobs. They plied trades of all kinds—butchers, bakers, tailors, shoemakers, jewelers, druggists, bricklayers, carpenters, farmers, gardeners, clerks, servants, engineers, and laborers.

Catch the Drift
The section of cheapest berths on a passenger ship is known as the **steerage**. This section was originally located in the rear of the ship near the rudder which steers it. There were two steerage sections on the *Titanic*, one at the stern, or rudder-end of the ship, the other all the way forward at the bow.

Steerage aboard the *Titanic* was separated into two sections of the ship, one at the bow, and one at the stern. When the starboard bow was punctured by the iceberg, many steerage cabins in the bow were quickly flooded with water. As a result, the passengers with berths in this section had an early warning of the danger the ship was in. Many of these passengers made it safely to lifeboats, unlike the steerage passengers in the stern, who didn't realize anything was wrong until the whole ship started tilting downward.

International Waters

Steerage passengers included Chinese, Russians, Armenians, Croatians, Syrians, Italians, Dutch, Scandinavians, and over 100 Irish. Reports indicate that, despite confusion caused by so many different languages, many steerage passengers had a good time on the journey right up until the final hours. Although they weren't allowed to use the gym, swimming pool, or the squash court, they got their exercise playing games, dancing, and even chasing rats.

Lifesavers
White Star Line provided the *Titanic* with a multi-lingual interpreter for easing communication difficulties among the passengers and crew—a German known as Herr Müller.

Song and Dance

Even though the famous band on board the *Titanic* played only for the first- and second-class passengers, there was plenty of music in steerage too, thanks to the passengers who brought their own instruments. In particular, there was a strolling bagpiper on board. (A bagpipe was found with the wreck decades later.) In addition, third class was furnished with its own piano.

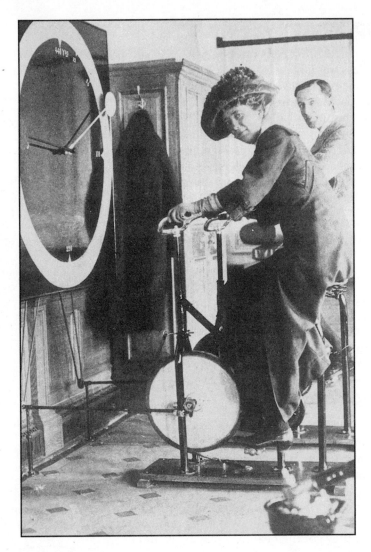

Titanic *passengers using the gym.*
Illustrated London News/Archive Photos

Blood Is Thicker Than Water

Among those on board the *Titanic* were many families, newlyweds returning from their honeymoons, and couples pretending to be married. Some couples and families were lost together; others parted as some died and others were saved. One of the strangest of all *Titanic*'s stories has to do with a mother and her baby who were separated—but only temporarily.

A view of the Titanic's *Boat Deck.*
Popperfoto/Archive Photos

Baby on Board

In the heat of the bustle and jostling for space in the lifeboats, little Frank "Filly" Aks was wrested from his mother's arms and tossed bodily into a lifeboat. Leah, his mother, was prevented from getting into the same boat by an officer who didn't understand what had happened. Fortunately, she managed to board a different boat. She was understandably distraught, however, at being separated from little Filly.

Meanwhile, the baby found himself in the arms of Elizabeth Nye, who was a good catch. She wrapped him in a blanket and held onto him. Eventually, the lifeboats were picked up by the *Carpathia*, where the survivors were able to walk around on deck.

SOS
All of the children from first- and second-class were saved. Out of a total of 109 children on board the *Titanic*, 52 were lost. All of these were booked as third-class passengers.

Here little Filly recognized his mother standing not far away, and reached out for her. She then saw him and claimed him as her own with great relief. Elizabeth Nye had maternal aspirations of her own, however, and refused to give up the tiny survivor. The captain of the *Carpathia*, Arthur Rostron, was called upon to settle the dispute. Captain Rostron didn't need the wisdom of Solomon, since Leah Aks knew her son had a strawberry birthmark on his chest, which proved she had put in some quality time with Filly already. So Leah and Filly were reunited.

Drifting Apart

Another mother temporarily separated from her children by the *Titanic* was Marcele Navratil, a French seamstress married to tailor Michel Navratil. The two were married when she was 17 and he 27. They lived in Nice and had two sons, Lolo and Momon, before their marriage got into trouble.

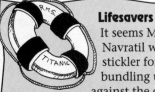

Lifesavers
It seems Michel Navratil was a stickler for bundling up against the cold. He is said to have stopped to help a teenage passenger—Madeleine Mellanger, whose arms were full—tie her shoes before fetching and bundling up his own kids.

Michel, the father, took the drastic measure of running off with his sons to America without telling anyone. He even adopted an assumed name, Hoffman, so he wouldn't be spotted and arrested for kidnapping. This is the name he used when he registered to board the *Titanic*.

When the ship began to go down, Hoffman (Navratil) bundled his children up carefully and put them in a lifeboat. They were saved, but he died of exposure. At that time, Lolo was almost 4 years old; Momon was 2.

One of the women in the boat with the two boys was Margaret Hays. She was a nice lady from New York who could speak French, so she started to get to know the kids right away. When no one claimed them, she took them home with her.

Paper Chase

As you might imagine, the papers made a big deal about the "orphans of the deep." When Margaret Hays took the kids shopping to get them clothes, the sales clerk recognized them from their picture in the paper and the store manager gave them free outfits. Meanwhile, offers to adopt them came pouring in.

Margaret held out, though, thinking that the mother might be around somewhere. In fact, news of the two little *Titanic* survivors ran in papers in Europe as well, so Marcele Navritil saw her kids' photos, got in touch with the authorities, and was given free passage on the *Oceanic* to go and get them. They returned safely to France with their mother.

The Least You Need to Know

➤ Along with the famous millionaires, *Titanic*'s first-class passengers included a number of artists, writers, and statesmen.

➤ Card-playing was a favorite activity. Passengers were warned to avoid professional gamblers and con-men.

➤ Many passengers joined in hymn-singing on Sunday evening before the disaster.

➤ Second- and third-class passengers fared much worse than first-class in terms of percentage saved.

➤ Many families were lost or separated by the disaster. Some were later reunited.

Captain Smith.

Leaks in Leadership?

In This Chapter

➤ The *Titanic*'s officers

➤ Why they didn't avoid the iceberg

➤ How they dealt with the catastrophe

➤ How Lightoller explained things later on

The captain and officers of the *Titanic* were experienced, knowledgeable seamen, among the best in their field. Some of them began their careers at an early age, serving on mail ships and doing military service before signing on with White Star Line. Some had been in shipwrecks prior to the *Titanic*. All were prepared to face the worst; they were used to danger and knew how to keep cool in tough situations.

This manly attitude was a real asset as the ship went down and the passengers relied on them for their safety. Unfortunately, that attitude may have helped cause the collision in the first place: None of those rugged sailors were afraid of icebergs—and they probably should have been!

Inquiries into the disaster found that the captain should have reduced speed in response to the ice warnings received by the ship. Even so, it seemed that the whole shipping industry failed to place enough emphasis on safety. Everyone was so confident in the big, fast, new steamships, they underestimated the threat posed by icebergs.

Who's in Charge Here?

Looking back, historians disagree about how well the officers of the *Titanic* did their job. Some are inclined to look for larger, overarching causes of the accident, including company policy, shipping industry practices, lax shipping regulations, and the new and still unfamiliar nature of enormous steamships. These broader explanations suggest that the *Titanic* disaster might have taken place with any set of officers in charge.

Captain Smith and the senior officers of the Titanic.
Popperfoto/Archive Photos

Others hold the *Titanic*'s officers largely responsible for the accident, as well as the confusion and uncertainty that set in after the accident occurred. According to this view, they should have known better than to have steamed toward ice without slowing down. They also should have had a better practical knowledge of the handling of the ship and the function of the lifeboats.

The Titanic's *Captain Smith as the ship sank.*
Hulton Getty/Tony Stone Images

Chain of Command

Here's a list of those in charge.

➤ **Captain Edward J. Smith**   Served as captain with White Star Line for 25 years before going down with his last ship at the age of 60.

➤ **Chief Officer Henry Wilde**   Assigned to the *Titanic* as an afterthought as a result of his experience on the *Olympic*, the *Titanic*'s sister ship. He went down with the ship.

➤ **First Officer William Murdoch**   In charge on the bridge when the iceberg was sighted by the lookouts. He gave the order "hard a-starboard!" in time to avoid a direct collision, but too late avoid a long, fatal scrape. He was lost with the ship.

➤ **Second Officer Charles Lightoller**   The highest ranking officer to survive. He supervised the loading of a number of lifeboats and was a stickler for "women and children first."

SOS
The *Titanic* only had enough life-boats to hold 1,178 of its 2,200-plus people on board. As precious as lifeboat space was, it wasn't utilized efficiently. Only a few more than 700 people survived the disaster. If the lifeboats had been filled, more than 400 additional people could have been saved.

➤ **Third Officer John Pittman**   Ordered to take charge of lifeboat #5 by Officer Murdoch after supervising its loading.

➤ **Fourth Officer Joseph Boxhall**   Survived the disaster and later served as a technical consultant for the making of the 1958 *Titanic* film, *A Night to Remember*. Boxhall's ashes were scattered at the site of *Titanic*'s sinking upon his death in 1967.

➤ **Fifth Officer Harold Lowe**   In charge of the only lifeboat to return for survivors after the *Titanic* sank. Lowe is also reported to have yelled, "Get the hell out of the way!" to White Star exec Ismay for inter-fering in the lowering of the lifeboats.

➤ **Sixth Officer James Moody**   Relayed the message from the lookout to Officer Murdoch that the iceberg had been sighted. He went down with the ship.

Top Sea Dog

Blow Me Down!
Captain Smith has been calculated to have sailed over 2 million miles before embarking on his final journey aboard the *Titanic*.

Captain Edward J. (E.J.) Smith was one of the most widely respected sea captains around. He started his seagoing career at the age of 16 as an apprentice and later served as com-mander in the Royal Navy reserve during the Boer War. Before taking the helm of the *Titanic*, he had been with White Star 30 years, 25 years as a captain.

Old Salt

When he took charge of the *Titanic*, Captain Smith was 59 years old. His officers respected him, and passengers admired him, too. In fact, his reassuring, authoritative manner and his salty white beard, together with his knowledge and experience, may have figured into his being selected for the *Titanic*'s maiden voyage. A big part of his job, after all, was to represent the White Star Line.

Even after the disaster, people continued to think well of him. Second Officer Lightoller remembered him decades after the disaster as "the best captain he ever knew." A big statue of the captain was put up in his native town of Southampton. Many important people attended the unveiling of this statue, including relatives of passengers who perished with the captain.

Fast Eddy

Despite his nearly perfect record at sea and the good reputation he enjoyed, historians tend to hold him at least partially responsible for the loss of the *Titanic*. Captain Smith was certainly aware that he was approaching icebergs the night of the collision; *Titanic* had received numerous ice warnings throughout the day. Icebergs in that region of the North Atlantic were common, especially in April, when spring thaws caused northern glaciers to drop big chunks of ice into the sea. Some say Captain Smith should have realized how dangerous the situation was and taken greater precautions by slowing down. As it happened, the ship was cruising along at more than 20 *knots*.

Catch the Drift
A **knot** is a unit of speed used at sea, roughly equivalent to 1.15 miles per hour.

The fact that the *Titanic* headed into icy regions at night at cruising speed has led to speculation that the captain was not thinking enough about the safety of the ship. He was extremely confident in the *Titanic*'s water-tight bulkheads and was quoted as having said, "I cannot conceive of any disaster happening to this vessel. Modern shipbuilding has gone beyond that." At the time of the collision, 11:40 p.m. on Sunday evening, Smith was in his quarters. He had left word to be notified if the weather changed.

SOS
Smith and Ismay had plans to run the *Titanic* at full speed for the first time ever on Monday, the day after the ship sank.

According to one story, he was trying to set a record, currently held by White Star's rivals, the Cunard Line, for making the trip in the least amount of time. This, however, seems unlikely. Cunard built smaller, speedy ships, whereas White Star was becoming famous for its slower, bigger vessels. If Captain Smith was trying to break a speed record, the *Titanic*, as big as it was, would not have been the ship to do it in.

Another bit of speculation is that J. Bruce Ismay, White Star's managing director who was aboard the *Titanic* at the time, was putting pressure on the captain to make a speedy run. In fact, in James Cameron's movie, *Titanic*, Ismay attempts to persuade Smith to go faster than Smith thinks prudent, saying that a fast journey would make headlines and be good for business.

Smith had a reputation for speed that was part of what made him a good captain in the eyes of White Star's management. Speed was a priority, not only for the convenience of passengers, but also because of the mail on board. Smith had lots of experience as captain of mail ships and *Titanic* was carrying lots of mail.

Blow Me Down!
As the *Titanic* sank, the order was given for a total of eight rockets to be fired as distress signals. The signals were spotted by the ship *Californian*, but the ship made no effort to come to *Titanic*'s assistance. This callous disregard for a sinking ship remains a mystery, but one explanation may be that the captain of the *Californian* was worried about running into icebergs himself!

Carried Away

While the real explanation for the speed of the *Titanic* remains something of a mystery, there is a good deal of evidence that it was common for steamers of the time to maintain cruising speed in areas known to have icebergs. This was Officer Lightoller's testimony when he took the stand during investigations into the disaster. The night was clear and all the officers seemed to think that any icebergs would be visible far enough away to avoid them. Other sea captains who were questioned said that they did not tend to slow down when approaching ice.

It seems that the entire shipping industry was too confident that steam liners would be able to avoid icebergs quickly. Captain Smith may well have been especially confident, believing that the *Titanic* was one of the sturdiest ships ever built. Evidently, he simply overestimated the ability of his officers and crew to steer clear of danger at that speed.

Mum's the Word

Once the collision took place, the captain was quick to assess the damage, but may have been slow to inform people of just how bad things were. This hesitation had both good and bad results. On the plus side, it prevented panic from setting in too soon. Most of the passengers were extremely calm until many of the lifeboats had already been launched.

The drawback was, the officers may not have realized the danger the ship was in. Their ignorance may have led them to lower many of the lifeboats with only a fraction of the number of passengers they could hold. If the officers had known from the start how desperate things were, they might have been able to save more people.

Ahoy There!

In a great emergency like that, where there are limited facilities, could you not have afforded to put more people into that [first] boat?

—Michigan Senator William Alden Smith, at the U.S. inquiry

I did not know it was urgent then. I had no idea it was urgent.

—Second Officer Charles Lightoller

Down with the Ship

Different stories have been told about how the captain spent his last hours. We know he inspected the damage and advised the passengers he saw to put on their life jackets and go up on deck. When he learned how bad the accident was, he gave the order to load the lifeboats. We also know that, when things were hopeless, he went into the ship's telegraph office and told the wireless operators that they had done their duty and should try to save themselves.

Many report the captain shouting, "Every man for himself!" as the last lifeboats were lowered into the sea. This, in effect, would have relieved the crew of its duty to the passengers. At that point he must have felt that there was little anyone could do to save the ship or those aboard.

There is no evidence that Captain Smith did anything inappropriate as captain of a sinking ship. Some have even romanticized his actions during the final moments. One story says that he swam to a lifeboat with a baby in his arms, and then disappeared. Another is that, instead of shouting, "Every man for himself," he shouted to his crew, "Be British!"

SOS
At one point, the captain checked the angle the ship had listed on a device called a commutator, which measures the ship's angle to the sea. He is reported to have said "Oh God!"

Tempest Tossed

One of the key figures in the history of the *Titanic* is Second Officer Lightoller. Before joining White Star, Lightoller lived a colorful and adventurous life. He went to sea at age 13 as his family's cotton-selling business dwindled off in the wake of the American Civil War. He had been wrecked at sea four times and, on another occasion, been on board a burning ship. In addition, he worked as a cowboy in Canada and prospected for gold in the Yukon.

*Second Officer
Charles
Lightoller.*
Mariners' Museum

MR. CHARLES LIGHTOLLER.

Walking a Fine Liner

Lightoller is especially important as far as the *Titanic* is concerned because he was the highest ranking officer to survive the disaster. Although he was not on duty when the collision occurred, he shouldered a lot of responsibility for getting people into the lifeboats in an orderly fashion. He was also one of the most important witnesses, giving testimony not only about what happened as the ship went down, but about what caused the disaster in the first place.

Lightoller was in a delicate position during inquiries into the disaster. On one hand, as an employee and representative of White Star, he didn't want to say anything that would place the blame on the company for the accident. On the other, as a high ranking officer, he didn't want to say anything that would blame the crew or its leadership. His take on the sinking—which he stuck to throughout the inquiries—was that no one was to blame.

Shipwrecks Happen

Lightoller claimed that an unusual set of circumstances was responsible for bringing about the catastrophe. He denied that the liner was going too fast, even though it was heading into an area filled with icebergs. Only under the most unusual circumstances would the crew and ship have been unable to respond in time to avoid icebergs. Thus, it wasn't Captain Smith's fault, nor the fault of the company, for setting the wrong speed.

Even so, Lightoller also claimed that the lookouts were not at fault for seeing the iceberg too late. For one thing, the ocean was unusually still. As a result, there were no *swells*, or small, rolling waves breaking against the iceberg. Ordinarily, according to Lightoller, the breaking swells would have stood out against the ocean, making the iceberg easier to spot. In addition, there was no moon to illuminate the berg.

Catch the Drift
A **swell** is a small, rolling wave that doesn't break unless it runs into something, such as a ship or an iceberg.

Another factor that, in Lightoller's view, prevented them from spotting the iceberg sooner was its dark color at the time. Lightoller explained that some icebergs turn blue temporarily when they roll over in the water, exposing a portion that has been submerged. The newly surfaced side of the berg looks blue until the water drains off it or freezes. Then it turns white again.

Lightoller said this must have happened to the iceberg that sank the *Titanic* right before the lookouts caught sight of it. By then it was too late to do anything about it. Ordinarily, however, there wouldn't have been a problem.

Second Guessing the Second Officer

Historians looking back at the disaster have raised doubts about both of these excuses. Although the sea was evidently calm the night of the sinking, a calm sea is not so unusual that the captain and crew should not have been prepared for it. After all, it's the captain's job to know how to handle the ship in all kinds of weather.

The "blue berg" excuse is controversial. Some authorities say icebergs do not turn blue and that it's extremely unlikely that the iceberg that hit the *Titanic* rolled over on its own in a calm sea. It was a big, solid mass of ice that didn't roll over when it was hit by a 46,000-ton ocean liner!

Steady as She Goes!

During the inquiries, Lightoller stuck to his guns under questioning, doing his best for White Star's reputation and the good name of the captain and crew. His behavior on the witness stand may have saved his job with the company, although his name would always be associated with White Star's biggest disaster.

Blow Me Down!
It was procedure on board the *Titanic* to run regular tests of the temperature of the sea in order to get an indication of how close the ship was getting to icebergs. Sea water was scooped up in a bucket and measured with a thermometer. A witness reported watching a sailor attempt to scoop water in a bucket on a rope that wouldn't reach far enough. After a few tries, he gave up, drew some tap water, and measured it instead! Maybe that sailor already knew what many seamen have come to believe: This isn't a very reliable way to test for ice.

Lifesavers
As Lightoller jumped from the ship, one of the funnels toppled over from the deck into the water. Although the funnel probably killed anyone it fell on, it may have made the difference between life and death for Lightoller. It stirred up a big wave that washed him away from the sinking ship and toward the collapsible boat where he stayed the night.

Catch the Drift
A **davit** is a kind of crane operated by a pulley used for lowering lifeboats into the water from the deck of a ship.

Blow Me Down!
Kenneth Moore plays an idealized Lightoller in Roy Ward Baker's 1958 docudrama, *A Night to Remember*. He has a wry sense of humor, a cool head on his shoulders, and a heart of gold. Near the end of the film, he is told by one of the men he has helped to save, "You've done all any man could do and more. You're not God, you know." To which Moore replies, "No seaman ever thinks he is."

Unfortunately, Lightoller's career with White Star didn't advance in the years to come. He never became captain of his own ship. He did, however, distinguish himself in military service during World War II. As a reserve officer, he commanded a Royal Navy destroyer that sank a German U-boat.

Coming Up Empty

It seems clear that Lightoller did his duty as an officer as the *Titanic* was sinking. He supervised the loading of several lifeboats until water washed up over the lifeboat deck. At that point, the ship sank fairly suddenly and he jumped and swam for his life. He was lucky enough to make it to one of the collapsible boats that was floating upside down in the water.

Looking back, however, many have questioned his actions in loading the lifeboats. Several of the first lifeboats Lightoller loaded were not even half full of passengers. Obviously, if the boats had been full, more people would have been saved. A number of explanations have been offered to account for the fact that so many underfilled lifeboats were lowered from the *Titanic*.

Taking Things Lightoller-ly

Lightoller himself claimed that he had sent some crewmen to arrange for passengers to climb from a lower deck into lifeboats that had already been lowered into the water. He said he felt it would be easier and safer this way. He also said he wasn't sure the lifeboats would hold up while being lowered at full capacity. He was afraid they would crack in the middle while hanging from the ship's new *davits* (a davit is the pulley-operated contraption used for lowering lifeboats). Lightoller's fears, however, were unjustified. Prior tests showed that the boats could be lowered filled with passengers.

Another possibility is that Lightoller may not have realized how serious the damage caused by the iceberg really was. He may have believed, at first, that loading the lifeboats was something of a formality, before it became clear that the ship was in real trouble.

The Titanic's *lifeboats in their davits.*
Hulton Getty/Tony Stone Images

All Handguns on Deck

In any case, Lightoller strictly adhered to the "women and children first" rule. His policy was to keep men off the lifeboats except for a couple of crewmen to row and steer. The second officer became especially severe as more passengers became aware of the danger. When some male passengers from steerage attempted to board one of the lifeboats, Lightoller brandished a handgun and ordered them to step back.

Several officers equipped themselves with guns to maintain control over unruly passengers. In fact, witnesses reported that First Officer Murdoch fired two shots into the air to keep frightened passengers from rushing the boats. These reports came to light within months of the sinking.

More recently however, eyewitness accounts of gunfire have emerged. These accounts tell a story that shows how desperate the situation was and how earnestly, if mistakenly, the officers tried to maintain order despite the danger. Two private letters, written independently of one another, tell of an officer who shot a passenger as he was trying to get into a lifeboat. The officer then turned the gun on himself and took his own life. Judging from the location of the shootings, the officer responsible could have been First Officer Murdoch or Chief Officer Wilde.

The Least You Need to Know

➤ Some blame broad, historical factors for the wreck of the *Titanic*. Others hold the captain and the officers at least partly responsible.

➤ The *Titanic* did not slow down as it approached the ice.

➤ Captain Smith seems not to have told his officers just how serious the damage was.

➤ Second Officer Lightoller defended the captain, the officers, and the lookouts from suspicion of wrong-doing.

➤ Lifeboats rowed away from the sinking *Titanic* with over 400 empty seats.

Salt-Water Staffers

The *Titanic* was staffed mostly with middle- and working-class types from England and Ireland. By today's standards, they were not well paid. Times were especially hard on working people, because industry was taking over, and labor organizations and government regulations to protect workers were slow to catch up with the new conditions.

Despite the growth of industry, jobs weren't always plentiful, so *Titanic* employees were mostly glad to have the work, despite the low pay—especially since it came with free room and board. They may also have been proud to work on such a spiffy ocean liner, and of their roles in helping to make it so spiffy.

Even so, when a ship hits an iceberg and starts sinking, that's when you might expect the ship's staff to say, "Don't ask me, I only work here." However, indications are that *Titanic* employees behaved like real pros in trying to make the best of a bad situation. Most of them stayed at their posts and took care of business.

The Gang's All Here

Catch the Drift
Firemen had the job of keeping the steam engines moving by shoveling coal into the boiler furnaces. **Trimmers** kept the firemen supplied with coal which they distributed in wheelbarrows. Firemen and trimmers were known as **"the black gang."**

SOS
In Queenstown, Ireland, where the *Titanic* picked up passengers, one of the stokers climbed to the top of one of the funnels from inside and looked out over the top, where his blackened face could be seen from below. A couple of the passengers thought this weird sight was a bad omen. One woman didn't undress for bed that night in order to be ready in case something went wrong.

A crew of about 900 were employed aboard the *Titanic*. Of these, fewer than 50 were actually seamen. The rest worked at just about everything else. Some were there to take care of the ship, others to take care of the passengers. The ship-types included lookouts, deck hands, engineers, electricians, pursers (ship's accountants) painters, *firemen* (they stoked the boiler furnaces with coal), and *trimmers* (they heaped the coal in piles for the firemen). The firemen and trimmers were called *"the black gang."*

Now We're Cookin'

The ship ran on steam produced by big tanks of boiling water. This was heated in coal-burning furnaces that were continually stoked by hand. Firemen, as they were called, shoveled coal around the clock. The trimmers moved back and forth with wheelbarrows, carrying loads of coal for the firemen.

The stokeholds where the firemen and trimmers worked were in the very bottom of the ship. They weren't pleasant places. For one thing, it was hot—often well over 100 degrees Fahrenheit. This would have made the physical labor especially difficult.

What's more, the air was thick with coal dust, and no one wore anything over their mouths and noses to filter the air. Today, people who work regularly in dusty conditions wear surgical masks to strain out floating particles. Not the men in the *Titanic's* stokehold.

Less of a health hazard, but undoubtedly unpleasant, is the tendency of drifting coal dust to stick to one's sweaty skin. In fact, stokehold workers were generally covered with the stuff, hence their common nickname of "the black gang."

Ahoy There!

Endless labor, joyless life; and yet the labor that gives life and movement to the whole ship. Up above are all the beautiful things. Up above are the people who rest and enjoy; down below are the people who sweat and suffer.

—Filson Young, describing work in the stokehold

Into the Drink

Although life was hard for the "black gang," a fairly high percentage managed to survive the disaster. Since it was located at the very bottom of the ship, the stokehold was among the first sections to be flooded. As a result, many of the firemen and trimmers were the first to realize the danger the ship was in. These men knew the layout of the ship and had no duties to attend to once the ship foundered, so they went straight for the lifeboats.

Of course, not all the members of the "black gang" made it off the ship in lifeboats. One who didn't was fireman Paddy Dillon from Belfast. A friend who survived reports that he and Paddy went to a bar, where they were giving liquor away. The deck was already sloping dangerously as Paddy downed three shots of whiskey. Then he grabbed a bottle of brandy and ran out on deck and fell overboard! Soon afterward, he was picked up by a lifeboat that was already in the water. They laid him on the bottom and threw a blanket over him. Someone found the bottle of brandy in his pocket and threw it over the side.

Service with a Smile

The workers aboard the *Titanic* who served the passengers included cooks, bakers, waiters, stewards, florists, barbers, a librarian, a nurse, two surgeons, a fitness instructor, and a squash pro. Many of these employees made good money despite getting low salaries, thanks to wealthy passengers' generous tips. Some rich passengers had favorite stewards and waiters who they already knew from other voyages on other ships.

Going Down Swinging

In addition to all of these *Titanic* staff-members was the eight-piece orchestra. The band aboard the *Titanic* has garnered lasting fame for sticking to their posts until the end and going down with the ship. They played sprightly tunes as the lifeboats were loaded in order to keep the passengers calm.

Blow Me Down!
Two *Titanic* movies, Cameron's 1997 film, and *A Night to Remember* (1958) include scenes showing crewmen plunging out of the stokehold with water gushing in. The last man to leave dives through the doorway just in time as the electric water-tight door slams shut.

SOS
Some people have all the luck. Not only did stewardess Violet Jessop and fireman John Priest survive the sinking of the *Titanic*, they were on board the big T's sister ship *Olympic* when it was crippled by a collision with the navy ship *Hawk* in 1911, and aboard the other sister ship, *Britannic*, when it was sunk in the Aegean in 1916.

Lunchtime in a Titanic *dining room.*
Archive Photos

Lifesavers
Chief Baker Charles Joughin supervised the loading of bread into the lifeboats upon orders by the captain when the berg hit. One report says Joughin and his helpers stocked the boats with over 500 pounds.

Their repertoire included popular ragtime arrangements, songs by Irving Berlin, tunes from the comic operettas of Gilbert and Sullivan, as well as classical favorites. Each piece—over 350 in all—was assigned a number and played by memory. Under ordinary circumstances, the band played during and after dinner. They also split up into trios during the day and played outside on deck.

Witnesses reported hearing music almost right up until the ship went under. Legend has it that the bandleader, Wallace Hartley, released the musicians from their duties as the deck began to slope and stayed himself to play a final tune on his violin. Rather than leave, the players joined the encore, and were washed over the side by a big wave as they finished.

THE ILLUSTRATED LONDON NEWS, APRIL 27, 1912.—636

BRAVE AS THE "BIRKENHEAD" BAND: THE "TITANIC'S" MUSICIAN HEROES.

1. MR. F. CLARKE, OF LIVERPOOL. 2. MR. P. C. TAYLOR, OF CLAPHAM.
3. MR. G. KRINS, OF BRIXTON, SOMETIME OF THE RITZ HOTEL ORCHESTRA. 4. MR. W. HARTLEY (BANDMASTER), OF DEWSBURY. 5. MR. W. T. BRAILEY, OF NOTTING HILL.
6. MR. J. HUME, OF DUMFRIES. 7. MR. J. W. WOODWARD, OF HEADINGTON, OXON.

The Titanic's *band played one of the most famous encores in history.*
Mary Evans Picture Library

There have been conflicting accounts about the final number they played. Some say their swan song was "Nearer My God to Thee," a hymn popular with church-goers on both sides of the Atlantic. This may, in fact, have been the band's final number. Like many

Lifesavers

Cameron's film, *Titanic* and Baker's film, *A Night to Remember* both include scenes depicting the band playing amid confusion on deck in which one of the musicians complains that no one is listening. The complaint is answered, "People don't listen when they're eating, but we play just the same."

SOS

The *Titanic's* musicians were not employed directly by White Star, but were hired by a booking agency. Officially speaking, they were not considered crew members but were signed aboard as second-class passengers. As a result, bereaved families of the band members could get no financial help from White Star or from the agency. Not until nine months later, when the *Titanic* Relief Fund decided to treat the musicians as regular crew members, did their families get support—no thanks to White Star.

hymns, however, this one is sung to more than one tune, two of which are popular in England, another in the U.S. As a result, even among those who agree that "Nearer My God to Thee" was the closing number, disagreement remains about which tune was played.

Another contender for the musical closer was a popular waltz, "Songe d'Automne" by Archibald Joyce. This tune was popular in England and is the song that wireless operator Harold Bride last heard. Thus evidence favors this number, although the sentimental favorite remains "Nearer My God to Thee."

Almost immediately after the disaster, appreciation for the band began to take on titanic proportions. The newspapers were full of stories celebrating their courage, and word of their final concert circulated all over Europe and America. People needed to find something good in the sinking of the *Titanic*, and the band provided the positive note they were looking for. Huge crowds turned out for bandleader Wallace Hartley's funeral in his home town of Lancashire, England. The funeral procession was half a mile long, and businesses closed for the day.

Big Senders

In addition to the band were two other employees hired by a separate company—wireless operators John Phillips and Harold Bride. Like the band, they too emerged as heroes in the aftermath of the disaster, remaining at their stations until the last possible moment, attempting to find help for the sinking ship.

Wireless Workload

Phillips and Bride were trained and employed by the Marconi Wireless Company, named after founder Guglielmo Marconi, inventor of the wireless telegraph. Their job consisted not only of sending and receiving official messages concerning the safety and navigation of the *Titanic* and other ships; they also sent personal telegrams for the passengers.

The two men were the only wireless operators working aboard the *Titanic*, and between them they worked nearly around the clock. The day of the collision was especially busy. There was the usual pile of messages to send, plus they had to be alert for the ice warnings that came in from other ships. The biggest job, though, was fixing a malfunction with the wireless equipment. This took several hours and produced a backlog of messages to send from passengers.

Awake at Their Posts

After they got the problem fixed, Bride, the assistant operator, went to bed while Phillips, the chief operator, tried to catch up on the work that had piled up. Bride had just got up to take over when the captain came in with the news about the collision. He told Phillips and Bride to send a message asking for help. It was time for Phillips to turn in for the night, but he stayed at the controls trying to summon help. He contacted the *Carpathia*, a steamer that agreed to come and help out, but was some four hours away. Then he continued to signal for someone closer.

Meanwhile, Bride relayed messages back and forth between Phillips and the captain. Phillips was so intent on his work that he didn't even get up to put on his coat or his life jacket. Bride helped him on with these while he remained at the wireless controls. Bride later reported that at one point, as he was returning from taking a message to the captain, he found a man had come into the wireless office and was trying to steal Phillips' life jacket while he was intent on his work. Bride hit him in the head with something heavy and knocked him out. Phillips just kept on working.

Finally, the captain came into the wireless office and told the operators they had done their duty and should fend for themselves. Even at that point, Phillips remained at the controls, trying to find someone nearby to receive *Titanic*'s distress signal. Bride went up to help with the last of the collapsible boats.

When the ship sank, both the wireless workers had to swim for their lives. They were picked up by survivors

SOS
One of the crucial ice warnings sent to the *Titanic* was jotted down by the wireless operator on duty, who failed to take it to the bridge. Instead, he continued with the pile of personal telegraph messages he was sending.

Blow Me Down!
You may already know that "SOS" is telegraph shorthand for "save our ship." An "S" is three dots, or short taps of the telegraph signaller; an "O" is three dashes, or long taps of the signaller. SOS, then, is ... / — / ... Actually, the SOS signal was only beginning to be used, and it's sometimes said that the *Titanic* actually sent the very first SOS. There is evidence, however, that other ships used the signal first. Most wireless operators, including the *Titanic*'s, still used the older signal, CQD (-.- . / —.- / -..). "CQ" is a handy way of saying "seek you." "D" stands for danger or distress.

SOS

In keeping with the policy of White Star Line, employees aboard the *Titanic* finished their assignments at the moment the ship went down. The iceberg, as it were, punched out everyone's time clock. As a result, they were paid only until the ship sank!

aboard the boat known as Collapsible "B." This boat was never loaded and launched properly, but fell into the sea as the ship sank, landing upside down.

Bride lay across the edge of the boat lying down with his feet wedged between some loose slats and with a man sitting on his legs. As he lay, waves occasionally washed up on his face. By the time they were finally picked up by the *Carpathia*, Bride was exhausted and his feet were badly injured. Even so, he came away better than Phillips, who died in the lifeboat from exposure. Bride believed that the long hours he had spent at the wireless were a contributing factor in his death.

A seaman's watch apparently stopped by seawater when the Titanic *went down.*
Bruce Dale/National Geographic Image Collection

Ahoy There!

The way the band kept playing was a noble thing. I heard it first while still we were working wireless, when there was a ragtime tune for us, and the last I saw of the band, when I was floating out in the sea with my lifebelt on, it was still on deck, playing "Autumn." How they ever did it I cannot imagine.

That and the way Phillips kept sending after the captain told him his life was his own, and to look out for himself, are two things that stand out in my mind over all the rest.

—Harold Bride

Back to Work

Bride was taken to the makeshift hospital aboard the *Carpathia,* where he slept all day. At night one of the *Carpathia*'s crew came in and asked if he could help the ship's exhausted wireless operator, who had been working alone without a break for hours, and was getting swamped with inquiries and requests to send messages to the families of *Titanic* passengers.

So, Bride went back to work! At this point, the newspapers in America were bursting to get the story of what happened to the *Titanic*. They kept questioning Bride over the wireless, trying to get the scoop. He refused. He felt it was more important to get word to the friends and families of survivors that their loved ones were safe. He spent the night sending off a pile of personal messages from *Titanic* passengers, ignoring the desperate requests of the newspapers.

The Least You Need to Know

➤ The *Titanic* employed about 900 crew and staff.

➤ The "black gang" kept the engines running.

➤ The band played, even after all the boats were lowered, and were lost with the ship.

➤ The wireless operators kept signaling for help even after the captain told them they could stop.

Part 2
Liner Notes

Steamships were a big thing in the decades leading up to—and beyond—the Titanic, *and the* Titanic *was the biggest of them all. To really appreciate what the* Titanic *was, it helps to know a little something about how and why it was built, as well as about steamers in general. They were the railroad trains of the sea, not only serving similar commercial and industrial functions, but also developing technologically at the same time as trains. They symbolized progress—the ability of people to do new things in new ways; and they symbolized power—the power of steam, but also the power of money and status.*

Big Boats, Big Business

It's natural to look into the conduct of the officers of the *Titanic* for problems that led to the disaster, or mistakes that made it worse. Problems with how the ship itself was run, however, were just the tip of the iceberg. Below the surface lies almost a century of steamship history during which disasters were just taken as a matter of course.

As ships got stronger and more powerful, they got faster and bigger. As more people took ships across the Atlantic, shipping companies got richer and built even bigger, stronger, faster boats. And as these big ships steamed ahead at unprecedented speed, they left concerns about safety behind.

There could have been more emphasis on safety in the shipping business, but there wasn't. This is partly because the industry had other priorities, and partly because regulations governing safety didn't keep pace with the other advances being made. One of the tragic results of this state of affairs was the *Titanic*.

Perilous Passage

Only gradually, and fairly recently, have people started to expect sea travel to be completely safe. Throughout much of the previous century, it was understood that whenever you set off on an ocean voyage, you took your chances. There was the danger of running into ice or rocks or other ships. Even more of a threat was bad weather.

Knock on Wood

Bad weather was especially worrisome in the days of the old wooden sailing ships. Dependent as they were on wind to blow them from place to place, it generally took at least four weeks to get from one side of the Atlantic to the other—if conditions were good. Of course, during those four weeks, you had to expect conditions to be bad at some point. Storms could drive a ship off course or sink it entirely, so delays at sea were common and sinkings not unusual.

Big Wheel

Blow Me Down!
When the *Savannah* was sighted off the coast of Ireland with smoke billowing out its funnels, it was thought to be on fire. The British cruiser *Kite* changed its course to rescue those on board, before they realized the smoke came from the *Savannah*'s furnace.

The use of steam engines to power ships made them safer by enabling them to move more steadily in bad weather, and, by making better time, lessened the odds of getting caught in *more* bad weather. Steam power was used tentatively at first, as a supplement to sailing. The first ship to cross the Atlantic with the help of steam was the *Savannah*, an American ship which made the voyage in 1819. The journey was made mostly under sail, but steam did part of the work. The *Savannah* used a paddle wheel, rather than the screw propellers used by the *Titanic*.

Not until late in the 1830s did ships start using more steam than sail in getting across the Atlantic. The innovation shortened the time required for the crossing, but also tended to cover everyone with soot spewed out by the coal-burning furnaces.

New Waves

In the 1840s, more shipping innovations were introduced. One was the screw propeller, which was less cumbersome than the old paddle wheel. Another was the use of iron in fashioning the hull. Iron ships are actually lighter and stronger than wooden ones, and therefore faster, too. By the end of the 1870s, iron was replaced by steel, which is even stronger.

Steel hulls made bigger ships possible, and bigger ships combined with speed created a new danger: A big, fast ship has a lot of momentum, so it's hard to stop or change its direction. Shipping engineers hadn't really considered this aspect of their new designs. Instead, they thought about how strong they were. The combination of increased size, strength, and speed was a mixed blessing in terms of safety. As the fate of the *Titanic* makes clear, strong does not mean "unsinkable."

An additional innovation that had a big, positive impact on safety was wireless. One of the first really big ships to cross the Atlantic was also one of the first to have wireless on board. This was German shipping company North German Lloyd's *Kaiser Wilhelm der Grosse*.

Unfortunately, the importance of wireless as a safety feature was sometimes overlooked. It was often thought of as a novelty and placed at the disposal of passengers for sending personal messages.

Blow Me Down!
The *Kaiser Wilhelm der Grosse* represents North German Lloyd's surprise attack on the shipping industry. It was built in secrecy to make an especially big splash. In fact, it really did make waves. Not only was it one of the first ships to be equipped with wireless, it won the Blue Riband for the fastest Atlantic crossing yet made. For a time, it garnered 25 percent of the passengers bound for America.

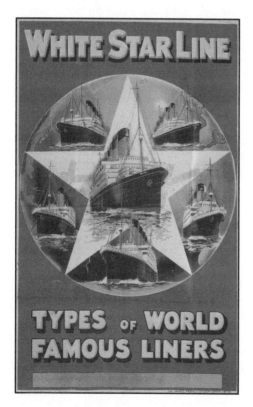

White Star advertisement.
Mariners' Museum

The Changing Shape of Shipping

Here's a list of historical developments that have changed the shipping industry through the years.

- ➤ **1819** The *Savannah* is the first steam-assisted ship to cross the Atlantic.
- ➤ **1838** The paddle-wheel steamship *Royal William* crosses the Atlantic within two weeks.
- ➤ **1843** The *Great Britain* is the first transatlantic steamer to have an iron hull and use a screw propeller.
- ➤ **1852** The *Pacific* crosses the Atlantic in 10 days.
- ➤ **1870s** Steel replaces iron in the construction of hulls.
- ➤ **1890s** Steamships drop the unnecessary precaution of carrying sails.
- ➤ **1900** The *Kaiser Wilhelm der Grosse* is the first ship to cross the Atlantic with wireless telegraph equipment.
- ➤ **1907** The *Mauretania* crosses the Atlantic in 4 days, 10 hours, and 42 minutes, setting a speed record that would last until 1929.
- ➤ **1912** The *Titanic*, the biggest ship yet built, sinks on her maiden voyage, prompting a review of safety regulations.
- ➤ **1950s** Transatlantic passenger shipping loses ground to commercial airlines and never recovers.

Dream Machines

As steamships became reasonably sturdy, fast, and reliable, more and more people wanted to make the journey between Europe and the U.S. Most were emigrants dreaming of a better life in America, and, year after year, their numbers increased. In 1905, a million people made the voyage.

Ships Coming In

By this time, a number of shipping companies were competing for customers. The Cunard Line started up in 1840 and dominated the North Atlantic run for decades. Even though the White Star Line, which later built the *Titanic*, started up during the 1850s, they didn't start sailing to America until 1870. Prior to that, White Star sailed between England and Australia, transporting prospectors who hoped to strike it rich in the Australian gold rush.

In 1871, White Star moved into the North Atlantic with the ship *Oceanic*. Although this ship was slower than the Cunard ships, it was larger and more luxurious, setting a White Star precedent that was taken to extremes years later with the *Titanic*. The *Oceanic* was a success and was followed by similar White Star vessels carrying immigrants and vacationers to and from America.

Lines in the Ocean

The North Atlantic shipping rivalry intensified as two German companies, North German Lloyd and HAPAG (Hamburg American Line) got a piece of the action. Other, smaller shipping lines did North Atlantic business too, but at the turn of the century, Cunard, White Star, HAPAG, and North German Lloyd dominated the industry and vied with one another for control of North Atlantic shipping. These companies built railroads and hotels to entice people who wanted to emigrate to America.

The competition got even hotter when American steel and railroad magnate J.P. Morgan muscled his way in. He bought out the Inman Line, one of the smaller British companies. The head of White Star at the time, T.H. Ismay, attempted to save Inman by organizing the British and German companies into a united front against the American interloper. His efforts, however, were unsuccessful and Morgan got a toe-hold in the shipping business.

Playing Hard Ball

As Morgan bought up smaller shipping companies, he put pressure on the larger ones. Morgan was sitting on the huge pile of money he'd made in American steel and railroads, so he could afford to stay in the shipping business without making a profit for as long as it took to drive out his competitors. He tried to do this by charging extremely low rates for third-class passage across the Atlantic.

> **SOS**
> The *Titanic* was not the first White Star ship to hit an iceberg. In April of 1864, the *Royal Standard* was badly damaged by a berg on the way back to Europe from Melbourne, Australia. The captain considered himself lucky that the ship didn't sink.
>
> The worst transatlantic disaster of the 19th century also took place on a White Star ship. In 1873, the *Atlantic* hit a rock off the coast of Nova Scotia. Of 942 people on board, 481 were lost.

> **Blow Me Down!**
> Morgan wanted a monopoly in the shipping business like the one he had in railroads. In fact, he became so associated with the concept of monopolies that the board game Monopoly modeled its cartoon mascot—with his top hat and droopy mustache—after Morgan.

This left the other shipping companies in a tough spot. They faced a choice: Either lose money by reducing their fares in order to compete with Morgan, or lose their customers. Morgan's main target was Cunard. Cunard fended off Morgan by getting help from the British government. Cunard persuaded the government that the well-being of the company was in the British national interest, and received subsidies that enabled it to stay afloat, despite Morgan and his money.

At around this time, in 1899, T.H. Ismay died, leaving White Star in the hands of his son, J. Bruce Ismay, who was relatively inexperienced. White Star was holding its own, but things looked bad with the savvy T.H. Ismay gone and Morgan breathing down J. Bruce Ismay's neck. This generated concern at Harland and Wolff, the company that built all of White Star's ships.

Selling Out

Harland and Wolff was run by William Pirrie, an engineer-turned-businessman who started with the company in 1862 as an apprentice at age 15. From there he rose through the ranks, becoming a partner in 1874 at age 27 and taking full control of the company in 1906. That same year he was made an English lord, and in 1909 he was made a baron.

Blow Me Down!
Pirrie had planned on taking *Titanic*'s maiden voyage, but was in bad health and had to cancel his arrangements. After the disaster, his friends tried to conceal the news from him, thinking it would worsen his condition.

Pirrie was worried about the future of White Star, since it was an important source of his company's business. He got together with J. Bruce Ismay and recommended an "if you can't beat 'em, join 'em" policy, persuading Ismay to sell White Star to Morgan to avoid going under. Pirrie was also hoping that the shipping trust Morgan wanted to put in place would send more business to Harland and Wolff.

So Morgan bought out White Star. He tried to keep his new company looking as British as possible by keeping Ismay as director. He also agreed to let the British government take over any of White Star's ships if it needed them during a time of war. Beyond that, he kept a low profile, and let Ismay and Pirrie take care of business. Morgan gave Pirrie the go-ahead to spare no expense in building the best ships.

Sparing No Expense

So the battle lines were drawn. Cunard became known for its sleek, fast ships, especially the *Mauretania* and the *Lusitania*, launched in 1907. White Star wanted to define itself differ-

Catch the Drift
A cost-plus contract means the manufacturer will be paid for whatever the work costs plus an agreed amount as profit. This is advantageous to the manufacturer, who doesn't have to bid on a job or worry about cutting corners in production.

ently, so that same year, Pirrie came up with the idea of building the biggest, most luxurious ships ever. Thomas Andrews, designer for Harland and Wolff, drew up the plans for the *Olympic*, the *Titanic*, and the *Britannic*. The idea was for one of these big ships to set off for America every week.

This plan allowed him to take full advantage of the money Morgan was making available to White Star. The *Titanic* and her sister ships were built under what is known as a *cost-plus* contract, meaning that, no matter how much it cost Harland and Wolff to build them, White Star would pay that cost plus a certain amount in addition. This enabled Harland and Wolff to pull out all the stops and build the most expensive ship they wanted to; they were assured of their profits.

Officers of the Olympic. *The man with the white beard is Captain Smith, who later took charge of the* Titanic.

Hulton Getty/Tony Stone Images

Four years later, the *Olympic* was launched. The *Titanic* followed soon afterward in 1912. Because these ships cost so much and were so big, strong, and carefully built, people believed they could not sink.

Pirrie was not aboard the *Titanic* for its maiden voyage, so he's not as well known to *Titanic* buffs as Ismay, who survived the disaster, and Andrews, who was lost with the ship he designed. Ironically, Pirrie and his company, Harland and Wolff, increased business after the sinking. At that time, many new ships were built to conform to new rules laid down to prevent more accidents.

The Sunken Survivor

Ismay has become a villain in many stories about the sinking of the *Titanic*. Some say he was to blame for the speed of the ship at the time of the accident, putting pressure on the captain to go fast for publicity. He sank even lower in popular estimation just for surviving.

Bad Press

Blow Me Down!
The *Titanic* sank on Ismay's 50th birthday. He was vilified in the press as "J. Brute Ismay." The *New York American* facetiously suggested, as a jab at Ismay, "that the emblem of the White Star Line be changed from a white star to a white liver."

The truth about how Ismay was saved is hard to know, because there are so many conflicting stories. Second Officer Lightoller said he was picked up and dumped into a lifeboat by Officer Wilde. Others say he got into a boat by shoving women and children out of the way. Still others said he ordered a boat for himself to be manned by experienced oarsmen to make extra certain of his own safety. His own claim was that there were no passengers around when what he thought was the last lifeboat (it was really the second-to-last) was being lowered, so he just stepped in.

Whatever happened, the very fact that he—the president of White Star—was saved in a lifeboat when so many passengers perished created a scandal. He was vilified in newspapers all over America. In fact, he probably realized what he was in for when he stepped into lifeboat "C."

Playing Dumb?

After the disaster, he avoided responsibility for the accident and for the survivors as much as he could. He made no attempt to explain what had happened or to see that the survivors were taken care of. On board the *Carpathia*, the ship that picked up the lifeboats, Ismay holed up in the doctor's quarters and tried to stay away from people.

Ismay appeared surprisingly ignorant of just about everything to do with ships. He said he knew nothing about the design of the *Titanic* or the proper speed it should have been going given the conditions. He even said he didn't know whether his room on the *Titanic* was on the port or starboard side.

It may be that Ismay really was uninformed about such things. After all, he was somewhat of a figurehead whose job was simply to maintain White Star's appearance as a British line. It may also be that he was faking his ignorance to avoid responsibility. The less he seemed to know the less he could be blamed. A third explanation is that he may have become a little deranged by the whole experience. He surely understood his own position of responsibility, even as he failed to live up to it.

The Titanic *never made this return trip.*
Mariners' Museum

Ahoy There!

I may say that at the time Mr. Ismay did not seem to me to be in a mental condition to decide anything…He was obsessed with the idea, and kept repeating that he ought to have gone down with the ship because he found that some women had gone down. I told him there was no such reason; I told him a very great deal; I tried to get the idea out of his head, but he was taken with it.

—Second Officer Herbert Lightoller

Learning the Lesson

Although Ismay became a scapegoat in the *Titanic* tragedy, government and industry officials recognized more general, widespread factors leading to the disaster. In response to the big sinking, new laws were passed requiring more lifeboats and stricter use of wireless. The sinking of the *Titanic* also gave rise to an important safety organization, the International Ice Patrol, which is still at work today monitoring ice in the North Atlantic to ensure the safety of oceangoing vessels.

The Least You Need to Know

➤ Steamships developed gradually over the century preceding the launch of the *Titanic*.

➤ Awareness of shipping hazards did not keep up with developing shipping technology.

➤ Tycoon J.P. Morgan bought out White Star Line as part of his attempt to start up a shipping trust.

➤ The *Titanic* was built in an atmosphere of intense competition among shipping companies.

➤ White Star Director J. Bruce Ismay faced severe criticism for choosing not to go down with the *Titanic*.

Building a Legend

The *Titanic* wasn't just big, it had all the bells and whistles. With its size came room to include all kinds of amenities, both for running the ship and for accommodating passengers in high style. Harland and Wolff, the company that built her, spared no expense to make the ship the sharpest thing on the waves.

The times were right for building ships like the *Titanic*. There was lots of demand for transportation by wealthy vacationers, businesspeople, and poor immigrants. Commercial airlines, which would later supplant ocean liners, were still far in the future. Technological advances allowed bigger ships and more convenient ways to take care of large numbers of passengers. And government was receptive to big enterprises like huge ships, which made them potentially profitable investments, to say the least.

Even so, although the time was ripe for big ships in many ways, people still had a lot to learn about getting safely across the Atlantic. They found out the hard way when, to everyone's shock and dismay, the *Titanic* sank, brand new and yet to break in all of its boilers.

The Big Three

The *Titanic* was the second of three ships built according to similar plans, intended to make staggered weekly departures back and forth between Ireland and America. The other two were the *Olympic* and the *Britannic* (the *Britannic* was originally to be named the *Gigantic*). The three are often referred to as the Olympic-class liners.

Anchors Aweigh!

Each one was an engineering feat. First the *Olympic*, and then the *Titanic*, were the largest man-made objects ever to move. What's more, they were equipped with lots of interesting gadgets. Trade journals at the time were full of features on how these ships were designed and built.

They used seven horses to carry the Olympic's *anchor to port.*
Ulster Folk & Transport Museum

The *Olympic* launched on October 20, 1910; the *Titanic* hit the water on May 31 of the following year. 100,000 spectators turned out, including J.P. Morgan himself. The *Britannic* followed in 1914, just in time for World War I. It was converted to a hospital ship and was sunk possibly by a mine or a torpedo. It was never used commercially. Recent investigations by Robert Ballard of Woods Hole Oceanographic Institute and an international expedition reveal that hull damage was blown outward, indicating a possible internal explosion aboard the *Brittanic*.

> **Lifesavers**
> The *Britannic* sunk more quickly than the *Titanic*—in under 60 minutes. Although she had about 1,100 on board, only 30 or so lives were lost. New attitudes towards the importance of lifeboats, adopted since the sinking of the *Titanic*, helped make a difference.

Old Reliable

The *Olympic* had the most illustrious career of the three ships. It ran successfully for years as a passenger steamer before being converted to a troop carrier during the war. During its military service it withstood attacks by German submarines. It even sank one sub by ramming it before it could submerge. The nickname "Old Reliable" was accorded the *Olympic* due to its many years of trouble-free service.

Soon after the war, the *Olympic*'s engines were converted to burn diesel instead of coal. In fact, it was the first big steamship to make this change. As a diesel-burning liner, it resumed its business of transporting passengers for more than 15 years before it was scrapped in 1935. By this time, White Star had merged with its arch-rival Cunard, and the new company was updating its fleet and getting rid of some of its older ships.

In the Works

The *Olympic* and the *Titanic* were built in the Belfast Queen's Island shipyard by Harland and Wolff. The shipyard was built on land that was piled up after Belfast Harbor was dredged to let bigger ships pass through in the 1840s. The shipyard was originally built by Robert Hickson and Company, which began making iron ships in 1853. A year later, Edward J. Harland came aboard as a manager. He took over the business in 1859. He joined forces with G.W. Wolff two years later and Harland and Wolff was born.

When the *Titanic* and *Olympic* were under construction, the shipyard had enough room to build eight ships at once. Prior to that, there was room for nine, but the two new liners were so big, they each required the building space of two ordinary ships. These building spaces—ships' garages, in effect—are known as *slips*. The *Titanic* was built in slip #3.

> **Catch the Drift**
> A **slip** is an enclosure in which a ship is built. Ships are built differently than cars. At the time, Henry Ford was perfecting the assembly line as a way of making lots of cars in a single space. In contrast, each ship is built in its own slip.

The Titanic *under construction in slip #3.*
Photofest

Harland and Wolff had to make additional changes in their shipyard in order to build Ti and Oly. They enlarged the steel workshop and built a new workshop for building the boilers. The shipbuilders weren't the only people who had to make changes to accommodate the big liners. A new dock had to be built in New York so they could load and unload. Shipping financier J.P. Morgan had to pull a few strings to get the city to pay for it!

On an Even Keel

Some 14,000 workers were employed at Harland and Wolff while Ti and Oly were built. Of these, somewhere from 3,000 to 4,000 worked full time on the big twins. Typical workmen were paid about two pounds per 49-hour week—with no paid vacations, and don't even think about a retirement plan! Even so, they were well paid in comparison with other shipbuilders. In fact, H&W had a waiting list of people wanting to work for them.

Harland and Wolff workers pose with two of the Titanic's *three propellers.*
Library of Congress

A Fitting Start

Work on the *Titanic* started March 31, 1909. The hull was put together on dry land, starting with the *keel*, the part that runs lengthwise along the bottom in the very center of the ship. Next, the frame of the hull was attached, a process completed in April of 1910. Six months later, the hull plates were put on. All this required an enormous scaffolding with moving platforms called a *gantry*. In fact, the gantry used for building Ti and Oly was the largest ever built.

Catch the Drift
The **keel** of a ship is, in effect, the breast bone—the bottom-most part running the length of the ship in the very center. A **gantry** is the bridge-like scaffolding used in shipbuilding that enables work to be done on the inside and outside of the hull.

SOS
It took 10 months for the *Titanic* to be fitted out, compared with only seven months for the *Olympic*. This is because Harland and Wolff interrupted work on the Ti in order to do some repairs on the *Olympic*, which was damaged when hit by the cruiser *Hawke*. Although it looked like the *Hawke* lost control and rammed the Oly, judges decided that the bigger ship sucked the smaller vessel into its wake and hence, was responsible.

At this point, framed and plated, the *Titanic* wasn't finished, but was ready to be launched and outfitted. The ship was slid into the water on runners extending 772 to the ocean. The runners were greased with 22 tons of tallow and soap, slathered on an inch thick. This sled ride to the sea took one minute and two seconds, coming off without a hitch with 100,000 watching.

Instead of the gantry used to build the ship on dry land, the fitting out required a huge, 200-ton floating crane, which could lift three quarters of its own weight 150 feet in the air. As big as it was, it still needed to do a lot of lifts to get the *Titanic* ready to roll.

Finishing Touches

The first stop was the graving dock. The propellers hadn't been put on yet, so tugboats were used, showing why they call 'em tugboats. At the graving dock, the ship was completed; the decks were put in, the props put on, and the electrical equipment installed, along with everything down to the wood paneling and carpeting in the first-class dining room. This process is known as fitting out.

During fitting out, some of the plans for the *Titanic* were modified, making it somewhat different from the *Olympic*. The infamous J. Bruce Ismay himself decided that the *Olympic* had too much deck space. He gave the order for excess deck space aboard the *Titanic* to be converted to additional berths for passengers.

Ismay also decided that the *Olympic*'s first-class reception room and dining saloon weren't big enough, and gave word for the *Titanic* to be altered accordingly. Other improvements over the *Olympic* were also built into the *Titanic*, including better carpeting, better paneling, better furniture, and better protection of the first-class decks from wind and rain. And one more egregious oversight was corrected—cigar holders were installed in the first-class bathrooms!

As a result of all of these changes, the *Titanic* ended up weighing about a thousand tons more than the *Olympic*. It could also hold up to 163 more passengers—mostly in first class. All in all, this made the *Titanic* the biggest ship floating, as well as the most luxurious.

The White Star Line's New Triple-screw Steamers
"OLYMPIC" ☆ "TITANIC"
LARGEST AND FINEST IN THE WORLD
(SEE OVER)

The Titanic *stands on tip-toe in this White Star ad.*
Ralph White/Corbis

Long Tall Ti

As you may have heard, the *Titanic* was big. How big was it?

➤ **852¹/₂ feet long** That's about a sixth of a mile, longer than the Singer Building is tall.

➤ **92¹/₂ feet wide** Okay, so it was a skinny ship.

➤ **175 feet high** From the keel to the top of the funnels.

➤ **46,328 tons** This was its registered weight.

➤ **52,310 tons displacement** This is the weight of the water that had to move out of the way when the *Titanic* was sitting in it.

Blow Me Down!
Among the features built into the *Titanic* that were absent on the *Olympic* were two first-class suites, which cost over $4,000 for one-way passage. One of these was built with J.P. Morgan in mind, who was planning to board the *Titanic* for its maiden voyage, but canceled due to illness.

What's more, the *Titanic* had four funnels, each with a diameter of 22 feet; three anchors, with an average weight of over 10 tons each; and a 101-ton rudder. This was so big it had to be cast in six different pieces.

Ahoy There!

Competition between the great shipping companies…has been very keen, and efforts to secure pre-eminence have been quickly followed by the endeavors of rival lines to "go one better." In this respect, the White Star Line…has always been in the first rank since the company was formed in 1869, and the building of the Olympic and Titanic makes it evident that the characteristic policy of enterprise and foresight is being worthily maintained.

—*The Shipbuilder,* 1911

Bells and Whistles

The *Titanic* had eight steel decks, counting the boat deck. There were also the Orlop and Lower Orlop decks, but these were at the bottom of the ship and were not full decks. All of these were serviced by four 50-horsepower electrical generators, which powered lights and machinery throughout the ship and produced 16,000 amps. These generators ran all the ship's gizmos: the ship's four elevators, the wireless apparatus, the switchboard that could handle 50 phones, the pumps, the refrigerators, the steam evaporators, the electric heaters, the clocks, the eight electric cargo cranes and winches, the electrical slicers and dicers in the four modern kitchens, and even the electric showers. They also powered the famous watertight doors. *Titanic* also carried a pair of auxiliary 30KW generator sets and was illuminated throughout by 10,000 incandescent lights.

Blow Me Down!
The electrical showers on board the *Titanic* consisted of enclosed coffin-sized wooden boxes through which water was pumped. To take a shower in one, you would lie down in it with your head sticking out!

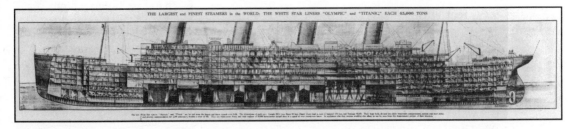

The Titanic *shows off its layered look in this illustration.*
Mariners' Museum

Good Intentions

The 12 watertight doors were a safety innovation that might have been just the thing if the *Titanic* had been damaged in a more ordinary way. They might have helped keep the ship afloat by closing off one or two of the 16 watertight compartments from the others. By design, the ship would have been able to stay afloat with any two of these compartments flooded. Unfortunately, the iceberg that ripped open the *Titanic*'s hull let water into five compartments. From there it was downhill all the way.

How Bad Can It Be?

The designers were thinking that the worst that could happen was for the ship to collide head-on with something big and hard, or to be rammed in the side—"broadsided"— by another ship. Had this happened, it would have let water into only one or two compartments.

The doors could be closed all at once by flipping a switch located on the *bridge*. They could also be closed manually, one at a time as needed. They could also close automatically. This was supposed to happen when a compartment filled with water, triggering a release mechanism. Each compartment had a ladder leading to a hatch in the top so no one would be trapped inside when the doors closed.

The watertight compartments were kept that way by 15 *bulkheads*—partitions on the ship. The bulkheads towards the bow and stern extended up through five decks. Those amidships (the center of the ship), extended up through four decks, about 10 feet above the water line. This turned out not to be high enough to keep water from spreading throughout the ship after it hit the iceberg. That was because the water filling the compartments dragged the bow down into the sea until water flowed over the bulkheads.

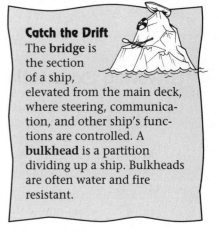

Catch the Drift
The **bridge** is the section of a ship, elevated from the main deck, where steering, communication, and other ship's functions are controlled. A **bulkhead** is a partition dividing up a ship. Bulkheads are often water and fire resistant.

Getting to the Bottom

The *Titanic* had a double-plated bottom. This was a special feature not found in most ships, although it was not unique to the Ti. In fact, the Ti's designers could have gone all out and double reinforced the sides, as had been done on some other ships. This would have taken away from space in the boiler room, however, so the sides were not as thick as they might have been. Too bad!

The bottom was five feet three inches thick throughout the ship except for the engine room, where it was a foot thicker. It contained cells that could be filled with water in order to level out the ship if it listed (tilted to one side) as a result of unevenly loaded cargo.

Coming to Power

On the double bottom of the *Titanic* rested 29 boilers, heated by coal furnaces. Twenty-four of these were bubbling away when the Ti steamed up against the iceberg that sank it. These boilers produced the steam that drove the ship's three engines.

Blow Me Down!
The inventor of the turbine engine used in steamers was Charles Parsons. He created a stir in 1897 when he steered his ship, *Turbinia,* among a fleet of British warships at an unimaginable 34 knots. The inventor intended his disruptive antics to draw attention to the power of his invention.

Two of the engines were of the reciprocating variety. In a reciprocating engine, the steam pushes alternating sets of pistons up and down to turn a crankshaft. The third engine, in the center, was a turbine engine. In this kind of engine, the steam pushes a circular, slanted blade around and around. Interestingly, the turbine engine ran on steam that was left over from the other two engines.

Together, these engines kicked out 50,000 horsepower—a lot, but not enough to set speed records. The smaller, speedier Cunard ships—the *Mauretania* and *Lusitania*—ran at 70,000 hp. Each engine was attached by a shaft to its own propeller. When the *Titanic* hit the iceberg and came to a stop, a number of passengers suspected that the ship had simply popped a prop.

Lowering Expectations

One new (but sadly underutilized) feature of the *Titanic* was its state-of-the-art davits—the pulley mechanisms for holding and lowering lifeboats. These were specially designed by the Welin Davit Company of Sweden in order to hold more than the usual number of lifeboats. In fact, the *Titanic*'s davits were equipped to carry over twice the number of boats it actually had on board.

The davits generally worked well for the boats that were lowered. One problem occurred, however, when one of the boats scraped against the side of the ship because the ship was leaning sideways. The davits themselves, however, proved strong enough to safely lower full lifeboats.

Unfortunately, not all the officers loading them realized this at first, so they were reluctant to fill them to capacity. The officers were not informed of the tests that had been conducted on the new davits by Harland and Wolff. In these tests, they successfully held boats chock full of burly workers.

Just One Thing Missing

The builders of the *Titanic* spared no expense in making it as luxurious and as modern as they could. Strength, power, size, elegance, and convenience were all part of the package. Everyone just assumed that safety went along with these other things. By virtue of its size and the expense of its construction, the general feeling was that the ship was unsinkable. It didn't take long for the world to find out otherwise.

The Least You Need to Know

➤ The *Titanic* was the second of three sister ships built according to similar specifications. The first was the *Olympic* and the third was the *Britannic*.

➤ The *Olympic* was the most successful of the three, running until it was scrapped in 1935.

➤ The *Titanic* became the largest ship afloat by virtue of additions and improvements made on the original *Olympic* design.

➤ The *Titanic* had a double-thick bottom, but not double-thick sides.

➤ The watertight bulkheads extended 10 feet above the water line, but not all the way to the top.

➤ The davits were capable of working better than the officers may have realized.

A Sea Full of Shipwrecks

Sometimes it's nice to know that no matter how bad things are, you're not alone. If misery loves company, those made miserable by shipwrecks have had a lot of what they love. It can help put the *Titanic* disaster in perspective to think about some of the other steamships that have ended up on the bottom of the sea.

The *Dictionary of Disasters at Sea During the Age of Steam*, which covers the period from 1824–1962, has thousands and thousands of entries. Before this, thousands and thousands more seagoing vessels were lost. The ocean is a dangerous place and all kinds of things can go wrong—bad weather, bad planning, bad navigation, bad leadership, war, mutiny, and piracy all contribute to the long list of the lost.

There are hundreds of shipwreck stories. Many were told as popular tales back in the days before radio and television; others made headline news. This chapter has just a few of the famous ones. The stories show that, when things go wrong at sea, they really go wrong.

Catch the Drift
A **frigate** is traditionally a medium-size sailing ship, traditionally used for war from the 1600s through the 1800s.

At Sea

One of the most pitiful disasters in all of seagoing history was the running aground of the *Medusa*, a French *frigate* bound for colonies in Africa in 1816 in the wake of the Napoleonic wars. The *Medusa* was not a steamer, but the story shows what can happen when the captain and officers don't look out for those on board. Damage to the ship was slight, and danger not very great, but leadership was in seriously short supply. Next to those in charge of the *Medusa*, J. Bruce Ismay looks like a gallant and selfless hero.

Land Lubber at the Helm

In charge of those on board was a governor who was not a seaman. On a strange whim, he placed control of the vessel in the hands of an inexperienced citizen, who proceeded to steer the ship into shallows well off the African coast. The tide came in and the ship floated free for a moment, but the man in charge was unable to find the way back to safe sailing, and the ship ran aground again.

This time, the hull was damaged and water leaked in, although not enough to sink the ship. The actual captain was curiously uninvolved in much of this. According to some accounts, he was preoccupied with his mistress at the time. In any case, once the damage was done, the captain and governor decided to abandon ship and strike out for shore in the lifeboats.

An Unkind Cut

There was room in the boats for only about 250 of the more than 400 aboard the ship, so a large raft was built for the rest. The plan was for the boats to tow the raft ashore, some 60 miles away. One hundred forty-seven climbed onto the raft, which had been hastily lashed together and failed to keep anyone but those at the very center anything close to dry. Seventeen stayed aboard the wreck.

The makeshift ferry didn't get far before the line attached to the captain's boat gave way. The captain later claimed it broke, although it was probably cut. In any case, the captain had given up responsibility for the fate of those aboard the vessel long before the raft was built. Outrageously, the other boats followed suit and dropped their lines. Now 147 people were left to drift.

The raft floated helplessly on the open sea for 12 days. The number of survivors rapidly diminished due to exposure, hunger, thirst, treachery, and despair. What's more, the raft turned out to be neither big nor strong enough for all of its passengers, and many were swept overboard and drowned.

Numerous fights broke out, as tempers became agitated by fear and wine. Those left alive eventually resorted to cannibalism. By the time the raft was saved by a ship, only 15 men were left alive. Of these, five died shortly after the rescue.

Meanwhile the lifeboats made it safely to shore. Belatedly, a ship was sent to look for those who remained on board the *Medusa*—and to salvage any goods still on board. They didn't find the wreck until more than seven weeks after it had been abandoned.

Blow Me Down!
The Raft of the "Medusa" is the title and subject of a famous painting by the neo-classic French painter Theodore Gericault. This dramatic depiction of helpless drifting hangs in the Louvre Museum in Paris.

Of the 17 who had been left, only three were still alive. Twelve had built a second raft and were lost trying to make it to shore. Another floated off on a chicken coup and perished. One more died on the wreck. The three remaining evidently survived in spite of one another, keeping to separate corners of the ship.

Two of these died shortly after their rescue. The third let on that he had damaging information about the incident and was subsequently murdered in his bed. The murderer was never found out. All in all, not a pretty story.

Standing Firm

More inspiring is the story of the *Birkenhead*. The actions of the captain and crew of the *Birkenhead* set a seagoing precedent that was foremost in the minds of the *Titanic* officers as they loaded the lifeboats "women and children first."

Flash Flood

The *Birkenhead* was a paddle steamer, built in 1845, used for troop transport during the colonial Kaffir wars in South Africa. She carried close to 640 people including the crew. Most of the passengers were noncommissioned officers. There were 25 women and 31 children on board.

Lifesavers
Frederick IV, the king of Prussia, had an account of the *Birkenhead* incident read to his regiments as a lesson in heroism. The English writer Rudyard Kipling celebrated the event in a poem called "Soldier and Sailor Too."

Off the coast of Cape Town at close to 2:00 in the morning, the *Birkenhead* ran into an uncharted rock. A hole was opened in the hull where many of the troops were sleeping, and water rushed in so quickly, and the way out was so small, that most of them were drowned. The rest of the passengers and crew scrambled on deck.

Coming Apart at the Seams

The captain ordered the pumps to be set working and the boats lowered. There were only eight lifeboats—not nearly enough for everyone on board. While the crew was loading the boats, the sea continued to drive the ship against the rocks until, only 10 minutes after the first collision, the ship broke in two. One of the funnels collapsed onto the deck, killing a number of crewmen.

Lifesavers
Among the army officers who gave orders to the troops to stand still were Major Seton of the 74th Highlanders and Captain Edward Wright of the 91st Queen's Regiment.

To make loading operations even more difficult, many horses were on board, and they started to panic. They had to be corralled off the ship into the sea, where they were attacked by sharks.

Standing for Courage

Three lifeboats were launched, one of which contained all the women and children on board. The rest were destroyed or capsized and were of no use. As the ship continued to break apart, the captain released the men of their duty, yelling "Every man for himself." Fearing the crowded lifeboats would be rushed and swamped, however, the officers in charge of the troops countermanded the captain, giving the order to stand pat. Only three men broke for the lifeboats. The rest remained in their ranks on deck.

SOS
Some critics have countered the hoopla elicited by the *Birkenhead* incident by pointing out that the brave soldiers who stood their ground may not have realized that the ship was going to sink. In contrast, the seamen—who had a better idea of the danger they were facing—made it into the lifeboats in higher proportions.

The ship sank 25 minutes after hitting the rock, as those in the lifeboats watched. All those in lifeboats were saved. In addition, 68 men saved themselves by clinging to floating wreckage. Forty others climbed the mast and were able to wait until help came. The rest were drowned or killed by sharks; 445 were lost and 193 were saved. Queen Victoria had a tablet put up in front of Chelsea Hospital inscribed with the names of all those who went down with the *Birkenhead*.

Smoke on the Water

The *Birkenhead* story shows that following orders can be a good thing. This is only true, however, when the orders are good. Sometimes, captain and crew try some pretty stupid things, as in the case of the passenger steamer *Austria*, a German HAPAG liner built in 1857 that was lost loaded with immigrants on their way to America. The ship was destroyed not by bad weather or a collision, but by an accident on board.

On September 2, 1858, the *Austria* left Hamburg. Like the *Titanic*, she made a stop in Southampton to pick up more passengers before heading west across the Atlantic. Altogether, the people on board numbered 538.

The ship had a fairly serious problem with vermin, so the ship's surgeon asked the captain to order that steerage be fumigated by dipping a red hot chain into a bucket of tar. Steam from the tar, it was hoped, would take care of whatever it was that was eating the passengers.

The hot chain turned out to be too hot and set the tar on fire, then the seaman dropped the chain and knocked the bucket over. Flaming tar spilled onto a mattress and fire spread until the whole steerage was in flames. Many of the crew were suffocated by the smoke. Confusion spread with the flames and many passengers jumped overboard.

SOS

So many of the crew of the *Austria* were suffocated by smoke, there weren't enough left to control the ship. She kept steaming along with the engines at half speed and no one at the wheel!

The ship was equipped with a fire hose, but unfortunately this had to be connected to a lead pipe to draw water from the sea, and the lead melted before it could be used. Only a few lifeboats could be launched before the ship's magazine exploded; 471 drowned or burned and only 67 were saved by passing ships.

On the Rocks

The first of a number of major White Star Line disasters was the foundering of the *Atlantic*, a steamer equipped with sails built by Harland and Wolff in 1871. The *Atlantic*, in fact, was one of the first White Star ships. She left Liverpool on March 20, 1873, with passengers—mostly immigrants—and crew totaling 931.

Angry Seas

The weather was bad for almost the entire crossing. On top of this, the ship was quite narrow and didn't stand up to rough weather very well. Attempting to steer out of the high winds, the captain changed course by heading northerly towards Halifax. On the stormy steers, the vessel lost its bearings as it approached the rocky coast of Nova Scotia.

Catch the Drift

A sailing ship's **rigging** consists of the ropes, chains, and other equipment that are used for maneuvering the masts and sails.

At 3:00 in the dark morning of April 1st, the *Atlantic* was steaming at full speed and crashed on some rocks near Meagher Island off the Nova Scotia coast. The sea was so rough that lifeboats were ripped from the ship and broken to pieces. One of the booms came loose and swung wildly from side to side, making things extremely dangerous on deck. The captain ordered the passengers to climb up into the *rigging*, beyond the reach of the high waves, to wait for rescue. The sea couldn't reach them, but they suffered from severe winds and bitter cold.

In the pounding surf, three crewman swam 150 yards to a rock, carrying a line tied to the ship. They secured the other end, enabling more crewmen to cross with more lines. Five lines were strung in all, providing a tenuous chance of escape from the battered ship. Only the hardiest—371—were able to pull themselves to safety along the ropes. Those who were too cold or too tired—560—were lost.

Damn the Torpedoes!

One of the finest ships of the Cunard Line was the *Lusitania*. Built in 1907, she remained in use as a passenger ship even after the start of World War I, making the North Atlantic run between Liverpool and New York five times without incident. On the return voyage of the sixth trip, as the *Lusitania* was nearing the coast of Ireland, Captain W.J. Turner received wireless warnings that German submarines (U-boats) were in St. George's channel, the narrow body of water between Ireland and Wales. The *Lusitania* was to steam through this channel on its way to Liverpool.

Ahoy There!

Travelers intending to embark for an Atlantic voyage are reminded that a state of war exists between Germany and her allies and Great Britain and her allies; that the zone of war includes the water adjacent to the British Isles, that…vessels flying the flag of Great Britain or any of her allies are liable to destruction in those waters; and that travelers sailing in the war-zone…do so at their own risk.

—Imperial German Embassy notice posted in New York newspapers, May 1, 1915, the day the *Lusitania* embarked on her final voyage from New York.

The first warning came on May 5, with subsequent warnings on the 6th and 7th. At 12:40 p.m. on the 7th, the captain altered course to steer clear of the subs, until he received word of submarine sightings behind him. At this point, believing he was in the clear, he got back on course.

At 2:15 in the afternoon, the ship was hit in the side by a torpedo. The engines failed immediately; one of the boilers evidently exploded. The ship carried on a little way under its momentum, but soon began listing to starboard and sinking. The list was severe enough to make the lifeboats difficult to launch, and there was very little time to lower them. The ship sank only 15 minutes after being hit.

Close to 1,200 people were lost, including 124 Americans, 291 women, and 94 children. 761 were saved—some by the ship's own lifeboats, others by the trawler *Bluebell*, which happened to be nearby. The German Navy was criticized not only by Britain and British allies, but by neutral countries as well.

Blast the Luck

One sea disaster was so bad, it killed many people on land! This was the collision of the French steamer *Mont Blanc* with the Norwegian steamer *Imo*. The *Mont Blanc* was headed to Halifax from New York with a cargo of 5,000 tons of powerful explosives. On December 6, 1917, the French steamer had nearly reached its destination and was steaming through the channel into port. Coming through the channel in the other direction was the *Imo*.

Hit or Miss

The weather was clear and the two ships spotted each other from two miles away. Yet, somehow, they got their signals crossed and bumped into each other at half speed. Under ordinary circumstances, the collision would not have been serious at all, prompting, at most, some angry international cursing. Even so, disaster might have been avoided.

The captain of the *Mont Blanc* actually had time to turn his ship to take the impact in the forward hold, which contained benzene, a flammable substance, but not one that explodes on impact. In fact, the collision did not cause an explosion—immediately. Instead, it set off a chain reaction.

Bad Chemistry

The benzene leaked and spilled onto a supply of picric acid stowed below, which caught fire. The optimistic crew tried to put the fire out. The smart thing to do, however, would have been to sink the ship immediately. By the time the crew realized that they would be unable to put out the fire and save the ship, it was too late to do anything but take to the lifeboats and row for it.

The lifeboats actually made it to shore. By then, about 20 minutes had passed since the *Mont Blanc* and the *Imo* bumped. At that point, the fire on board the French ship reached the main cargo hold, filled with thousands of tons of TNT.

> **Blow Me Down!**
> The sinking of *Lusitania* created a serious international scandal and may have played a role in the decision of the U.S. to enter World War I.

> **Blow Me Down!**
> Some sea disasters have yet to be explained. The famous brigantine *Mary Celeste* was found off the coast of Gibraltar in 1872. She was completely seaworthy, but not a soul was aboard. Fifty years later, the schooner *Carroll A. Deering* was found off Cape Hatteras, North Carolina. The only ones aboard were two cats!

The explosion was so powerful, it picked the *Imo* up out of the water and blew it all the way to shore across the harbor from Halifax. Halifax itself, however, took the brunt of the explosion. Thousands of people were buried in their houses, which collapsed with the force of the explosion, or were flayed by flying glass.

Casualties were enormous: 1,500 were reported killed, 2,000 were missing and 8,000 injured; 3,000 houses were destroyed, as well as a good number of ships in the harbor.

"EVERY ATTENTION GIVEN TO THE COMFORT AND SAFETY OF OUR PASSENGERS."

NEPTUNE.—You ought to go slower, my friend; there are many dangers about you!
TRANS-ATLANTIC CAPTAIN OF THE PERIOD.—Can't help it; I'm bound to make the fastest trip on record, and don't you forget it!

Some things go in one ear and out the other.
Mary Evans Picture Library

One of a Kind

Despite the number of disasters that have occurred down through the history of ships, the *Titanic* stands out as especially significant. The *Titanic* disaster wasn't the biggest in terms of loss of life, or in terms of lost property. There was no obvious negligence or malice on the part of an individual or group leading to the disaster. Instead, what sets the *Titanic* apart is the fact that its loss was so unexpected. Prior to the *Titanic*, most people went to sea realizing the danger. Those on board the *Titanic* steamed off thinking nothing bad could happen.

The Least You Need to Know

➤ One of the most horrible stories in seagoing history is the tale of the *Medusa*.

➤ The troops on board the *Birkenhead* have become models for discipline in the face of danger.

➤ The *Austria* caught fire and went down as a result of a badly botched fumigation.

➤ White Star's *Atlantic* steamed off course and was wrecked on rocks off Nova Scotia.

➤ Cunard's *Lusitania* was a passenger liner sunk by a torpedo during World War I.

Part 3
Cruisin' for a Bruisin'

The icy heart of the Titanic story, of course, is the run-in with the iceberg. As simple as this basic fact may seem, there were a surprising number of contributing factors that led to the collision. After the collision took place, the situation determining who was saved and how was equally complex, and historians have been debating the circumstances ever since.

Chapter 9

The Tip of the Iceberg

They knew what it was; they were experienced and had traveled the North Atlantic before. They knew it was out there; it was the right time of year, and there were warnings indicating a specific area. They knew it could cause trouble; other ships had been badly damaged in recent memory. They thought they could steer around it. They were wrong.

When the *Titanic* shipped off for America, the seagoing world hadn't really faced up to the dangers frozen water represented to the new, faster steamers. Other, more dramatic, perils of the sea had been practically eliminated by the big steamships. Shipping seemed safer than ever, and those involved were too busy congratulating themselves to worry about mere chunks of ice drifting around.

The details leading up to the disaster are not unusual: Things were pretty much business as usual aboard the *Titanic*. The irony is that such a catastrophe could result from a such an ordinary series of events.

Anchors Aweigh!

After the *Titanic* was fitted out at the graving dock at Harland and Wolff, it went for a test run in Belfast Lough. British Board of Trade inspectors paid it over 2,000 visits to make sure everything was ship shape. With the OK of the BOT, it steamed off to its first stop at Southampton.

Arriving in Southampton on April 2, 1912, the Ti picked up supplies, crew, cargo, and its first passengers. Many of the crew, including Captain Smith, were from Southampton; *Titanic* was a major source of jobs for the town.

All Hopped Up

A crucial—and scarce—supply at the time was coal. A big coal strike had been going on, so there wasn't enough to go around. The *Titanic* would burn 650 tons every day. Just to be sure of having plenty, she stocked up on 6,000 tons for the journey.

To get enough coal for the *Titanic*, White Star had to cancel the voyages of some of its other ships—the *Oceanic* and the *Adriatic*—and dump their coal into the *Titanic*'s hoppers. Even a ship from another line, the *Philadelphia*, contributed coal to the *Titanic*. In what would prove to be a painful twist of fate, the passengers scheduled to depart on these ships embarked on the *Titanic* instead.

A Powerful Attraction

All that coal gave the Ti a lot of power. So much, in fact, that it created a huge suction as it steamed out of the harbor. This nearly caused an accident involving the *New York*, a liner sitting in the harbor, out of commission as a result of the coal strike.

Blow Me Down!
The suction produced by the wake of the *Titanic* was so strong, it dragged the wreck of a sunken barge 800 yards along the bottom of the harbor as it was leaving Southampton.

As the *Titanic* steamed passed, the steel hawsers anchoring the *New York* snapped and the ship was sucked toward the *Titanic* by its wake. Just in time, Captain Smith nudged the *Titanic* towards the wayward ship, producing a wave big enough to float the *New York* out of harm's way. The tug boats came on the scene and secured the drifting ship once more.

A similar occurrence took place earlier, when the cruiser *Hawke* was sucked in by the wake of the *Olympic* and collided with the bigger ship. The *Olympic* had to be taken to the graving dock for repairs.

A close call as the New York *drifts near the* Titanic.
Brown Brothers

Going with the Floe

The weather was fine for the start of *Titanic*'s maiden voyage and stayed fine right until the end. It had been warm enough that spring to melt a large number of icebergs loose from the glaciers of Greenland, where they drifted into the Labrador Current and into the North Atlantic shipping lanes.

The routes customarily taken by steamers changed every year with the season. Of the two main routes, the northern was more direct, but was also more likely to be obstructed by icebergs. The course of the *Titanic* was charted along the more southerly route. (Since the *Titanic* went down, the southerly route has been moved even farther south.)

SOS
There is a rumor that the *Titanic* actually took the more dangerous northern route to save time and energy because she was short on coal as a result of the coal strike. This is not true.

Cold, Hard Facts

The ice in icebergs is made of highly compacted snow. On average, this snow has been mashed into place over a period of about 3,000 years, becoming extremely rock-like. They can be huge—weighing as much as six million tons. The berg that sank the *Titanic* weighed about 500,000 tons. This is not enormous as icebergs go, but is still over 10 times the weight of the ship.

A North Atlantic berg like the one that sank the Titanic.
Topham/The Image Works

➤ **Iceberg** A large, floating piece of ice broken off from a glacier. "Berg" is Scandinavian for "mountain."

➤ **Growlers** Small icebergs under 15 feet high and 50 feet long.

➤ **Pack ice** Frozen sea water that has packed together over sizable stretches of the Polar Sea.

➤ **Ice floe** A large, flat body of ice.

➤ **Field ice** An especially large, field-size ice floe.

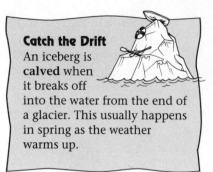

Catch the Drift
An iceberg is **calved** when it breaks off into the water from the end of a glacier. This usually happens in spring as the weather warms up.

➤ **Blue bergs and black bergs** Icebergs that appear blue or black as a result of having recently rolled over in the sea. Some experts doubt whether they actually exist.

Chips Off the Old Block

Icebergs that break off from glaciers are said to be *calved*, as if they were big animals being born. Anywhere from 10 to 15 thousand icebergs are calved by about 100 glaciers each year. Of these, about 1,000 a year make it into the shipping lanes.

Chilling Encounters

With all that ice out there, it wasn't unheard of for steamships to run into icebergs. At least three known steamer accidents took place before the *Titanic* called everyone's attention to the problem. And that's just the tip of the iceberg: No one knows how many other ships that were lost without a trace sank after colliding with ice.

Crushed Ice

The first of these accidents involved the liner *Arizona*. This ship was the largest liner in 1879, the year she plowed straight into a big berg off the coast of Newfoundland. Fortunately, the ship didn't sink and no one was killed. Her bow was completely crushed, however, and she had to hobble into port for some serious body work.

In 1907, North German Lloyd's *Kronprinz Wilhelm* dented its bow on an iceberg. This collision, like the ones involving the *Arizona* and the *Titanic*, took place at night. Another iceberg accident took place in foggy conditions. In 1911, the *Columbia* ran into a berg near Cape Race. The crash injured a passenger and a number of the crew, and seriously crushed the bow of the ship.

Despite their collisions, none of these ships sank and there were no fatalities. As a result, the shipping

SOS
Observers pointed to the *Arizona* collision as evidence of how hard it was to sink an ocean liner. Too bad they didn't look at it as evidence of how easy it was to run into an iceberg!

industry in general, and the captain and crew of the *Titanic* in particular, seem to have underestimated the danger posed by ice. It is very likely, however, that many ships had hit icebergs and sank without anyone's knowing. Before the invention of wireless, many ships simply disappeared without a trace. Ice may well have caused the disappearance of some of these ships.

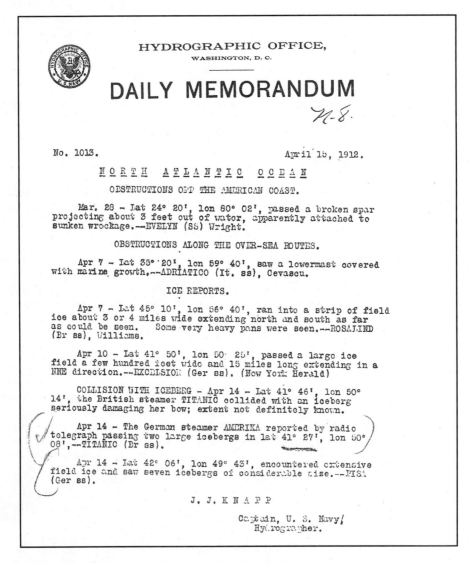

Ice reports recorded by the U.S. Navy, including one received by the Titanic.
National Archives

Icy Exchanges

In any case, no one seemed terribly concerned by the numerous ice warnings picked up by the *Titanic*'s wireless operators:

➤ The first warning came late afternoon on Friday, April 12, from the French liner, *Touraine*. There was ice over 1,000 miles ahead, and well north of the *Titanic*'s route. Officer Boxhall marked the site on the *Titanic*'s chart.

➤ The next warning came on the night of the 13th, not on wireless but on a Morse blinker from the *Rappahannock*. This ship had actually run into ice and got a dent in her bow and a bend in her rudder.

➤ The third warning came on the 14th at 9:00 in the morning from the Cunard liner, *Caronia*. The ship sent a wireless of "bergs, growlers, and field ice" up ahead. Officer Boxhall marked the location on the ship's chart and posted the note "ice" above the chart. Captain Smith gave the complete message to Officer Lightoller early that afternoon.

➤ At 11:40 that same morning, the Dutch liner *Noordan* warned of "much ice" in the same area. Captain Smith acknowledged the warning, but it is not known whether he posted the message for the officers.

➤ That same afternoon, at 1:42, White Star's *Baltic* warned of "icebergs and a large quantity of field ice 250 miles ahead." Captain Smith gave the note to White Star Director J. Bruce Ismay, and later read it to some passengers, Mrs. Thayer and Mrs. Ryerson. That evening, Captain Smith took the message back from Ismay, saying he wanted to post it for the officers. We don't know whether he did, in fact, post it.

➤ Just three minutes later, the German liner *Amerika* transmitted a wireless about two big bergs it had seen. This message was intended for the U.S. Hydrographic Office, but the *Amerika* didn't have the sending power to get the message all the way there, so the *Titanic* relayed it along. We don't know whether any of the *Titanic*'s officers saw this message.

➤ At 7:30 that evening, the *Californian* reported "three large bergs" 50 miles ahead of the *Titanic*. Wireless operator Harold Bride said he gave the warning to someone on the bridge, but did not know who it was.

➤ The last warning came at 9:40 that night, Sunday, April 14, exactly two hours before the *Titanic* ran into a berg. This message was sent by the liner *Mesaba*, reporting "much heavy pack ice and great number large icebergs, also field ice." The coordinates locating this ice defined an area that included the *Titanic*'s position at the time. In his memoirs years later, Lightoller said that Jack Phillips, the wireless operator who wrote down the message, told him as the ship was sinking that he simply stuck the warning underneath a paperweight and continued sending personal messages for the passengers.

Blow Me Down!
Wireless signals carry much farther at night than they do during the day. As a result, many personal messages to be sent from the *Titanic* were saved up and sent after sundown.

Catch the Drift
A crow's nest is the elevated part of the ship where the lookout stands. In sailing ships, the crow's nest may be attached to one of the masts. On the *Titanic*, the crow's nest was a high platform.

Blow Me Down!
Fleet recounted the events following his sighting of the iceberg in the U.S. Senate inquiry. His statement that Moody said "Thank you" made a big impression on the spectators. Some newspapers that featured Fleet's testimony used the words "Thank you" as a headline.

➤ There was, in addition, another message about ice from the *Californian*, a ship that had sent a warning earlier that evening. This new message, sent at 11:00 that night, was not so much an official warning, but some casual chit-chat from the *Californian's* wireless operator. He broke in on the *Titanic's* frequency and said "I say, old man, we're stopped and surrounded by ice." Jack Phillips, the *Titanic's* chief wireless operator responded: "Shut up, shut up, I'm busy. I'm working Cape Race." (Cape Race is a relay station in Nova Scotia.)

The Watch Runs Down

Despite the many warnings, the officers and crew of the *Titanic* took no special precautions to avoid icebergs the night of the collision. They maintained a cruising speed of about 22 knots, and the usual number of lookouts (two) were scheduled for duty. There were no special alerts given to the officers or lookouts. Instead, word of ice was passed along casually among some of the officers.

Captain Smith and Second Officer Lightoller remarked on the situation on the bridge at about 9:00 p.m. They agreed that the sea was a "flat calm." The weather was cold, but the sky was clear. There was no wind and no moon, but the stars were out. Just before going to his quarters, Smith told Lightoller to contact him if there was any change in the weather.

First Officer Murdoch replaced Lightoller on the bridge at 10:00 p.m. The two commented on the cold and Lightoller mentioned that the ship was approaching ice and passed along the captain's instructions to be awakened if the weather changed. He also mentioned the lookouts had been told to watch carefully for ice. Then Lightoller went off duty.

See No Evil

The *Titanic* employed a total of six trained lookouts who took turns working in pairs. Shifts lasted for two hours and lookouts got four hours off between shifts. Shifts were spent in the *crow's nest*, an elevated part of the ship that provides a 360-degree view of the horizon. The *Titanic's* crow's nest was equipped with a bell that could be rung by hand as a warning, and a telephone with which to call the officer in charge on the bridge.

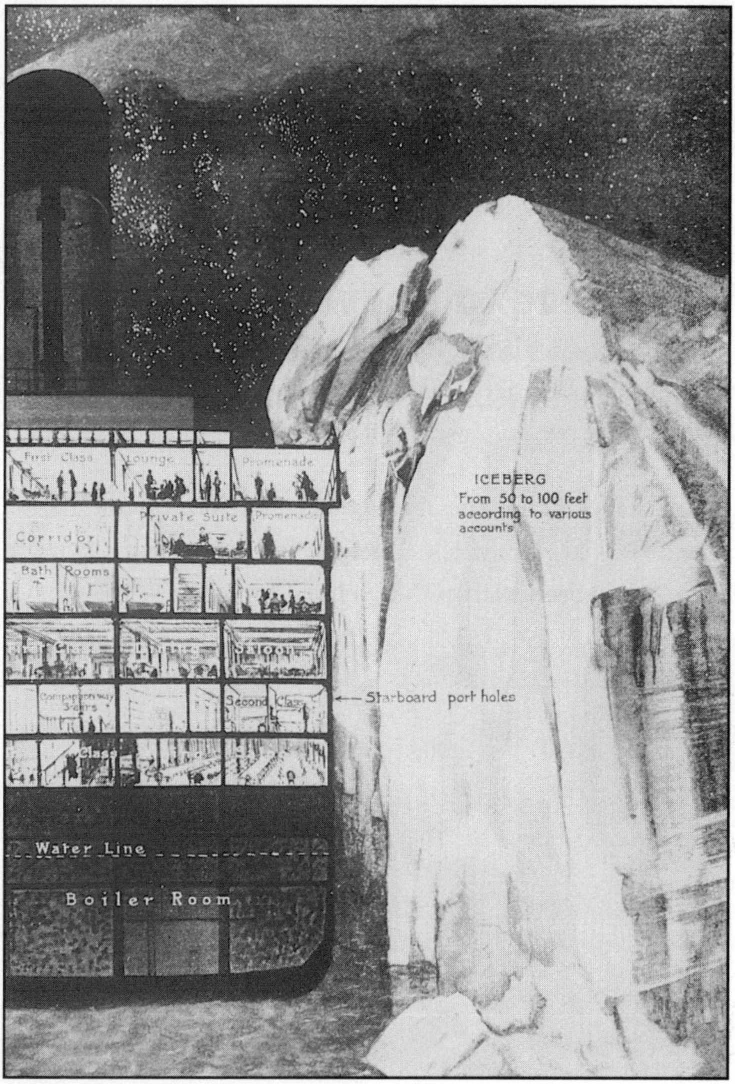
First Class
Lounge
Promenade
Private Suite
Promenade
Corridor
Bath Rooms
Second Class
ICEBERG
From 50 to 100 feet
according to various
accounts
Starboard port holes
Water Line
Boiler Room

The insides of the ship; the outside of the berg.
Illustrated London News/Archive Photos

The lookouts on duty at the time of the collision were Reginald Lee and Fred Fleet. It was Fleet who first spotted the iceberg. First he said to Lee, "There's ice ahead. Then he rang the bell three times by jerking the bellpull. Next he picked up the phone and called the bridge. The phone was answered promptly by Sixth Officer James Moody. "Iceberg right ahead," said Fleet. Moody said "Thank you."

Crunching Numbers

Calculations from tests later conducted on the *Olympic* indicate that the iceberg was just 500 yards away when Fleet spotted it. At a speed of about 22 knots, the *Titanic* was moving about 38 feet per second and reached the iceberg 37 seconds after the berg was sighted.

Then it hit.

The Least You Need to Know

➤ As the *Titanic* prepared to leave Southampton, many other steamers were delayed as a result of the coal strike. Their passengers were diverted to the Ti.

➤ The *Titanic's* wake was so powerful, it snapped the moorings of the steamship *New York*.

➤ The iceberg that sunk the *Titanic* weighed about 500,000 tons.

➤ The *Titanic* received eight wireless messages mentioning ice.

➤ The lookouts had been warned to watch out for ice.

Chapter 10

A Bad Scrape

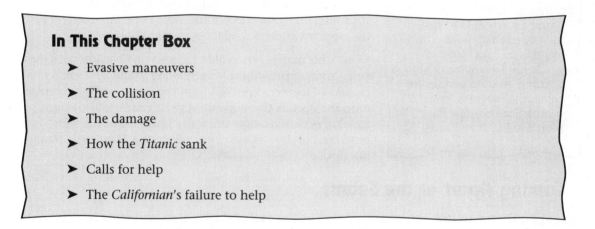

In This Chapter Box

➤ Evasive maneuvers

➤ The collision

➤ The damage

➤ How the *Titanic* sank

➤ Calls for help

➤ The *Californian*'s failure to help

If you've ever taken a dip in cold water, you may have noticed that it's easier to plunge right in than to slip in gradually. It's cold either way, but if you go slowly, you're only prolonging the agony! The *Titanic* sank slowly, a little at a time, over about two and a half hours. During this time, there wasn't a lot most people could do but grit their teeth and wait.

Many people involved with the *Titanic* disaster did their utmost to make a difference. Some officers loaded the lifeboats; others, together with the wireless operators, sent messages for help; the engineers kept the lights working; many passengers encouraged one another, prayed, or resigned themselves to their fate.

Unfortunately and mysteriously, some of those who were in the best position to be the most help did nothing. Although the wireless operators did all they could to signal for help, the only contacts they made were with ships too far away to save passengers who didn't make it into the lifeboats. One ship, the *Californian*, was quite close and might have arrived in time to rescue people in the water, if only the crew had realized what was going on.

SOS

Murdoch took the proper actions to avoid the iceberg and minimize the damage, but in retrospect different actions might have saved the ship. Had he kept the engines at full speed ahead, the rudder would have turned the ship more sharply. Alternatively, had he plowed straight into the iceberg, the ship probably would not have sunk; despite a jarring collision and serious damage to the bow, fewer compartments would have been flooded.

A Turn for the Worse

"Hard a-starboard," ordered First Officer Murdoch at the bridge, immediately upon hearing of the iceberg dead ahead. (This is the order to make a sharp left turn.) Quartermaster Robert Hitchens cranked the steering wheel, and the rudder bit in against the sea and the ship moved $22\frac{1}{2}$ degrees to port (the left).

Murdoch signaled the engine room: "Stop. Full speed astern." (This is the signal to cut the power going forward and blast off backward—the closest you can come in a steamship to slamming on the brakes.) At the same time, Murdoch flipped the electric switch closing the watertight doors.

Murdoch's maneuvers avoided a head-on collision with the berg. Instead, the ship skimmed along to the left. Some small chunks of ice were knocked from the upper part of the berg onto the deck as the ship edged past. The serious damage, though, occurred below the water line. Part of the berg jutted out under the water just where the *Titanic* was steaming through.

Coming Apart at the Seams

Under the surface, the iceberg opened up the hull of the big ship, and water started streaming in. There are a number of ideas about exactly how this happened. At first, on piecing together the evidence, it was thought that the iceberg opened a big gash in the steel plating of the hull, extending 100 yards along the starboard bow. Calculations at the time indicated that 16,000 gallons of water was coming in through the hull during the first 40 minutes of the disaster.

Since this theory was formulated, the wreck has been found at the bottom of the sea. The part of the hull that was damaged is buried under upwards of 50 feet of silt and mud on the ocean floor. Even though we can't see this part of the ship, sonar tests indicate six long slits *between* the steel hull plates.

What evidently happened was that the iceberg caused a number of the plates to bend sharply, popping the rivets that held them and allowing water to rush in. These rivets may have been made of a poor-quality iron, making them especially vulnerable to the force exerted by the bending plates.

Softly in the Night

The collision was not tremendously shocking. The ship vibrated somewhat for about 10 seconds, but did not lurch to one side or stop suddenly. Many who were asleep did not even wake up. Some heard a scraping noise. Some thought one of the ship's propellers had fallen off.

The captain was among those who sensed something funny had just taken place. He came out onto the bridge and got the bad news from Officer Murdoch. At that point, Fourth Officer Boxhall came on the scene, and the captain sent him below to look for damage. Boxhall reported that water was entering the ship on G Deck into the mail sorting room. The postal clerks were busy moving mail to a dry location.

Blow Me Down!
Until he was summoned by Captain Smith, ship designer Thomas Andrews had no idea there had been an accident. He had been working on his notes for improving the ship—the press in the galley didn't work properly and the state-room hat racks had too many screws!

Ahoy There!

She heeled slightly to port as she struck along the starboard side. There was the sound of rending metal right away.

—Lookout Reginald Lee

We felt a sort of stopping, a sort of, not exactly shock, but a sort of slowing down, and then we felt a sort of a rip that gave a sort of a slight twist to the whole room.

—Hugh Woolner, passenger

If I had had a brimful glass of water in my hand, not a drop would have been spilled.

—Jack Thayer, passenger

[It was] as though someone had drawn a giant finger all along the side of the boat.

—Lady Lucile Duff-Gordon, passenger

It did not seem to me there was any great impact at all. It was as though we went over about a thousand marbles.

—Mrs. J. Stuart White, passenger

Other reports of water coming into the ship came from the first three cargo holds, from the fifth and sixth boiler rooms, and from the firemen's berth. Smith went with Harland and Wolff's managing director, Thomas Andrews, to investigate. Andrews was chief designer of the ship and was intimately familiar with its construction.

Andrews knew the ship could stay afloat with any 2 of 16 compartments flooded, or any 3 of the first 5. His inspection revealed five compartments taking in water. After only 10 minutes, it was already 14 feet deep. There was no hope. Andrews estimated the ship had about another hour and a half before going under.

Cries in the Dark

When he realized the serious danger the ship was in, Captain Smith went to the wireless room and ordered a call for help: "CQD," the signal for distress, along with the ship's position as Boxhall had calculated it.

Rescue Radio

At that moment, Harold Cottam, the wireless operator aboard the passenger steamship, *Carpathia*, was trying to reach the *Titanic*. He had been listening for messages from Cape Cod and learned that the Cape Cod relay station had been trying to get through to the *Titanic* with messages, but couldn't reach her. So Cottam thought he'd let the *Titanic* know.

Lifesavers
Captain Arthur Rostron of the *Carpathia* was hailed as a hero for his decisive actions in coming to the aid of the *Titanic*. He was awarded a $1,000 gold medal by decree of the U.S. Senate.

Titanic wireless operator Jack Phillips sent the distress message: *Titanic* had hit an iceberg and was sinking and needed help immediately. Cottam sent word to the *Carpathia*'s captain, Arthur Rostron, who ordered his ship around to help the *Titanic*.

The *Carpathia* was headed to the Mediterranean from New York and was 58 miles southeast of the *Titanic* when the distress signal arrived. Going all-out at 14 knots, Rostron estimated it would take the *Carpathia* four hours to reach the *Titanic*. He knew when he got there the survivors would be shocked and freezing, so he ordered the ship's doctors to get ready to treat the sick and the stewards to make hot coffee and soup. Rostron also saw that plenty of blankets were on hand.

Frozen in Her Tracks

The *Carpathia* was not the only ship in the area. The steam freighter *Californian* was even closer to the accident—so close, in fact, the *Titanic* and the *Californian* were even in sight of one another. Captain Smith attempted to signal this ship, giving the order to Boxhall to send up distress rockets. The rockets were fired every five minutes beginning at 12:45 a.m.

The *Californian* was the same ship that had broken in on Wireless Operator Phillips earlier that same evening as he was trying to catch up with the pile of messages to be sent to America. By the time the *Titanic* hit the iceberg, the *Californian*'s only wireless operator, Cyril Evans, had gone to bed for the night. Evans lay in bed as the *Titanic* was sinking. The *Californian* itself was drifting with its engines shut down, since the captain had decided that there was too much ice in the area to risk trying to move.

Ships in the Night

Californian's Third Officer Charles Groves was on watch that evening from 8:00 to 12:00. He noticed the *Titanic* at about 11:00, just 40 minutes before the collision, but didn't know what ship it was. At 11:40, when the *Titanic* hit the iceberg, Groves noticed the big ship on the horizon had stopped. The *Californian* had been using a *Morse* lamp to try to signal the *Titanic*, but got no response.

After ending his watch at 12:00, Groves went down to the wireless room. He was interested in the contraption and sometimes liked to experiment with it, but did not know how to work the equipment on his own. He played with some dials in case he could pick up a message, but was unable to hear anything over the receiver, so he gave up. Although he was curious about the *Titanic*, he didn't know anything serious had happened, so he didn't bother to wake Wireless Operator Evans!

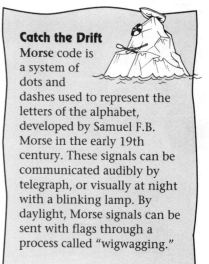

Catch the Drift
Morse code is a system of dots and dashes used to represent the letters of the alphabet, developed by Samuel F.B. Morse in the early 19th century. These signals can be communicated audibly by telegraph, or visually at night with a blinking lamp. By daylight, Morse signals can be sent with flags through a process called "wigwagging."

A Flare for Disaster

Second Officer Herbert Stone was on the bridge of the *Californian* when the *Titanic* sent up the first distress rockets. After he saw five rockets go off, he notified Captain Stanley Lord, who had been resting in the chart room. Lord said to keep trying to contact the ship with the Morse lamp.

The *Californian* didn't get a response to their Morse lamp messages. Perhaps the two ships were too far away. Lord would later claim the ship his officers saw was not the *Titanic*! In any case, the *Titanic* kept firing more rockets. *Californian* crew members sighted eight rockets in all between 12:45 and 1:40. Finally, it appeared to Officer Stone that the mysterious ship was leaving. He sent word to the captain that the ship that had been firing rockets was now moving away. In retrospect, it appears the ship was the *Titanic* sinking.

SOS
Thanks to the *Titanic* disaster, it became illegal to send up signal rockets at sea for reasons other than to signal distress.

Asleep at the Wheel

Captain Lord later claimed that he had been asleep when his crewmen tried to tell him the third time about the ship they had seen. He didn't remember what they said, only that someone came in, spoke a few words, and left. Crewmen later claimed that Captain Lord was awake and responded to the information. They said the captain wanted to know what color the rockets were. Lord may have been uncertain whether the rockets were actually distress signals or not.

That Sinking Feeling

The *Titanic* was equipped with watertight doors to seal off any or all of the 16 compartments in case any were flooded. In case of an accident, the undamaged portions of the ship would remain dry and buoyant. As we mentioned, Murdoch closed these doors almost as soon as the iceberg was sighted, well before the collision took place.

Lifesavers
In the Broadway show, *Titanic*, Thomas Andrews, designer of the ship, reviews the Ti's blueprints as she sinks. Realizing that watertight bulkheads reaching to the top deck would have saved the ship, he wildly erases and redraws the lines!

As far as we know today, the watertight doors worked fine. Unfortunately, the compartments they sealed off were only watertight on the bottom and sides. The waterproof bulkheads didn't reach to the top deck of the ship, enabling water to pour into undamaged compartments from above.

Water Weight

Five of the *Titanic*'s compartments at the starboard bow were damaged by the iceberg and began to fill with water. As they flooded, the bow-end of the ship sank, slowly pulling the rest of the ship down with it. Eventually, compartments that were dry and sealed off were pulled down far enough that seawater poured in over the watertight bulkheads. As more and more compartments were flooded, the ship listed farther and farther towards the bow, while the stern was lifted up out of the water.

Blow Me Down!
The stern half of the ship sank practically straight into the water while the bow sank at an angle. The two halves landed almost 2,000 feet apart. Afterwards, additional debris continued to drift down for several hours.

During this time, the lifeboats were loaded and passengers and crew came out on deck. The wireless operators remained at their stations, trying to contact help. The postal workers continued their attempts to keep the mail dry. In addition, the ship's engineers kept the electricity flowing throughout the ship; the lights and the wireless equipment continued working almost until the end. Unfortunately, none of the engineers were saved after their good work.

State-of-the-art special effects from 1953 depict the Titanic *sinking in 20th Century Fox's movie* The Titanic.

Everett Collection

Finally, the pressure of gravity pulling down on the stern as it was lifted out of the water cracked the ship in the middle. Survivors recall hearing loud cracking sounds as the steel holding the ship together broke, as well as booms as some of the boilers exploded. The back half of the ship crashed down and seemed to right itself, twisted around in the water for a moment, and then followed the front half down into the water. The two halves of the *Titanic* would not be seen again until 73 years later when the wreck was found on the ocean bottom.

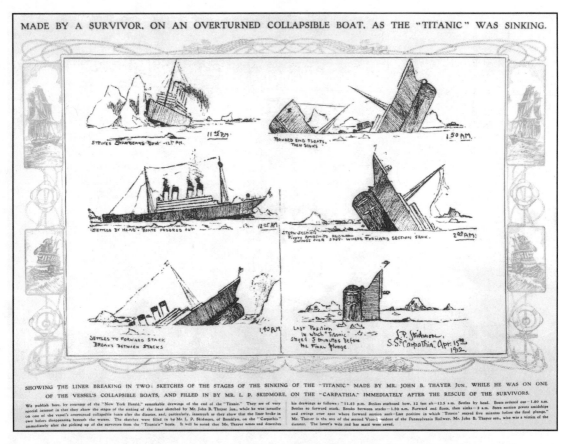

Survivor John B. Thayer gave his account of the sinking ship, which was later sketched by an artist. The sketch was published in the Illustrated London News, *May 4, 1912.*

Topham/The Image Works

Ahoy There!

She tilted slowly up, revolving apparently about a center of gravity just astern of midship until she attained a vertically upright position; and there she remained—motionless! As she swung up, her lights, which had shone without a flicker all night, went out suddenly, came on again for a single flash, then went out altogether…Then, first sinking back a little at the stern, I thought, she slid slowly forwards through the water and dived slantingly down; the sea closed over her and we had seen the last of the beautiful ship.

—Passenger Lawrence Beesley

Too Little Too Late

Hours later, at 3:20 a.m., another ship became visible over the horizon from the deck of the *Californian*. This ship was also firing rockets. This was the *Carpathia*, which had finally arrived on the scene to rescue the survivors of the *Titanic*. The rockets were fired to let them know that help was on the way. Officer Stone didn't bother to wake Captain Lord to tell him about the new ship.

Finally, at 5:20 in the morning, one of the *Californian*'s officers decided to wake up Wireless Operator Evans to find out what happened. As soon as Evans picked up the receiver, the news came pouring in from other ships. The *Titanic* had gone down less than 19 miles away. The *Carpathia* was on the scene picking survivors in lifeboats.

Only at this point did the captain and crew of the *Californian* try to help out. They arrived at 8:30, when the *Carpathia* was picking up survivors from the very last of the *Titanic*'s lifeboats. The two ships exchanged messages and worked out a plan. The *Carpathia* turned back for New York with the survivors while the *Californian* stayed to hunt for more survivors and for bodies of victims. All they found, however, were odds and ends of the disaster and some empty lifeboats.

The Least You Need to Know

➤ The *Titanic* was damaged underneath the surface. Evidently, the iceberg bent the steel plates of the hull, causing rivets to pop.

➤ The *Titanic*'s watertight bulkheads did not extend all the way to the top deck, allowing water to rush in over the top.

➤ The *Titanic* sank slowly over a period of about two and a half hours.

➤ Distress signals sent by wireless summoned the *Carpathia*, which picked up the *Titanic*'s lifeboats.

➤ Wireless and rockets failed to summon the *Californian*, which was less than 19 miles away.

Going Under

The most dramatic events of the *Titanic* tragedy centered around the lifeboats. Since there were only enough to hold a little over half of those on board, they became the central focus of the ship's last hours. A number of dramatic events took place around the lifeboats while they were being loaded. Other scenes occurred below the Boat Deck, where passengers were trying to get to the boats.

Perhaps the most significant actions of all, however, were carried out after the ship sank. While hundreds of people floated helplessly in the freezing sea with only their life-jackets to help them, a lucky few were in lifeboats, faced with an important decision: Turn back to pull a few doomed men and women from the icy sea and risk being tipped over themselves, or stand clear, watching and listening as their fellow passengers and crew members cried for their lives.

Room on Board

Aboard the *Titanic* were 2,228 passengers and crew, and 20 lifeboats with a combined capacity of 1,178. Over the side of the *Titanic* was an ocean full of frigid water—just below freezing. The sad, simple facts were that lifeboats were necessary to the survival of those on the ship, and there were not enough lifeboats. There was no way all of these people could be saved.

Some of the lucky ones who survived the disaster in a lifeboat.
NARA—Northeast Region

Even so, many more might have been saved. Only about 700 people actually made it into the boats, leaving room for about 475 more. There are a number of explanations for all those empty seats in the lifeboats. One of the main reasons was that people couldn't believe what was happening until it was too late.

Fall Guys

Not until 12:45 a.m. was the first lifeboat loaded with people—over an hour after the collision with the iceberg. This was lifeboat #7, with a 65-person capacity. It was lowered into the water with only 28 on board, and many of them got into the boat reluctantly, thinking they would be safer on the big ship than in the little boat.

The boat was lowered from the Boat Deck, the uppermost deck, towering some 75 feet above the water, on ropes and pulleys called *falls* that had to be cranked from the deck. Before they were convinced that the *Titanic* was in serious trouble, few passengers liked the idea of dangling from a rope in a boat high above the ice-cold ocean at midnight. The ship, after all, was still afloat, with its heaters and electric lights working.

If you were a passenger aboard the Titanic, *would you feel safer on deck or on one of these boats hanging high over the water?*
Topham/The Image Works

Catch the Drift
Falls are the ropes and pulleys used for raising and lowering boats and cargo to and from the deck of a ship.

Lifesavers
As boat #6 was lowered, a crewman yelled that there were not enough seamen to manage it. Canadian Arthur Peuchen offered to help, saying he was a yachtsman. Captain Smith told him to go down to the Promenade Deck, break a window, and climb in the boat. Instead, Peuchen grabbed a rope and lowered himself, hand over hand. In the process, his wallet fell out of his pocket—to be found decades later on the bottom of the ocean.

Ten minutes later, the next boat, lifeboat #5, was lowered with 41 passengers and crew—and 24 empty seats. Boats #7 and #5 were loaded and lowered from the starboard side under the supervision of First Officer Murdoch. Murdoch gave preference to women and children, but allowed men into the lifeboats, too. A number of men got into these first two boats together with women.

Boats loaded on the port side of the ship were supervised by Second Officer Lightoller. He refused to allow men into the lifeboats, except for crewmen to man the oars and the tiller. He lowered boat #6 with 28 aboard, and boat #8 with 39.

Heavy Loads

Lightoller thought it might be easier to load some of the boats from the Promenade Deck, one deck lower than the Boat Deck. The Promenade Deck, however, was enclosed by windows that were not easy to open. Some passengers had to walk up and down the stairs between the Boat Deck and the Promenade Deck until the officers and crew figured out how best to deal with the situation.

Other passengers waited on the Promenade Deck for over an hour to get into lifeboat #4. At first, the windows were closed. By the time they were opened, the officers in charge of loading had moved on to other boats on the Boat Deck. By the time the passengers were loaded into boat #4 from the Promenade Deck, it was almost 2:00 and the ship had sunk until the water was just ten feet below the deck. The boat was loaded in a rush, leaving 20 empty seats.

Lightoller also had the idea of loading boats that were already in the water from the gangway of a lower deck. This helps explain why he lowered so many boats only partially full. He sent off a group of seamen to open the gangway, but they disappeared somewhere in the lower decks of the boat. They may have been swept up and drowned in seawater as it rushed into the ship.

Touch and Go

You may sleep or read your newspaper on an airplane while the stewardess explains the safety/evacuation procedures, but if the worst happened, you'd be glad there was a system to follow. *Titanic* had no established, coordinated procedure for loading the lifeboats; the officers in charge all had different ideas about how to go about it, and much of the loading was haphazard. Many people managed to get on boats just because they were in the right place at the right time. Many others were denied access to boats that had room for more people.

Two boats, collapsibles "A" and "B," were not ready in time to be loaded properly. They were tied away on top of the bridge and the crew had a hard time cutting them loose. To make things worse, the ship was listing so much that the falls couldn't work properly. When the *Titanic* sank, these boats ended up in the water without anyone in them at first. "B" was overturned and "A" had water in it.

Blow Me Down!
Passenger Eugene Daly tried to board a lifeboat, but was told to step back by an officer with a gun. As the *Titanic* sank, Daly jumped into the sea. He was later pulled out of the water and into the same boat he had tried to board earlier from the deck of the ship!

Skimming Off the Top

Despite all the confusion, the lifeboat loading wasn't simply arbitrary. Statistics clearly indicate that certain groups of people had a better chance of making it than others. In general, first-class women and children came out much better than everyone else. Second- and third-class male passengers fared the worst. See Appendix D for a complete list of all passengers' names.)

	Lost	Survived
First-class men	118	57
First-class women	4	140
First-class children	0	6
Second-class men	154	14
Second-class women	13	80
Second-class children	0	24
Third-class men	387	75
Third-class women	89	76
Third-class children	52	27
Male crew members	670	192
Female crew members	3	20
Total men on board	1,329	338
Total women on board	109	316
Total children on board	52	57

Overall, higher percentages of women were saved because of the "women and children first" convention. Although lots of men tried to get around this unwritten, generally recognized rule, few complained that women and children ought to have first crack at the lifeboats. It seemed like the civilized way to do things.

As for those men who objected, they had the officers and crew to contend with. These seamen formed rings around the lifeboats and controlled who boarded them. As we mentioned in Chapter 4, the officers had guns and used them to prevent men from

Blow Me Down!
Legend has it that millionaire J.J. Astor was standing by as a 13-year-old boy was denied a seat on one of the boats. He put a girl's hat on the boy's head and said "Now you're a girl and can go."

SOS
Some *Titanic* movies show steerage passengers using axes to break down the gates separating them from the Boat Deck. We don't know whether this actually happened. Explorations of the sunken wreck show that some gates are still intact on the bottom of the sea, and they are still locked!

rushing the last boats during the final minutes. Reports disagree as to whether one of the officers shot a passenger before shooting himself.

Lockdown

The officers and their guns were merely the last of several obstacles keeping lower-class passengers from the safety of the lifeboats. Many passengers from steerage seem to have been kept behind locked gates below the Boat Deck until all the lifeboats were gone. Some may well have drowned without even getting off the ship.

Separating steerage from the Boat Deck were two Promenade Decks that were ordinarily restricted to first-class passengers. These remained locked during much of the boat-loading, with stewards standing behind them. Passengers were told to wait behind these gates until their boats were ready. An hour after the first lifeboat was loaded, a few groups of women were finally led through the gates, up to the Boat Deck, and into lifeboats. The gates were opened to let them through and locked again behind them.

Slipping Through

Some women managed to persuade stewards to open the gate to let them through. Of course, the many passengers who couldn't speak English couldn't do this. Other women from steerage were allowed through the gates only after men who were with them complained and argued with the steward who kept the key.

Some men from steerage—who knew about the accident right away because their rooms were flooded—may have made it to the boats before the gates were locked. Other men climbed over a high railing into one of the first-class areas on a crane.

Last Gasps

Many boats were instructed to wait near the ship in case more passengers could be loaded from gangways on lower decks. This never happened. Instead, people in the boats watched as the ship went under.

One of the big funnels collapsed as the ship broke into two halves. The bow-half filled with water and sank completely under, pulling the stern-half higher and higher out of the water as it broke free. The stern rested a moment, almost perfectly flat upon the sea. Hundreds clung to the railings or balanced on the upturned hull. Many fell a considerable distance into the sea, where hundreds more were already moaning and calling for help in the icy water.

Finally the stern pivoted and sank straight down. Many were sucked below in its downward wake. The rest, kept afloat by their life jackets, faced a lingering death from *hypothermia,* also known as freezing to death.

Catch the Drift
Hypothermia is the medical condition commonly known as freezing to death.

Slow Boats

Unfortunately, only a few boats made an effort to pick up additional passengers after the ship sank. Many were afraid of being overturned by too many desperate people in the water. Compounding the problem was the fact that many of the seamen put in charge of the boats had little experience in controlling them and in leading people. A number of boats drifted aimlessly while others rowed off in the direction of lights that turned out to be stars or reflected starlight.

Ahoy There!

Unprepared as we were for such a thing, the cries of the drowning floating across the quiet sea filled us with stupefaction: We longed to return and rescue at least some of the drowning, but we knew it was impossible. The boat was filled to standing-room, and to return would mean the swamping of us all, and so the captain-stoker told his crew to row away from the cries.

—Lawrence Beesley

Pulling for Survivors

Some boats, however, did go back to pull survivors out of the water. One of these was boat #4, commanded by Quartermaster Walter Perkis. Perkis was later criticized for his incompetence by some of the passengers in the boat, but he did manage to get it in position to pull several people out of the water.

Another boat that rescued survivors in the water was #14, led by Fifth Officer Lowe. Before setting off in his boat, Lowe organized a group of four partially full boats. He tied them together for added stability and rearranged passengers to empty his boat and make room for more survivors. Lowe had a salty, seamanlike manner: when one of the women passengers was slow in moving from one boat to another, he yelled, "Jump, goddamn you, jump!"

Lowe didn't act immediately to rescue survivors in the water. He evidently felt that it would be dangerous to take a lifeboat among the desperate crowd of floating people. The boat might be *swamped*—pulled over and filled with water.

Catch the Drift
A boat is **swamped** when it gets so full of water that it can't be rowed properly. Although a swamped boat may not sink, it's effectively useless.

SOS
One boat actually was swamped by people in the water trying to get in. Collapsible "A," which had not been loaded before the ship went under, ended up in the midst of many people in the sea. As more and more tried to get on, it filled up with water, but didn't sink.

Lowe waited until the people in the water were too cold to pose a threat to his boat. Unfortunately, he waited too long. By the time he and his crew finally rowed among the people floating in the water, most had frozen to death! Lowe and his crew were able to save just three additional people.

There was debate aboard many boats between those who wanted to go back and those who didn't. Seaman Thomas Jones, in charge of boat #8, wanted to go back but was shouted down by the passengers. One passenger who wanted to go back for more survivors was "Unsinkable" Molly Brown in boat #6. Although unsuccessful in persuading Quartermaster Hitchens at the tiller to turn the boat around, she succeeded in organizing some of the women in the boat to row in order to keep warm.

Better Late Than Never

It took over an hour for the cries of the dying to fade away. Some boats rowed, others drifted, but all were basically powerless, awaiting rescue. Finally, at about 4:00 a.m., rescue arrived. The *Carpathia* made it to the scene of the disaster after receiving the *Titanic*'s wireless distress signal three-and-a-half hours earlier. Although the *Californian* might have arrived sooner had its captain and crew taken action, the ship remained adrift for the night.

One by one, the boats were found and the passengers hauled on board. Many had to be hauled on board inside cargo nets. Once on deck, they were offered hot soup and warm blankets. Despite their ordeal, many passengers, anxious to know the fate of their loved ones, were unable to rest. They searched among their fellow survivors until the last boat was picked up at 8:30 that morning.

The Least You Need to Know

➤ Only 705 people made it into the lifeboats, which could have held 1,178—still only half of the *Titanic*'s 2,228 passengers and crew.

➤ The boats had to be lowered 75 feet into the water. Boats were lowered partially full for many reasons, including the false expectation that they could be filled from the lower decks once they were in the water.

➤ Many passengers from steerage were denied access to the Boat Deck.

➤ Once in the water, only a few boats returned to pull people out of the water.

➤ The *Carpathia* arrived at 4:00 a.m. to rescue survivors in the lifeboats.

In the Wake of Disaster

In This Chapter

➤ Recovering bodies from the sea

➤ Identification and burial

➤ The bereaved and bereft

➤ Memorials and relief efforts

It was difficult for people to get information on exactly what happened to the *Titanic* after the first news that it had hit an iceberg. It was difficult to face the possibility that something had gone seriously wrong for the world's mightiest ocean liner. Once the news came in, it was difficult to accept.

It was difficult to recover the bodies of the victims and to make arrangements for their burials. For many, it was difficult to get by financially as a result of the loss of family breadwinners on board the *Titanic*. And it was difficult to get compensation out of White Star Line.

As hard as it was, all of these difficulties were overcome. The bad news sank in, bodies were recovered, memorial services were conducted, monuments were put up, government inquiries were held, and relief efforts were organized. Life went on, even though, for many, it would never be the same.

Sea Hearses

In the days following the disaster, White Star made arrangements for recovering the bodies of the victims from the site of the disaster. The first ship to search for bodies was the *Mackay-Bennett*, which arrived on the scene on Saturday, April 20, equipped with embalming equipment, tons of ice, and over 100 coffins.

Blow Me Down!
The day after the sinking of the *Titanic*, an eclipse of the sun was visible throughout much of Canada.

Before the *Mackay-Bennett* arrived to begin its work, a North German Lloyd passenger ship passed by the scene. Wreckage and bodies—kept afloat by their lifejackets—were visible from the deck. A passenger reported seeing the body of a woman holding her dead baby, another woman holding a dog. There were also the bodies of about a dozen men clinging to one another.

When the *Mackay-Bennett* arrived, the sea was choppy, with large, breaking waves. In spite of the rough weather, 51 bodies were recovered the first day. A record was kept for each victim, including a physical description and descriptions of any possessions found with them. Each body was numbered.

Ahoy There!

Fortunately, the scene that followed was shrouded in darkness. Less fortunately, the calm, still silence carried every sound with startling distinctness. To enter into a description of those heartrending, never-to-be-forgotten sounds would serve no useful purpose. I never allowed my thoughts to dwell on them, and there are some that would be alive and well today had they just determined to erase from their minds all memory of those ghastly moments, or at least until time had somewhat dimmed the memory of that awful tragedy.

—Second Officer Lightoller

Some of the bodies were embalmed on the ship. Others were put on ice to be embalmed later on shore. Some bodies were badly damaged, perhaps by the ship as it sank or by sea creatures. These were buried at sea.

In the days that followed, the *Mackay-Bennett* recovered 306 bodies. Of these, 116 were buried at sea. As the ship started running out of supplies, it was joined by the *Minia* on Friday, April 26th. The *Minia* took over as the *Mackay-Bennett* returned to Halifax with its cold cargo. The *Minia* found only 17 bodies; the captain said the rest of the victims had been swept off by the gulf stream. A final effort was made by the steamer *Montmagny*, which found only three more bodies.

A whaling boat used to recover the body of a Titanic *victim.*
Joseph H. Bailey/National Geographic Image Collection

Resting Places

The bodies were taken to Halifax, where room was made in the Mayflower Curling Rink for them to be embalmed and identified. A number of family members came to identify victims. Those that were not identified were photographed in case they could be identified later. Of 328 bodies, fewer than 100 were identified. 119 were buried at sea. Approximately 1,300 other victims were never found; they sank with the ship or were swept away by the Gulf Stream. The 17 bodies recovered by the *Minia* underwent autopsies performed by the ship's surgeon, Dr. Mosher. Of these bodies, only one had lungs filled with water, indicating the victim had drowned. The others perished of hypothermia.

Blow Me Down!
Collapsible "A" was found almost a month after the *Titanic* sank. Inside were three bodies—a crewman, a stoker, and a first-class passenger dressed in formal evening attire.

129

Horse-drawn hearses taking bodies from the Titanic *disaster to Halifax, Nova Scotia, where many of them were buried.*
Joseph H. Bailey/National Geographic Image Collection

Some friends and families made their own arrangements for burial. Most, however, were buried in one of three cemeteries in Halifax—a Catholic cemetery, a Jewish cemetery, and one that was non-sectarian. In many cases, it was a matter of guesswork to decide which cemetery a body should be buried in. There was even some confusion and squabbling about some of the unclaimed bodies as to whether they belonged in the Jewish cemetery or the Catholic one!

Remains of the Day

One of the first bodies to be identified and claimed was that of millionaire John Jacob Astor. Although the body was covered with soot from one of the *Titanic*'s broken funnels, his clothes, jewelry, and the large amounts of money he carried made him easy to recognize. He had coins and bank notes in U.S., British, and French currency.

Another body attracted a great deal of attention, even though it could not be identified. This was the body of a two-year-old boy, the fourth body found by the crew of the *Mackay-Bennett*. When people found out about the unidentified baby, there were many offers to pay for the burial. One of these offers, the one that was finally accepted, came from the captain and crew of the *Mackay-Bennett*. Six seamen from the ship carried the little coffin to its grave.

Rites of Passage

A service for all of *Titanic*'s dead was held in Halifax on May 4th. It was not the first, or last, *Titanic* memorial service. A national day of mourning was observed in England on Friday, April 19. On Sunday, April 21, churches were packed full on both sides of the Atlantic. Many people had difficulty accepting the disaster, and couldn't understand why it happened.

Written in Stone

Among the places most devastated by the sinking of the *Titanic* was the town of Southampton, England, where the *Titanic* embarked. Many of the staff and crew aboard the ship came from Southampton, and a huge proportion of the town lost relatives who were employed on the ship.

Blow Me Down!
When the body of John Jacob Astor was pulled out of the sea, he had a gold watch, gold and diamond cufflinks, a diamond ring, 225 pounds in English paper money, $2,440 in American bills, five pounds in gold, five 10-franc pieces, and a gold pencil.

Blow Me Down!
White Star executive Alexander Carlisle, who helped design the ship, attended a memorial service during which he fainted.

Southampton has erected a number of memorials in their memory; the largest is the Engineer's Memorial in Andrew's Park, unveiled in front of a huge crowd on April 22, 1914. The Crew's Memorial, in honor of those who worked below decks on the *Titanic*, was unveiled on July 27, 1915, on Southampton Common. This was moved to Holyrood Church in 1972.

The Musician's Memorial was unveiled in Southampton Library on April 19, 1913. Unfortunately, the library and the memorial were destroyed during World War II. A plaque in memory of the staff of *Titanic*'s restaurant was hung in St. Joseph's Church in Southampton. The staff included the manager, Mr. L. Gatti, and 10 of his cousins, all of whom were lost when the ship sank. Dozens of other Gatti employees died in the disaster due to the heavy recruitment of his London restaurant staff.

A procession in Southampton, England, during a memorial service for the victims of the Titanic.
Brown Brothers

The Titanic *Engineer's Memorial in Southampton, England.*
Morgan Collection/Archive Photos

Other *Titanic* memorials include a statue in Belfast, where the ship was built; a second monument to the engineers was erected in Liverpool. A larger-than-life statue of Captain Smith stands in Lichfield in Staffordshire, England. Wireless Operator John Phillips is remembered with a stone tablet in his hometown of Godalming in Surrey, England.

The statue memorializing the Titanic *in Belfast, Ireland, where the ship was built.*
Hulton Getty/Tony Stone Images

More Memories

In America, the *Titanic* Memorial Lighthouse was built on top of the Seaman's Church Institute building in New York City. The lighthouse now stands in the city's South Street Seaport, where it was moved after the Seaman's building was torn down in the 1960s. Also in New York City is a fountain memorializing passengers Isidor and Ida Straus, located on Broadway and West 106th Street.

Lifesavers
Ida Straus has been touted for her decision to go down with her husband on the *Titanic* both as a champion of traditional marriage values *and* as a champion of women's equality with men!

A number of Jews throughout the U.S. expressed interest in building a memorial to the Strauses, and to Ida Straus in particular. They looked upon her decision to remain on the sinking ship with her husband as a potential source of inspiration to other married Jews. Many were concerned about the growing divorce rate among Jews and hoped that a monument to Ida Straus would encourage married couples to stay together.

Women's Issues

In 1931, the *Titanic* Women's Memorial was dedicated to the men who bravely abided the "women-and-children-first" rule. The 15-foot memorial was erected by a women's group and presented by Mrs. Taft, widow of President Taft. This memorial stands in Washington, D.C.

The monument quickly became a subject of controversy between those who took a traditional view of the role of women and those who felt women should have greater independence and responsibility. The monument came to symbolize other controversial issues as well.

Well-to-do women were most active in raising funds for the memorial and for emphasizing the messages that went along with it. The memorial fund also became a popular cause among conservative regional women's groups. Fund-raising began shortly after the disaster, but it wasn't until after World War I, near the start of the Great Depression, that it was actually built. By then, many of the ideals it stood for weren't quite so popular. These ideals included the separation of the male-dominated workplace from the women-centered home. During the depression, many women had to go to work outside the house. As a result, the idea of men making sacrifices for women didn't ring true.

What's more, many felt that the *Titanic* Women's Memorial implicity glorified the rich, but not the poor, and the Anglo-Americans, but not other races and nationalities. It was wealthy Anglo-American women who did the most fund-raising to build the memorial.

The memorial was criticized in newspapers run by ethnic groups, by socialists, and by feminists. Of course, debates about the memorial were only a small cross-section of the debates about the disaster as a whole. People have continued to squabble over who deserves praise and who should be blamed since the ship went down.

Sadly, pretty much everyone who survived has been at least indirectly criticized. This includes married women who became widows as a result of the disaster. They have been faulted, together with the "women-and-children-first" rule, on account of the men who died.

Lost Leader

Perhaps the most widely attended memorial service was held for bandleader Wallace Hartley, whose body was recovered from the sea and shipped back to his hometown of Colne in Lancashire, England. An estimated 30,000 mourners came to pay their respects on Saturday, May 18th, as businesses closed for the day. The funeral procession marched through town on foot, extending half a mile. Hartley's casket was escorted to his grave with the music of seven bands.

Collection box in London for donations to Titanic *relief.*
Hulton Getty/Tony Stone Images

Pitching In

A number of victims' dependents were thrown into serious financial trouble with the loss of their bread-winning relatives. White Star was slow to settle insurance claims, and when claimants were able to collect, they got only a small percentage of what they asked for. What's more, White Star did not provide for the next of kin of deceased employees.

To help these people, the *Titanic* Relief Fund was organized. The fund raised money by soliciting donations, selling *Titanic* memorabilia, and sponsoring events. Memorabilia included postcards and musical recordings of songs about the disaster. Events included concerts, shows, and sporting events. Dependents of lost crew members could also get help from the British Seafarer's Union. Three hundred union members died during the disaster.

The crew of the Carpathia, *the ship that rescued the* Titanic *survivors, organized a football (soccer) team and played to benefit the* Titanic *fund.*
Brown Brothers

Ahoy There!

Yes, it's true...husband and son have gone and left eleven of us. It was the first time that Arthur and his father had been at sea together and it wouldn't have happened if Arthur hadn't been out of work because of the coal strike. He tried to get a job ashore but failed and he had his wife and baby to keep. So he signed on aboard the Titanic *as a fireman. His father shouldn't have been on the* Titanic *but a bad leg kept him from going on his own ship, the* Britannia. *Now they're gone and there are eleven of us. The eldest boy, nineteen, makes a few shillings a week by odd jobs. My own youngest baby is six months old.*

—Mrs. May of Southampton, in a statement to the *Daily Mail*, April 18, 1912

The Least You Need to Know

➤ Only a small percentage of the bodies of victims were recovered; many of these were never identified.

➤ Most of the bodies were buried in the seaport town of Halifax, Nova Scotia, Canada.

➤ Among the more famous *Titanic* memorials are the Engineers Memorial in Southampton, England, and the Women's Memorial in Washington, D.C.

➤ The *Titanic* Relief Fund was organized to help families of passengers and crew who experienced financial hardship as a result of the disaster.

Life Goes On

Of the 700 or so people who survived the *Titanic* disaster, most have preferred to live fairly quiet lives, despite painful memories and attention from the media. While some attempted to forget the experience altogether, others have helped keep the memory alive in various ways—by telling their stories, keeping souvenirs, and through political action and fund-raising.

Survivors have found themselves at the center of attention at various times since the disaster, including quite recently as a result of James Cameron's hit movie *Titanic*. As of now, there are fewer than six known survivors, and most of them have been interviewed in newspapers and on TV. The vast majority of survivors, however, managed to stay out of the spotlight for most of their lives.

Some passengers who survived were understandably reluctant to travel by sea again. Most of the crew, however, continued to pursue their careers at sea. Many distinguished themselves in military service, and many stayed on as employees of White Star Line.

Mixed Feelings

When the *Carpathia* arrived in New York Harbor with the *Titanic* survivors, a huge crowd was gathered, among them many friends and relatives of those who had been aboard the big ship. Many didn't know whether their loved ones had survived, and a good number found out the hard way as the ones they waited for never disembarked from the *Carpathia*. They were not shy about expressing their grief.

A crowd greets the survivors as they disembark from the Carpathia *in New York Harbor.*

Hulton Getty/Tony Stone Images

THE ARRIVAL OF THE "SHIP OF SORROW" AT NEW YORK
SURVIVORS OF THE TITANIC MEETING FRIENDS AND RELATIVES ON THE PIER

Others, however, were overjoyed to learn their loved ones had survived. Many happy reunions took place in port. The sound of laughing and happy greetings could be heard together with weeping and moaning.

Back to Normal

A number of *Titanic* survivors lost loved ones they were traveling with. Among these was Edith Brown Haisman, who lived to be the oldest survivor at age 100 until her death January 20, 1997. Edith was 15 years old at the time of her *Titanic* voyage. She remembers many details of the disaster, but one of her most significant memories is of her father as he said good-bye from the deck of the sinking ship. He had a glass of brandy in his hand, and he said "I'll see you in New York."

Edith later married Frederick Haisman of South Africa. They had 10 children and 30 grandchildren.

Kids in Tow

Many *Titanic* survivors seem to have been largely unaffected by the disaster, aside from their lingering painful memories. Nellie Becker and her three children were returning on the *Titanic* to America from India, where Nellie's husband, Allen, was working for the Lutheran Church as a missionary. Their son, 2-year-old Richard Becker, was seriously ill and needed medical treatment in the States. So Nellie took Richard and her other children, 12-year-old Ruth and baby Marion, back with her to the States, while Allen finished his work in India.

Fortunately, the three Beckers survived the *Titanic* disaster and moved to Benton Harbor, Michigan, where they were eventually reunited with Allen. Family members said, however, that Nellie remained disturbed by the experience of escaping from the sinking ship, preferring not to talk about it, and becoming upset whenever it was mentioned.

Oldest daughter Ruth went on to graduate from college in Ohio and became a school teacher. Richard became a singer and later, a social worker. Marion contracted tuberculosis at an early age. She died in 1944. Nellie died in 1961, Richard died in 1975, and Ruth, in 1990.

SOS
Ruth Becker remembers being on board the *Carpathia* when it suddenly stopped. She says many passengers became afraid that this ship, too, had hit an iceberg and was going to sink. In fact, the ship stopped for a brief funeral service for victims who had died in the lifeboats.

The Reverend Roger Anderson, who conducted a burial service on board the Carpathia, *together with one of the* Carpathia's officers.
Brown Brothers

Camera Shy

Many survivors were courted by the media, and many were reluctant to participate in the hoopla even years after the disaster. Passenger Anna Turja, from Finland, was coming to America on the *Titanic* in order to work at her brother-in-law's store in Ashtabula, Ohio. After surviving the wreck, she arrived in New York unable to speak English, but was directed to a train for Ashtabula, where she was greeted by a crowd as a celebrity.

Anna was invited as a special guest to attend a screening of the 1953 film *Titanic*, starring Clifton Webb and Barbara Stanwyck. After the movie, a reporter asked her if she thought the film was realistic. Anna responded through a translator, saying "If they were close enough to film it, why didn't they help?"

Anna was invited to appear on two TV shows, the game show, *I've Got a Secret*, and *The Ed Sullivan Show*. She turned these offers down, partly because she was uncomfortable with English, which she never learned. She had seven children and died in 1982 at the age of 89.

A New Direction

In recent years, survivors of the disaster have been much sought after, especially following the success of James Cameron's 1997 film, *Titanic*. Among these was Eleanor Johnson Shuman, who met with the director and saw a special pre-release screening of his film together with movie critics Siskel and Ebert. She has seen the movie twice since then and says she cried each time.

Eleanor was 18 months old as a *Titanic* passenger. She was scheduled to board a different ship with her mother and 4-year-old brother, Harold, but, like many passengers bound for America, they ended up on the *Titanic* as a result of the coal strike. They signed on as third-class passengers and made the journey with two teenage Swedish girls whom they had befriended in Sweden.

Blow Me Down!
Titanic survivors did not have to go through customs, unlike most steamship passengers arriving in the U.S. As a result, Anna Turja had no record of ever having arrived in America. This became a temporary problem for one of her children, who needed clearance for doing government business.

Her mother later told her that the Swedish girls were among those playing with the ice that had been knocked on board by the collision until an officer told them to return to their cabins. The whole party was later summoned by a steward, who evidently liked them and gave them preferential treatment, leading them to the lifeboats.

They all made it into the last lifeboat to be loaded, except for one of the Swedish girls, who handed Eleanor's little brother into the boat from the deck. This girl was the only member of the group who did not survive.

Ahoy There!

Mr. Buckley: *They tried to keep us down at first on our steerage deck. They did not want us to go up to the first-class place at all.*

Senator Smith: *Who tried to do that?*

Mr. Buckley: *I cannot say who they were. I think they were sailors.*

Senator Smith: *What happened then? Did the steerage passengers try to get out?*

Mr. Buckley: *Yes, they did. There was one steerage passenger there, and he was getting up the steps, and just as he was going in a little gate, a fellow came along and chucked him down; threw him down into the steerage place.*

—U.S. Senate Inquiry

Eleanor grew up in Charles, Illinois. She later took a job with the Elgin Watch Company and worked after that as a telephone operator. She got married to Delbert Shuman in 1934; they remained together until his death in 1981.

In 1958, Eleanor and Harold attended the New York premiere of *A Night to Remember*. She kept a photo of the two of them taken outside the theater. She also collected *Titanic* books, and a painting of the ship, as well as a photo of herself with James Cameron.

She returned to the site of the sinking in 1996 to take part in a memorial service for the victims. Just before her death in 1998, she was one of only six known survivors still living.

Eleanor Johnson Shuman and Louise Pope, Titanic *survivors at a convention in Boston.*
Morgan Collection

Lifestyles of the Rich and Famous

Perhaps the survivor who obtained the most notoriety as a result of her *Titanic* experience was Margaret "Unsinkable Molly" Brown. Molly was already known as a social-climbing millionaire whose husband, J.J. Brown, struck it rich in a Colorado gold mine. Afterwards, her energy and outspokenness made her a center of attention. She later became the subject of a Broadway musical and a movie, both called *The Unsinkable Molly Brown.*

SOS
Molly Brown once said that J. Bruce Ismay caused the *Titanic* collision by ordering the captain to go as fast as he could so that the ship would arrive in New York in time for Ismay to attend a dinner party!

Rising to the Top

Molly was born Margaret Tobin in Hannibal, Missouri, in 1867, the daughter of an Irish immigrant. She claimed to be well-acquainted with the writer Mark Twain, who was also from Hannibal, but this is somewhat doubtful. She married her husband in 1886. He was a poor miner at the time, but became wealthy within the next 30 years.

After J.J. struck gold, he and Molly gradually became estranged. He did not share her interest in high society, so she often went off on her own. She was touring the Mediterranean when she received word that her grandson was ill and booked passage back to the states on board the *Titanic.*

She claimed she was not at all afraid as the ship was sinking and she was picked up and dropped four feet into a lifeboat that was already being lowered. Once in the boat, she was critical of Quartermaster Hitchens, who refused to row and refused to go back to pick up survivors in the water. She took on some of the rowing duties herself, and stripped off some of her clothes to help keep other passengers warm.

After the disaster, she became politically active, attempting to run for Congress. She voiced her opposition to the "women and children first" rule, since it split up so many families and left many women and children destitute. She also lobbied in favor of the Equal Rights Amendment.

Blow Me Down!
Thanks to her strong public image and her reputation for doing charitable work, Molly Brown is in advertisements for U.S. Savings Bonds and for the National Advertising Council.

When her husband died without a will in 1922, Molly became involved in a lengthy squabble with her two children about the estate. Molly wound up with a modest settlement and eventually moved into a hotel in New York City, where she died in 1932 at the age of 65 with very little money. She was buried next to her husband on Long Island.

Wealthy Widow

Another millionaire who survived the *Titanic* sinking was Madeleine Astor, the young bride of John Jacob Astor, who was lost with the ship. The couple had been married only a short time when they boarded the ship, returning to the States on account of Madeleine's pregnancy. She eventually had a son and named him John Jacob after his father.

Madeleine inherited a $5 million trust fund and the use of two mansions, one in Newport, Rhode Island, and the other on Fifth Avenue in Manhattan. She lost the use of these mansions when she married New Yorker William K. Dick during World War I. She gave birth to two sons by her second husband but divorced him in 1933 in Reno, Nevada.

That same year she married professional boxer Enzo Firemonte, but her third marriage lasted only five years before it, too, ended in divorce. She died in 1940 in Palm Beach, Florida, at the age of 47.

Divided Duties

A fairly high percentage of *Titanic* survivors were crew members. This drew criticism from some observers, who felt that the crew had a duty to look out for passengers ahead of themselves. The surviving crew, however, were not alone in taking flack for staying alive. Male passengers had to deal with suspicion that they had taken seats from women, even if they were pulled out of the water. Some women—namely suffragette groups—criticized women survivors for taking seats on the lifeboats. Any way you look at it, the *Titanic* was a no-win situation.

Blow Me Down!
Canadian yachtsman Major Arthur Peuchen (who lost his wallet descending to a lifeboat in need of a steersman) was later so concerned about damage to his reputation that he obtained a signed statement from Second Officer Charles Lightoller saying he had been told to board the lifeboat by the captain.

One passenger who faced harsh criticism just for surviving while others perished was Masabumi Hosono, who served in Japan's Ministry of Transportation. He was fired from his job and personally disgraced for failing to live up to his country's strict code of honor. He was even disparaged in a school text book.

Hosono avoided speaking of the disaster and died in 1939. In 1997, his diary came to light, together with memorabilia including notes written on *Titanic* stationary shortly after the sinking. His descendents hope that public interest in the diary will help restore his good name.

Some crew members were assigned to lifeboats in order to row, steer, or take charge of the passengers. Others were pulled, or pulled themselves, out of the water. And others simply happened to be around when lifeboats with extra room were being lowered.

Titanic survivors reunite with family in Southampton, England.
Brown Brothers

A Seasoned Sailor

One crew member assigned to take charge of a lifeboat was Fourth Officer Joseph Boxhall. At the age of 28, Boxhall had already been a seaman for 13 years before signing on with the *Titanic*. He remained a seaman for another 28 after the *Titanic* went down, having the longest career of all of the junior officers.

Boxhall served on White Star's *Adriatic* for a short time until World War I, when he served as a sub-lieutenant on a battleship with the Naval Reserve. He was later assigned command of a torpedo boat. After the war he went back to work for White Star.

After White Star merged with rival Cunard in 1934, Boxhall served as first officer aboard the *Ausonia*, the *Scythia*, and the *Antonia*. He retired in 1940 as his health declined. In 1958, he was a technical advisor for the film *A Night to Remember*, although he was critical of the way the movie depicted the disaster. Boxhall died in 1967. His ashes were scattered at sea at the site where the *Titanic* went down.

Ahoy There!

Mr. Boxhall: *I have the position.*

Senator Smith: *Have you a memorandum of it?*

Mr. Boxhall: *No, I have it in my head.*

Senator Smith: *Give it to the reporter.*

Mr. Boxhall: *Forty-one, forty-six, fifty, fifteen.*

Senator Smith: *Was that the last time the ship's position was taken?*

Mr. Boxhall: *That is the position I worked out.*

Senator Smith: *Was that the last time it was taken so far as you know?*

Mr. Boxhall: *Yes, that was the position at the time she struck.*

—U.S. Senate Inquiry

The Pride of the Fleet

Another crewman assigned to a lifeboat was lookout Frederick Fleet, who was the first to sight the iceberg that sank the ship. He helped row lifeboat #6 along with yachtsman Major Peuchen and passenger Molly Brown. After the disaster, Fleet testified with great reluctance at the Senate inquiry.

At the inquiry, he was worried that people would try to blame him for the collision, so he was unwilling to give full answers to questions. In self-defense, he pointed out that the *Titanic* lookouts had no binoculars, a fact the inquiry seized on as especially significant, since it showed the negligence of White Star Line. The surviving *Titanic* senior officers held this disclosure against him later on.

Fleet remained a seaman until the 1930s, when he had trouble finding work during the Depression. In 1936, he went to work for Harland and Wolff, the company that built the *Titanic*. He worked as a nightwatchman for another shipping company, and later sold newspapers in Southampton. In 1965, at the age of 76, he was devastated by the death of his wife and hanged himself.

Too Loyal for His Own Good?

One crew member who was saved after jumping into the water was Second Officer Charles Lightoller. Lightoller continued to work for White Star following the *Titanic* disaster, but never became captain, even though he defended the company as a key witness. It could be that people felt Lightoller's association with the *Titanic* would make passengers uncomfortable with him as captain. It could also be that Lightoller fell out of favor by sticking up for the unpopular J. Bruce Ismay.

Lightoller served in the Navy during World War I, after which he returned to White Star. After he retired, Lightoller and his son were among the many private boaters who heroically rescued soldiers from the beaches of Dunkirk during World War II. Taking his 60-foot yacht, *Sundowner*, Lightoller rescued 130 soldiers, taking them across the English Channel in the midst of enemy fire.

It is said that one of the soldiers Lightoller rescued was disturbed to learn he had been an officer on board the *Titanic* and threatened to jump overboard rather than take his chances with such an ill-fated skipper. A companion replied by surmising anyone who could survive the *Titanic* disaster could get them safely across the English Channel.

Lightoller died in 1952 at 78 years of age.

Bashful Bride

Junior Wireless Operator Harold Bride was pulled out of the water aboard collapsible "A" when the *Titanic* sank. He was the first survivor to make money from the disaster, accepting $1,000 from newspapers for his account of what happened. He disappeared from the public eye during the following years. During World War I, he worked as a wireless operator aboard the steamship *Mona's Isle*, and later worked as a traveling salesman. He died in 1956.

SOS
Although they all stayed on with White Star, none of the surviving officers ever became captain of a White Star ship. Lightoller, Boxhall, and Lowe did become captains in the Royal Navy during World War I.

Lying Ashore

You've already learned that Harold Bride went right back to work sending wireless messages on the *Carpathia*, the ship that rescued the *Titanic*'s lifeboats. One of the passengers went right back to work on the *Carpathia* as well. This was George Brayton, a con man. Two days after the survivors had been picked up by the *Carpathia*, as the ship was sailing back to New York, Brayton was wandering around the deck looking miserable. A fellow survivor asked him what was the matter.

Brayton said he had to get to Los Angeles, but lost all his money on the *Titanic*. The fellow survivor, leather manufacturer Harry Stengel, suggested that Brayton call the White Star office to get traveling expenses from them. Soon after the *Carpathia* landed, Stengel got a phone call from Brayton, thanking him for his advice and saying that White Star came through with the money. As the conversation continued, Brayton managed to finagle a dinner invitation at Stengel's house in Newark, New Jersey.

At dinner, Brayton told Stengel about a deal involving his brother-in-law, who supposedly worked for Western Union, the telegraph company. Stengel expressed interest and heard nothing more for several weeks. Finally, Brayton called again. Brayton and Stengel arranged to meet with the "brother-in-law" in a New York hotel room.

The "brother-in-law" said that his job at Western Union involved transmitting results of horse races. He said he could hold up the results of certain races and tell Stengel which horses won in time for Stengel to place bets on the winning horses. In exchange, the "brother-in-law" wanted $1,000 from Stengel.

Fortunately for him, Stengel did not have rice pudding for brains. He saw through the scheme and went to the police, but Brayton and his partner escaped.

The Least You Need to Know

- ➤ As of today, fewer than six known *Titanic* survivors are still living.
- ➤ The oldest survivor was Edith Brown Haisman, who was a passenger on the *Titanic* at age 15 and who died at 100 years of age in 1997.
- ➤ Eleanor Johnson Shuman met with film director James Cameron and attended a special screening of the 1997 movie *Titanic* with movie critics Siskel and Ebert.
- ➤ Anna Turja turned down offers to appear on TV shows *I've Got a Secret* and *The Ed Sullivan Show*.
- ➤ Fourth Officer Joseph Boxhall was a technical advisor for the 1958 movie, *A Night to Remember*.

Part 4
Lowering the Boom

Crowds gathered on both sides of the Atlantic to find out about the Titanic and try to figure out what should be done. The people, the newspapers, and the governments of Britain and the U.S. complained, argued, cast blame, and came up with suggestions for preventing similar disasters in the future. Much valuable safety legislation has emerged in the wake of the ship, but several controversies surrounding the Titanic itself remain unresolved.

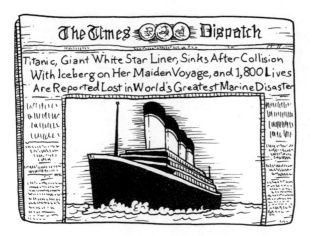

Chapter 14

Making Waves

In This Chapter

➤ Newspaper reports of the disaster

➤ Confusion on shore and false stories in print

➤ The first report of the disaster and the sensation it caused

➤ Attempts to profit from the exclusive story

The *Titanic* disaster made front-page news for weeks. Even though the presidential primary race between William Howard Taft and Teddy Roosevelt was heating up, it was pushed completely aside when word came in that the *Titanic* was in trouble. Everyone wanted an explanation for how the impossible had happened.

The explanation was long in coming. As wireless operators across the Atlantic searched the airwaves for news to send back to shore, they found only vague hints and garbled messages. This didn't stop the papers from printing stories, however. In the absence of solid information, they filled their pages with conjecture, resulting in general confusion and frustration.

People's hopes went up and down like yo-yos with each new bit of information. Even the Navy was on the job, trying to find out what happened. As the whole country was in turmoil, wireless operator Harold Bride sat at the transmitter aboard the *Carpathia*, keeping a tight lid on the story.

It took some time for the whole story to reach shore, but the sinking of the Titanic *was one of the biggest stories of the century.*

Hulton Getty/Tony Stone Images

Bad News Travels Fast

Even before the wreck of the *Titanic* was resting peacefully on the bottom of the ocean, word of the disaster came in over wireless at the office of *The New York Times*. At 1:20 in the morning, the *Times* wireless operator picked up a message relayed from Cape Race, Newfoundland, that the *Titanic* had hit an iceberg, was sinking, and required immediate assistance.

Blow Me Down!
The *New York Times* broke the news of the *Titanic*'s sinking on April 15. On that same day, the paper carried an ad for the *Titanic*'s return voyage to England!

Sink or Swim

Needless to say, the *Times* ran the story on the front page that morning, but only news of the ship's calls for help was available. No one on shore knew whether the ship had stayed afloat since messages over the wireless were slow in coming.

The White Star office in New York City was swamped with phone calls and visitors. Vice President P.A.S. Franklin was reassuring, saying he was certain that all those aboard the *Titanic* were safe. He went on to claim that the ship was "practically unsinkable." By the time he said this, however, the *Titanic* had already gone down!

Crowd gathered outside the White Star office in New York City wanting news of the disaster.
Mary Evans Picture Library

No News Is Good News

Later that same morning, another wireless message came in from Cape Race saying that the *Titanic* was being towed into Halifax by the steamer, *Virginian*, and that everyone on board was safe! The White Star office began making preparations to receive the passengers and transport them to New York, the *Titanic*'s original destination.

Later that afternoon, more reassuring reports came in over wireless. Newspapers printed the good news in the headlines! People even started criticizing *The New York Times* for running its discouraging story that morning.

> **SOS**
> It has been said that as the news about the *Titanic* looked bad, then improved, insurance rates on the ship's cargo and White Star stock went down, then up in value.

LINER TITANIC IS AFLOAT AND ON WAY TO HALIFAX

GIANT STEAMER CRASHES INTO ICEBERG

THE EVENING NEWS.

Many newspapers missed the boat on the Titanic *disaster, printing erroneous news that the passengers were safe.*

Mariners' Museum

Who started these hopeful rumors, and why, was a mystery. Some speculated that they were started by owners of White Star stock who wanted to keep stock prices high until they could sell their shares. Eventually it appeared that the false news that the *Titanic* passengers were safe resulted from two garbled wireless messages that had been spliced together.

One of these messages was actually a question asking if the ship was safe. The other message had nothing to do with the *Titanic* at all, but concerned an oil tanker that was being towed to Halifax. Someone confused the tanker with the *Titanic* and assumed that she was safe.

On top of this confusion, wireless operators, White Star executives, and the press became frustrated about not hearing any word on the ship. Faced with incomplete information and the desire to think positive thoughts, they made hasty assumptions about what happened.

Rumors continued to be reported even as new information came to light. Some papers reported numerous ships had converged on the scene in time. Others reported that all the women and children aboard were saved.

Throwing Cold Water

The first definitive report of the sinking of the *Titanic* came in at 4:35 in the afternoon over radio-receiving equipment at Wanamaker's department store in New York City, which had one of the most powerful radio stations in the country. The wireless operator who received the message, 21-year-old David Sarnoff, became instantly famous, and eventually rich.

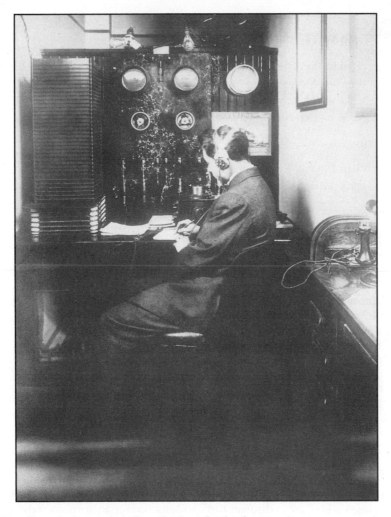

David Sarnoff at the wireless controls, relaying the bad news.
Sarnoff Research Center/National Geographic Image Collection

The wireless message was sent by White Star's *Olympic*, the *Titanic*'s sister ship from the site of the disaster 1,400 miles away. It said that the *Titanic* had gone down and that only about 675 people had been saved aboard the *Carpathia*, which was steaming for New York. Sarnoff is said to have stayed at his wireless controls for 72 hours straight relaying messages to the friends and families of survivors.

Ahoy There!

Senator Smith: *With the right to exact compensation for an exclusive story detailing the horrors of the greatest sea disaster that ever occurred in the history of the world, do you mean that an operator under your company's direction shall have the right to prevent the public from knowing of that calamity?*

Mr. Marconi: *No.*

Senator Smith: *Hold on for a moment. From knowing of that calamity except through the exclusive appropriation of the facts by the operator who is cognizant of them?*

Mr. Marconi: *I say, not at all. I gave no instructions to withhold information.*

—U.S. Senate Inquiry

Lifesavers

Sarnoff was one of the first to envision the potential of radio to broadcast music. He had the idea in 1916 before radio broadcasting had caught on.

Blow Me Down!

Harold Bride was badly injured in his struggle to save himself. He had to be carried to the witness stand to testify at the Senate inquiry. It has been said that his hair turned white shortly after the incident, even though he was in his early twenties!

Sarnoff went on to become a big cheese in the world of radio. Shortly after the *Titanic* incident, he became chief inspector for the Marconi company. Years later, after World War I, the American branch of the Marconi Company was bought out by General Electric. This new division of GE was called the Radio Corporation of America (RCA). In 1926, Sarnoff was made general manager of RCA. He became the company's third president in 1930. He attributed his professional success to his luck in first picking up the radio signal about the *Titanic*.

Radio Silence

Only later did people start wondering why word of the disaster took so long to reach shore and why the news came from the *Olympic* and not from the *Carpathia*. In fact, the *Carpathia* was swamped with questions about the disaster, wired in from the papers and the U.S. Navy. At the time, these questions went mysteriously unanswered.

As we mentioned in Chapter 5, *Titanic* wireless operator Harold Bride, working on board the *Carpathia* after the disaster, did not respond to any inquiries from the press. Not only that, he refused to answer questions wired to the *Carpathia* by U.S. Navy cruisers. Bride's mysterious silence led to an important line of questioning days later at the inquiry conducted by the U.S. Senate.

Wireless Operator Harold Bride being carried off the Carpathia *in New York Harbor.*

Mariners' Museum

Friend or Foe?

The Navy wanted information about Major Archibald Butt, who, as you may remember from Chapter 3, was a close friend and advisor to President Taft. Before working for Taft, Butt had been an advisor to Taft's predecessor, Teddy Roosevelt. Now Taft and Roosevelt, once close allies themselves, were squaring up to compete against one another in the upcoming Republican primaries and both contenders wanted Archie Butt in their corner.

Archie was torn between the two. He felt loyalty toward both, and realized that if he sided with one of them, the other would feel betrayed. He needed some time to think, so he took a vacation in Europe to sort things out. No one knows what he finally decided. He scheduled his return trip to the States on board the *Titanic* and was lost with the ship.

President Taft was eager to learn what became of his advisor. He ordered the Navy to ask the *Carpathia* if Butt were still alive. Harold Bride was working the wireless on board the *Carpathia* at the time, giving the ship's only paid operator, Harold Cottam, a rest from an extra-long shift. Bride acknowledged that he received the Navy's questions, but pretended that he couldn't understand what they were asking.

No Re-Morse

Bride was later questioned at the Senate inquiry about his radio silence—his refusal to respond to the Navy and to the press. Bride's excuse was that the Navy operators were incompetent and did not understand continental (European) Morse signals well enough. The Navy later denied this, saying their operators were fully trained in continental Morse.

SOS
In the middle of Bride's testimony at the Senate inquiry into the *Titanic* disaster, an unidentified woman entered the room in tears, wanting to know what had happened to Officer Murdoch, who had been lost with the ship.

Bride also had an excuse for not answering the press. He said he felt his first duty was to the *Titanic* survivors on board the *Carpathia*. Many of them had telegrams they wanted to send to loved ones on shore. Bride gave these telegrams priority over questions from the press.

If this really was Bride's motivation for ignoring the press, it didn't have the helpful effects he intended. Most people on shore had only the press to rely on for information; by not communicating with the press, Bride prolonged the painful suspense for people who had loved ones aboard the *Titanic*.

Inside Line

Bride may not have told the whole truth about his actions while operating the *Carpathia*'s wireless equipment. The wireless industry in general, and wireless operators in particular, were known to take advantage of their privileged access to information for their own benefit and the benefit of their companies.

Bride may have snubbed the Navy on account of the wireless system they used, which was designed by a company in competition with the Marconi company, which operated the *Titanic*'s wireless and employed Harold Bride. Marconi wireless operators had instructions to boycott other companies except in an emergency. The *Titanic* disaster obviously qualifies as an emergency, but Bride may have felt that the disaster was over, and may not have realized that the Navy was requesting vital information for the president of the United States.

It seems this sort of behavior was fairly typical among wireless operators at sea. Looking out primarily for their own, and their company's interests, they often exhibited hostility toward others, even to the point of interfering with important work. Wireless workers were known to drown out the signals being sent by rival operators by setting a book on the telegraph key. By making noise in this way, they could disrupt important messages!

Some of this competitive attitude came into play when the *Titanic*'s chief wireless operator, Jack Phillips, was signaling the *Carpathia* for help. The wireless operator for another ship, the *Frankfurt*, broke in, wanting to know what the matter was. Phillips responded by signaling, "You fool. Stand by and keep out." The *Frankfurt* did not use Marconi wireless, but the rival Telfunken system.

Dialing for Dollars

There is still another explanation besides wireless rivalry for Bride's silence. Evidently, he was actually instructed to keep quiet by the Marconi company, which had worked out a deal with *The New York Times*. Guglielmo Marconi, founder and president of the Marconi Wireless Company and inventor of the wireless telegraph, understood the importance of wireless as a tool for spreading news, and wanted to take advantage of the value of wireless to the press.

Marconi evidently had an arrangement with Carr Van Anda, editor of *The New York Times*, who was willing to pay for exclusive, inside information on the *Titanic* disaster. As it turned out, a *Times* reporter, Jim Speers, was the first—and only—reporter to get to Harold Bride. He came aboard the *Carpathia* almost as soon as it docked as part of Marconi's entourage, while thousands of bystanders were kept behind police barricades. Bride gave the reporter his story and was paid $1,000 by the paper. Bride's account ran on the *Times'* front page the following day.

Other reporters for other papers were desperate to get a good story. They waited for the *Carpathia* to arrive in New York Harbor on the pier and in boats. One reporter who tried to force his way onto the *Carpathia* to interview survivors was punched in the jaw by *Carpathia*'s Third Officer Rees. Another reporter tried to trick his way on board by putting a foamy substance in this mouth and asking to see his sister! When this didn't work, he tried to bribe his way on board.

Marconi was asked about his relations with *The New York Times* during the Senate inquiry. He denied having any secret deal with the paper and was taken at his word. After all, it was thanks to Marconi's invention that any *Titanic* survivors were rescued, and he enjoyed a boost in prestige and popularity as a result of the disaster.

Even so, there is strong evidence that he had, in fact, cut a deal with the *Times*. The Navy intercepted a couple of wireless messages sent to Harold Bride by the Marconi Company. The messages promised Bride "big money" for hushing up the story. It seems the *Times* editor, Carr Van Anda, contacted Marconi to arrange for the interview with Bride.

Ahoy There!

Say old man, Marconi Company taking good care of you. Keep your mouth shut, and hold your story. It is fixed for you so will get big money. Now please do your best to clear.

Arranged for your exclusive story for dollars in four figures. Mr. Marconi agreeing. Say nothing until you see me. Where are you now?

—Wireless messages intercepted by the U.S. Navy, sent by the Marconi Company to Harold Bride on the *Carpathia*

Both Bride and Marconi were later called to testify at the U.S. Senate inquiry, where they were asked why the signals sent to the *Carpathia* by Navy cruisers were not answered. Both men denied knowledge of a cover-up. Bride, who was injured during his *Titanic* ordeal, looked tired and sick. As a result, his questioners were reluctant to put pressure on him. Marconi was widely considered a hero for inventing the wireless telegraph, so he too was spared probing interrogation.

Crowd Control

When the *Titanic* story finally broke, the crowd outside the White Star office grew, and police reinforcements were sent in to keep things from getting out of hand. People wanted to know what happened and whether their loved ones were among those who survived. An even larger crowd, estimated at about 4,000 people, gathered in Times Square, where *The New York Times* posted the news on a big bulletin board.

Crowds gathered in Times Square in New York as news of the disaster was posted.
Brown Brothers

It was hard to believe. People had come to place a great deal of trust in progress and technology, and now their faith was shaken. What seemed like one of humanity's biggest triumphs turned out to be one of humanity's biggest mistakes.

The Least You Need to Know

➤ Many early wireless messages and newspapers falsely reported that all *Titanic* passengers were safe.

➤ The bad news was first picked up late in the afternoon by Wanamaker's department store wireless operator, David Sarnoff.

➤ News of the disaster was slow to reach the shore, possibly because wireless operator Harold Bride was offered money for an exclusive story.

➤ Huge crowds gathered in New York outside the White Star office and at Times Square, hoping to learn the truth about the disaster.

Burning Questions

Looking for dirt at sea isn't easy, especially if you're a land-lubber who doesn't know much about ships and sailing. But the chance to pounce on the survivors of one of the most heart-wrenching disasters of all time and ask them what happened doesn't come around very often. When it came in April 1912, the U.S. Senate was ready.

Wild ideas flew about who did what as the ship went down as people tried to put various spins on the disaster. Blame shifted back and forth. One group's heroes were another group's villains. Many people were sincerely convinced that more could have been done to save the victims. Others simply wanted to know what happened.

The Senate inquiry into the *Titanic* disaster was the focus of an international controversy. It was conducted on the spur of the moment on a shoestring budget. Ultimately, it led to important changes in shipping laws, and became one of the most important sources of information on the disaster.

Something Fishy Going On

Even before the *Carpathia* landed in New York Harbor with the *Titanic* survivors on board, White Star Director J. Bruce Ismay was already making plans to get himself and the surviving crew back to England as soon as possible. Meanwhile in America, a senator from Michigan named William Alden Smith was making plans to find out what happened to the *Titanic* and why. Smith was responding to a growing outcry from the public. People were complaining that information about the disaster was being hushed up and that not enough had been done to save the victims.

Catch the Drift
A populist has political views that favor the interests of ordinary people as opposed to industry, trade, or specialized interests.

Smith was a *populist*—someone who believed in looking out for the interests of ordinary people whose rights were often overlooked in favor of the rich and powerful. He had experience fighting against J.P. Morgan and his railroad monopoly to ensure better working conditions for employees and safer accommodations for passengers. Now Smith had a hunch that Morgan and his business methods were at least indirectly responsible for the *Titanic* disaster, and he wanted to prove his hunch right.

Drifting on a Sea of Troubles

Senator Smith called the White House to find out what President Taft planned to do about the *Titanic*. A personal friend and close advisor to Taft, Major Archibald Butt, was among the passengers on board. As you'll remember from the last chapter, Taft had the Navy contact the *Carpathia* to ask whether Butt had survived. Strangely, the Navy wireless operator was unable to get an answer to the president's question.

Taft was not known for decisive action. He was concerned about his friend, but had no immediate plans to get involved with the circumstances surrounding the *Titanic*. Meanwhile, public concern and confusion increased, thanks to erroneous newspaper reports that all of the passengers were safe. When these reports were proven wrong, people around the country were upset.

Well-Laid Plans

Smith proposed a resolution in the Senate to investigate the disaster, find out what caused the accident, and, based on the findings, propose international guidelines for the safety of ships at sea. Beyond the resolution's stated purpose, Smith wanted to see if he could hold Morgan's company, International Mercantile Marine, which owned White Star Line, legally responsible for the loss of life and property.

The Carpathia *arriving in New York Harbor with the* Titanic *survivors on board and her flags flying at half-mast in honor of the dead.*
Brown Brothers

Smith was in a good position to propose the resolution and lead the inquiry for a number of reasons. He served on the Senate's committee on commerce, and therefore had a duty to look into the way trade influenced the course of events leading to the disaster. He also served on the Senate's committee on international relations, so he had a stake in the *Titanic* as a multinational problem. Smith's resolution focused on both these issues.

The resolution was immediately adopted by a unanimous vote in the Senate on April 17. Soon afterward, Smith was informed of telegrams sent by Ismay to the White Star office in New York from the Carpathia.

Lifesavers
Among the many resolutions Smith posed during his political career was one to make the birthday of his hero, Abraham Lincoln, a national holiday. The resolution was eventually passed into law.

These had been intercepted by the Navy. The messages arranged for Ismay and the surviving *Titanic* crew members to return immediately to England without even setting foot in the United States. We know now that it was Officer Lightoller who suggested this course of action.

Smith acted fast to prevent Ismay and the others from slipping away. He lost no time, traveling to New York to request the cooperation of White Star in the inquiry. He acted quickly enough to meet the *Carpathia* in person to arrange for witnesses to testify. The resolution gave Smith the power to subpoena witnesses, including Ismay and the officers and crew of the *Titanic*. Ismay, in particular, was reluctant, but agreed to appear at the inquiry. The inquiry began just two days later on April 19.

J. Bruce Ismay, director of White Star Line and survivor of the Titanic *disaster.*

Topham/The Image Works

Risky Business

The Senate inquiry was risky, because the *Titanic* disaster was an international problem. Although White Star was part of an American conglomerate, it was run by British executives, just as the *Titanic* itself was designed and built by British shipbuilders and run by British officers and crew. Even though many victims and survivors were American, and the whole country wanted an explanation for what happened, many people—especially those in the shipping industry—felt that the inquiry was interfering where it didn't belong.

What's more, to subpoena British citizens was a drastic and unusual step that risked damaging relations between the United States and England. This was especially so because Senator Smith himself had brushed up against British national interests in the past.

Prior to the *Titanic* disaster, the British wanted to establish a peace agreement between the two countries but Senator Smith opposed it. At the time, just before World War I, the countries of Europe were intensely nationalistic. England sought economic and political support from the U.S. in its rivalry with France and Germany. Smith argued against a treaty between England and the U.S. because it excluded Germany and France and therefore defeated the peaceful purpose of the agreement. Largely as a result of Smith's opposition, the agreement failed.

Clowning at the Funeral

Even aside from the political tensions, there were issues of national pride at stake. The British didn't want the Americans blaming the whole disaster on them, and many thought Senator Smith was trying to do just that. The papers in England made fun of Smith, portraying him as a buffoon who was acting foolishly in the face of tragedy. As the inquiry proceeded, they made fun of him especially for his ignorance of nautical matters.

Smith's purpose, however, was not simply to find out what happened, but to satisfy the public by addressing their concerns. As soon as people found out about the disaster, they began writing to the White House with ideas, suggestions, and anxieties. When the inquiry got under way, people started sending their letters to Smith instead. Before long, Smith received hundreds of letters. He asked his son, William Alden, Jr., to come to Washington to help him read them all so he would know what was on people's minds, and some of the letters did reveal people's ignorance about ships and seamanship.

For example, Smith received letters from people who had heard about the *Titanic*'s famous watertight compartments and were worried that people might still

SOS

The owner of the Hippodrome, a vaudeville theater in London, started a popular act including a clown who pretended to be Senator Smith. The theater owner pushed the joke even further by inviting Smith himself to come to give a speech on nautical subjects—suggesting that such a speech would be hilarious!

Blow Me Down!
The British press made fun of Senator Smith for asking whether passengers could be trapped under the sea inside the *Titanic*'s watertight compartments. He was also teased for not knowing which end of the ship the bow is on, and for asking what an iceberg is made of. (The answer to his question was, of course, "ice.")

Blow Me Down!
Carr Van Anda, editor of *The New York Times*, was an ancient-Egypt buff. Years after the *Titanic* incident, he caused a stir by translating Egyptian hieroglyphics that were discovered inside King Tut's tomb.

be trapped inside them at the bottom of the sea. Obviously, this reflects a misunderstanding of how the compartments were supposed to work. In fact, the compartments were only watertight on the sides and bottom. (See Chapter 7 for an explanation of the watertight doors and watertight compartments.)

Despite the risk and the criticism, Smith's concern about the disaster was in tune with many people around the country, and most people approved enthusiastically. Senator Smith took into account the doubts and worries people expressed in their letters and tried to satisfy them through his investigation.

Bad Press

Unlike the British press, the American press was generally supportive of Smith and the Senate inquiry, but not always. Smith had political enemies who felt he had lost sight of the dignity involved in being a senator. They believed he was plowing thoughtlessly into complicated matters, and their opinions found their way into the papers.

One paper that was especially down on Senator Smith was *The New York Times*. The *Times* was unhappy with Smith bringing Guglielmo Marconi to the stand and accusing him of having an inside deal with the paper. Carr Van Anda, the paper's editor, got revenge by printing editorials critical of Smith. He even had his reporters check into Smith's background for a way to embarrass him in public.

Looking for Mr. Wrong

The most important witness throughout the hearing was Bruce Ismay, White Star Director and survivor of the *Titanic* disaster. Smith wanted to prove either that Ismay interfered with Captain Smith in a way that led to the accident, or that Ismay knew of *Titanic* officers who were guilty of negligence. If he could prove either one, it would give survivors and families of victims the right to sue White Star for damages.

J. Bruce Ismay at the Senate inquiry into the sinking of the Titanic.
Topham/The Image Works

Straw Man

Ismay had already been targeted by the press as the villain responsible for the whole disaster. Ismay was able to defend himself well enough so that Smith could not prove he was at fault. He remained guilty, however, in the eyes of newspapers and the public. Many felt that even if he didn't do anything that led to the disaster, he was still at fault simply for saving himself.

171

Ahoy There!

What do you think I am? Do you believe I'm the sort that would have left the ship as long as there were any women and children aboard her? That's the thing that hurts, and it hurts all the more because it's so false and baseless…I have searched my mind with deepest care. I have thought long over each single incident that I could recall of the wreck. I am sure nothing wrong was done—that I did nothing that I should not have done. My conscience is clear, and I have not been a lenient judge of my own acts.

—J. Bruce Ismay, White Star director, at the U.S. Senate inquiry

Ismay asked repeatedly to be allowed to leave the country and go back to England. Senator Smith denied his request each time. Ismay complained to the British embassy, and International Mercantile Marine complained on his behalf to Congress. All to no avail. Ismay had to stay as long as Smith thought there was a chance of negligence.

Getting to the Bottom

Smith arranged to have a sheriff go undercover and spend time with members of the *Titanic*'s crew to see if any of them had any knowledge of what might have gone wrong. The sheriff came up with a list of 29 names of crew members who had stories to tell about the disaster. Smith ordered subpoenas for all of them. Later on, five more names emerged of crew members who might know something. These crew members were already on their way back to England on the *Lapland*. Smith had a Navy cruiser intercept the *Lapland* to subpoena them and bring them to the inquiry. Since the crew members were still in U.S. territorial waters, they had to return for questioning.

SOS
Even while trying to dig up incriminating evidence, Smith had to weed out some tall tales. One report given to Smith claimed that the *Titanic*'s lookout was asleep and the crew were all drunk the night of the disaster.

Although many crew members were frank in describing what happened and in offering their views of why things went wrong, Smith wanted to avoid getting an account of the disaster that was slanted toward the perspective of the crew. In addition to officers and crew, he also heard testimony from surviving passengers.

In this the Senate inquiry differed from the British Board of Trade inquiry that took place later in England. The British inquiry focused more heavily on questions concerned with ship design and leadership procedure, preferring to deal directly with those responsible for these things—nautical experts and the officers involved. The Senate inquiry was concerned with clarifying the disaster for the sake of ordinary people.

Despite the criticism Smith underwent throughout the inquiry, most people were impressed with his accomplishment. He managed to get a complete account of the disaster from dozens of witnesses—82 in all—while the event was still fresh in their minds, and make recommendations for new legislation.

In fact, the inquiry was remarkably fast, beginning on April 19, the day after the *Carpathia* landed in New York with survivors. The crew members who testified returned to England on the *Adriatic* on the 29th of April. The whole thing was wrapped up in a little over a month. Smith gave a speech in the Senate on May 28, summing up the inquiry and proposing legislation to avoid similar disasters from taking place in the future.

The Least You Need to Know

➤ Senator William Alden Smith launched the inquiry to develop new international shipping laws and to find out if anyone involved was guilty of negligence. Negligence would have allowed people to sue International Mercantile Marine.

➤ In general, Smith was ridiculed in the British papers but praised in America.

➤ As a result of being served with a subpoena by the Senate, Ismay had to delay his return to England. He appeared at the inquiry against his will.

➤ Ismay defended himself against suspicion of negligence and interference but remained a villain in the eyes of the American press.

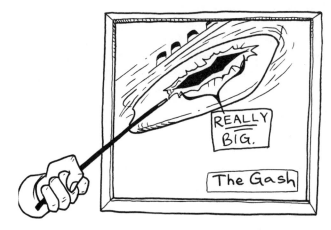

Chapter 16

Holes in the System

Before the Senate investigation in America finished, another inquiry in England started up, going over similar ground, but in a different way. The experts and lawyers were called out in full force.

For many of the smart set in English society, the *Titanic* inquiry was a fashionable event, and spectators turned out in their finest. They got a good show—about 100 witnesses were put on the stand and grilled by some of the sharpest lawyers in England. Running the show was one of the sharpest of all, Commissioner Lord Mersey, known in court for his satirical wit.

Through its painstaking efforts, the inquiry ferreted out the many human errors that led to the disaster, identified those responsible—and, in the end, let them off with a talking-to. It seemed that there were so many factors involving so many people, all contributing to the disaster, that it was pointless to hold anyone to blame. This seemed to satisfy most people at the time, but before long it was challenged with completely different results.

BOT-ching Things Up

The organization responsible for British shipping regulations followed by the *Titanic* and other ships of the day was the Board of Trade. The BOT not only made the rules, they enforced them. As the *Titanic* was being fitted out in Belfast, BOT inspectors made thousands of trips on board, making sure everything was ship shape.

Bad Show

SOS
The Board of Trade passed a rule in 1894 saying that all ships over 10,000 tons had to have at least 16 lifeboats. This was applied to the 46,000-ton *Titanic*, even though no ships anywhere near this big existed when the rule was passed.

It reflected badly on the BOT that the *Titanic* sank and so many people died. The most glaring BOT problem that came to light with the *Titanic* disaster was how lax the lifeboat rules were. The *Titanic* complied with BOT regulations, but BOT regulations turned out not to be good enough to prevent catastrophe.

The BOT required only a fraction of the lifeboat space necessary to accommodate everyone on board. What's more, the BOT was casual about enforcing tests and drills to make sure the crew knew how to load and lower the boats. It appeared that many officials in the BOT had the attitude that safety decisions should be left up to the owners of ships, rather than the government. This attitude encouraged owners to sacrifice safety considerations for profit.

Mersey Dotes

The U.S. Senate inquiry uncovered information that suggested it was time to lower the boom on the BOT. One big—if not *the* biggest—culprit in the disaster was the system of safety regulation, a system for which the BOT was chiefly responsible. Before the American investigation ended, the British inquiry began, going over much of the same ground, but in more meticulous detail. The BOT, however, had no reason to be shaking in its shoes. They were the group conducting the inquiry!

The fact that the group who investigated the disaster was also one of the groups most in need of investigation led some people to expect very little, especially since the person in charge, John Charles Bigham, Lord Mersey, Commissioner of the Wreck, played a key role in a notorious cover-up in the past.

Ahoy There!

The BOT had passed that ship as in all respects fit for the sea, in every sense of the word, with sufficient margin of safety for everyone on board. Now the BOT was holding an inquiry into the loss of that ship—hence the whitewash brush. Personally, I had no desire that blame should be attributed either to the BOT or the White Star Line, though in all conscience it was a difficult task, when handled by some of the cleverest legal minds in England, striving tooth and nail to prove the inadequacy here, the lack there, when one had known, full well, and for many years, the ever-present possibility of such a disaster.

—Charles Lightoller, looking back at the British inquiry

John Charles Bigham, Lord Mersey, head of the British Court of inquiry into the Titanic *disaster.*

Topham/The Image Works

Keeping a Lid on It

Lord Mersey was highly experienced in almost every aspect of British law, including nautical matters. By the time he was appointed to head the inquiry, he had served as the president of several divisions of the High Court in England, including the Admiralty. He also served in the House of Commons, where he had investigated the scandal of the Jameson raid.

Blow Me Down!
Senator Smith, who conducted the U.S. Senate inquiry, knew about Mersey's role in the Jameson raid investigation. Smith had many Dutch-American constituents in his home state of Michigan, and supported the Boers during the war. When he found out Mersey would lead the British inquiry, he was all the more determined to do a thorough job in his own inquiry!

Prior to the Boer War, fought at the turn of the century in South Africa between British and Dutch colonialists, the British were suspected of involvement in a failed attempt to overthrow the Dutch president of the Transvaal, Peter Kreuger. This was a serious affront to the Dutch, and aggravated the heightening tensions between Dutch and British. Lord Mersey's committee was in charge of looking into the incident to see if the British were, in fact, involved.

To most people's surprise, and many people's irritation, the committee found the British innocent of any wrongdoing. The Jameson raid inquiry was labeled a "whitewash." Many expected another whitewash from Lord Mersey in his investigation of the *Titanic* disaster.

Bellying Up to the Bar

Not only was Mersey in charge of the investigation, he got to decide who could participate. At first he refused a number of groups who wanted to be in on the proceedings, including the Seafarers' Union, the Imperial Merchant Service Guild, and the National Union of Stewards. Later he allowed these groups to be represented. Lawyers for these groups would make it more difficult for blame to be placed specifically on the officers, crew, and staff of the *Titanic*.

Numerous other groups hired lawyers to look out for their interests. In fact, some 50 lawyers participated. Here's a list of some of the key counselors in the British inquiry:

➤ **Sir Rufus Isaacs** for the Board of Trade

➤ **Mr. Raymond Asquith** also for the Board of Trade

➤ **Sir Robert Finlay** for White Star Line

➤ **Mr. W.D. Harbinson** for the third-class passengers

➤ **Mr. Thomas Scanlon** for the National Sailors and Fireman's Union

➤ **Mr. C. Robertson Dunlop** for the captain and officers of the *Californian* (the ship that failed to respond to the *Titanic*'s distress signals)

➤ **Mr. Henry Duke** for Sir Cosmo and Lady Lucile Duff-Gordon

Money Talks

Critics of the inquiry later complained that it cost so much—over 20,000 pounds. Included in the cost to the nation were the salaries of the lawyers for the Board of Trade, each of whom made close to 2,500 pounds. In contrast, lawyers representing seamen, stewards, and third-class passengers made less than a third of this amount.

This disparity in lawyer's fees helps account for the fact that no third-class passengers were called to testify. In the absence of the testimony of anyone who was there, the court ruled that third-class passengers were not restricted in any way from equal access to the lifeboats on the first-class decks. Abundant evidence suggests that this ruling is false.

Know-It-Alls

Assisting Lord Mersey as his secretary was his son, Clive Bigham, who rented the Scottish Drill Hall in London to be used as the court. Also on hand was a panel of five experts on shipping, ship design, and navigation. A special model of the *Titanic*, 20 feet long, was built and displayed in the hall, with a white mark on the hull at the spot where the ship first hit the iceberg.

Workmen put finishing touches on the 20-foot model of the Titanic *used during the British inquiry.*
Brown Brothers

Lifesavers

Among the experts was Professor J.H. Biles of Glasgow University who had designed ships himself and studied the design of the *Titanic*. He brought it to the Board of Trade's attention that one reason the *Titanic* sunk was that the watertight bulkheads did not extend all the way to the top deck.

Clearing the Air

The British inquiry heard from only two passengers, who asked to appear in order to clear themselves of suspected wrongdoing: Sir Cosmo and Lady Lucile Duff-Gordon. They escaped from the sinking ship in a lifeboat that was less than half full, and when the ship sank, their boat did not go back to try to pull more survivors out of the water.

Sir Cosmo was suspected of bribing the boatmen in their lifeboat to keep away from survivors in the water for fear the boat would be swamped. He and Lady Duff-Gordon were cleared by Lord Mersey, who accepted their story that the money Sir Cosmo gave the boatmen was to replace the luggage they had lost on the ship. Lord Mersey did point out, however, that Sir Cosmo might have tried to do more for the survivors in the water.

Forgive and Forget

Lord Mersey's treatment of the Duff-Gordons was similar to his approach to all those who were suspected of wrong-doing in the disaster. In general, Lord Mersey found that, although many people involved clearly could have done a better job, no one in particular had done anything seriously wrong. This attitude applied especially to Mersey's assessment of Captain Smith.

Ahoy There!

He made a mistake, a very grievous mistake, but one which, in face of the practice and of past experience negligence cannot be said to have had any part; and in absence of negligence it is, in my opinion, impossible to fix Captain Smith with blame.

—Lord Mersey, speaking at the British inquiry on Captain Smith

Another example is Alexander Carlisle, who served as Harland and Wolff's managing director when the *Olympic* and the *Titanic* were built. Even before either ship ever sailed, Carlisle was uneasy about how few lifeboats they were intended to carry. He felt, quite logically, that since these ships were so big, they ought to carry more lifeboats.

He even acted on his feeling by talking with the Welin Davit Company, getting them to design davits for the big ships that would hold up to 48 boats. He shared the design with J. Bruce Ismay and suggested that the *Titanic* and the *Olympic* be equipped with extra boats. Carlisle's suggestion was disregarded by Ismay and the White Star owners. Carlisle made no complaint.

What's more, Carlisle even signed some recommendations intended for the Board of Trade saying that there was no need to increase the number of lifeboats on new ships. He later admitted under questioning at the British inquiry that, even at the time, he personally disagreed with the recommendations he had signed. Clearly, Carlisle might have done more to prevent the tragedy. Even so, Lord Mersey did not rule that he was responsible for what happened.

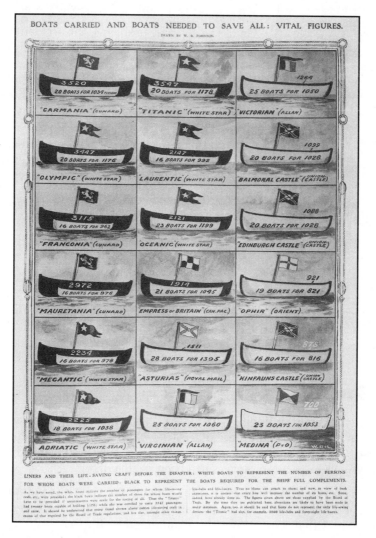

A news feature from 1912 showing the inadequacy of lifeboats for steamships of the time.
Topham/The Image Works

Off the Hook

SOS

A scandal stemming from the *Titanic* disaster involving Board of Trade Attorney Rufus Isaacs came to light early in 1913. The day after the ship went down, Isaacs bought numerous shares of stock in the Marconi Wireless Company of America. As a result, he stood to benefit from the good reputation of Marconi himself. Despite this interest, he participated in the British inquiry's questioning of Marconi and drew suspicion of helping Marconi look good in court.

Despite concerns that the inquisition was only going to whitewash the *Titanic* incident, the investigation did bring important facts to light. Many of the inquiry's findings confirmed conclusions drawn by the U.S. Senate inquiry, including problems with the ship's leadership, problems with the Board of Trade, problems with White Star's owners, and problems with the building and design of the ship, as well as problems with the way wireless was used on board.

On top of all these problems, the accident seemed to have been caused by plain old bad luck. Finally, Lord Mersey was extremely reluctant to blame anyone or anything in particular for the disaster. He avoided finding fault with Captain Smith, who obviously could not defend himself. He did not place special blame on Ismay, judging that he did not exert any pressure on the captain to maintain a high speed through the dangerous, icy region. Neither did he blame the officers or the lookouts, ruling that they had acted as they were supposed to under the circumstances.

The court concluded that there was no negligence involved. Since no negligence was involved, White Star Line could not be sued.

New Suits

Not everyone was persuaded by the court's ruling. One person in particular, an Irish farmer named Thomas Ryan, had lost his son Patrick to the disaster. He wasn't willing to abide by the decision without a fight, so he sued the British High Court, arguing that White Star was, in fact, negligent, and therefore responsible for the disaster and liable for damages.

A Knotty Problem

The case went to court on June 20, 1913. Unlike the investigation, Ryan's lawsuit was tried in front of a jury. The purpose of the trial was not to learn, in general, about why the accident occurred and whether anyone was particularly to blame, but to decide whether White Star or its employees had been negligent.

The lawyers for White Star argued that the captain and crew had followed established procedure, and therefore could not be held accountable for the disaster. They provided evidence to show that most steamships maintained high speed, even in icy regions, as long as the weather was clear.

Expert witnesses testified that they would not have reduced speed under the circumstances. These witnesses suggested that the speed of the *Titanic* as it approached the iceberg—21^1/$_2$ knots—was appropriate under the circumstances. The officers were therefore justified in assuming that an iceberg would be visible from far enough away to be avoided, even though that turned out not be the case.

A Case of Black and White

Ryan's lawyer, John Campbell, argued that White Star either should have taken better precautions against the ice they knew was in the area, or should have been able to avoid the ice. He referred specifically to the question, raised throughout the trial, of whether the side of the iceberg facing the ship had been black.

Lifesavers
One expert witness called by White Star to testify gave testimony damaging to White Star. This was Captain E.G. Cannons, who said that if he had received as many ice warnings as the *Titanic* had received, he would have added extra lookouts until he reached the ice; then he would have slowed down.

Campbell said White Star was negligent either way you looked at it. If the iceberg had been black and difficult to see, it shows that the ship was going too fast under those conditions. If it had been white and clearly visible, then the lookouts should have seen it soon enough to avoid it. Thus the officers and crew should have been better prepared to stay out of danger, or better able to avoid it at the moment of crisis.

Campbell's arguments persuaded the jury. They ruled that White Star and its employees were negligent in contributing to the disaster, overturning Lord Mersey's decision at the British inquiry. They awarded Ryan 125 pounds. White Star appealed the decision, but the ruling in favor of Ryan held up.

Back Seat Driver

Ryan's victory prompted others to sue White Star as well. Some were Americans who sued in British courts, where they thought they would have better luck than at home. Eventually in America, the case against White Star was reopened by other private suits. This case was opened on June 22, 1915.

Blow Me Down!
Total claims against White Star came to around $16 million. The amount seems low for many reasons, including inflation and that fact that many people who could have sued didn't.

Just as J. Bruce Ismay was central to the U.S. Senate investigation, he was central to the arguments of those suing White Star in America. They claimed that Ismay influenced the captain to maintain high speeds. Their evidence for this consisted largely of the fact that Captain Smith handed Ismay a note with one of the ice warnings on it the day of the collision.

Getting Settled

After each side presented its arguments, the lawyers rested their cases and it was left to the judge to decide. He never had to make a decision. Instead, White Star decided to settle out of court. They agreed to pay the claimants a total of $664,000 to be divided among them. In return, the claimants would drop their suit. This agreement protected White Star from future suits, both in America and England. The arrangement seemed to satisfy most of those involved. White Star had to pay, but not nearly as much as they were being sued for.

The Least You Need to Know

➤ The British investigation conducted by the Board of Trade has been labeled a "whitewash."

➤ Lord Mersey, who led the investigation, ruled that there was no negligence on the part of White Star.

➤ Mersey's ruling was overturned in later private suits.

➤ Ultimately, White Star settled out of court with claimants.

Cold Judgments

In This Chapter

➤ *Titanic* controversies

➤ The debate over precautions

➤ The Ismay question

➤ Captain Lord versus the inquiries

➤ Steerage rights

➤ Looking for heroes and villains

Points of view abound about what caused the *Titanic* disaster, what was done about it at the time, and its significance. Many debates conducted by *Titanic* experts, concern questions of fact and involve the careful sifting of evidence that has piled up over the decades. Much of this evidence is contradictory, suggesting that we may never know the answers to some of the event's most burning questions.

Other points of view involve matters of personal or group pride. Who gets blamed and who gets praised for their actions often depends on who's doing the blaming and praising. For example, although not all of the lifeboats were fully loaded when they were lowered from the *Titanic*, why they weren't has always been a loaded question. Possible answers to the question say a lot about human nature and Western civilization.

As the years go by, and the *Titanic* disaster remains a source of fascination, it becomes increasingly possible to gain a better historical perspective on the sinking. It was a terrible thing for everyone involved. Many people might have done more to prevent or minimize the harm done, but no one acted with extraordinary negligence or cowardice. By the same token, many people did fine things in the heat of the moment, but no single group stands out as particularly noble.

Fault Lines

The British and U.S. Senate inquiries managed to reach many of the same conclusions. This impressive accomplishment suggests the results were fair and reliable. Finally, however, the inquiries failed to satisfy everyone, and a number of questions continue to arouse disagreement. Most have to do with who, if anyone, was at fault, and how some were saved and so many weren't.

Some of the Titanic's *lifeboats after the disaster. These were repainted and used again on different White Star ships.*
Brown Brothers

Testimony That Floats

One of the star witnesses in both investigations was Second Officer Lightoller. He was one of the most convincing—and, according to some, most deceptive—of them all. He was the highest ranking officer to survive the disaster, an articulate speaker and an experienced and knowledgeable seaman. These attributes made it hard for his questioners to trip him up.

What's more, he offered a point of view that those who might be held responsible were most happy with: No one was to blame. Lightoller testified that everyone in charge behaved just as they should have, both before and after the collision. According to him, the disaster was caused by a combination of unlikely and unforeseeable circumstances.

For one thing, the sea was unusually calm. According to Lightoller, this meant there were no waves breaking against the iceberg, which would have made it easier to see. For another thing, there was no moon. In addition, said Lightoller, the side of the iceberg itself was unusually blue or black, making it still less visible.

Blow Me Down!
Second Officer Lightoller was questioned at the U.S. inquiry for three and a half hours on the lowering of the lifeboats alone!

Lightoller's point was that no one could have predicted these circumstances, hence no one could be blamed for the accident. Both inquiries basically accepted this point of view, but doubts remained. Some question Lightoller's claim that the circumstances were really so unusual. People also point out that the danger of ice was known ahead of time, yet no special precautions were taken.

Speed Readings

Perhaps the most burning question surrounding responsibility for the collision has to do with the effect J. Bruce Ismay had on the speed of the ship. He managed to clear himself at the inquiries of the suspicion that he influenced Captain Smith's judgment, but many *Titanic* experts find it hard to accept that he was "just another passenger," as he claimed to be.

SOS
Margaret Brown, better known as "Unsinkable Molly" Brown, told reporters that Ismay wanted the *Titanic* to get to New York as fast as possible so he could be there in time for a fashionable dinner party!

As we mentioned, Ismay was harshly blamed in American newspapers, and many wild stories have been told about him that don't have much basis in fact. One popular story is that Ismay was trying to break the record for the fastest transatlantic crossing and was pressuring Captain Smith to go faster than he should have. We know this couldn't be true, because the *Titanic* was not built to be fast enough to break the record, held by the smaller, faster Cunard ship, the *Lusitania*.

It is quite possible, though, that Ismay wanted the *Titanic*'s crossing to be faster than that previously made by her sister ship, the *Olympic*. If so, he may have tried to influence the captain to go fast. In fact, there is an incident that suggests Ismay did have some influence on the captain.

The afternoon before the ship hit the iceberg, Captain Smith gave Ismay a piece of paper with one of the ice warnings written on it. Ismay later gave the note back to the captain. Why did the captain want Ismay to know about the ice warning? We'll never know. He may have simply wanted to pique Ismay's interest in the voyage. On the other hand, giving Ismay the note may have been a way of saying "maybe we should rethink our plan to go so fast."

Ismay and the captain did, in fact, plan to speed up the following day. Of course, they never got a chance. It remains a mystery whether Ismay was pushing the captain to reach greater speed in order to attract more publicity for the *Titanic*.

Could Have, Should Have

Although the British and U.S. Senate inquiries did not find that gross negligence had been committed leading up to the disaster, or blame Ismay for his actions, they did single out, and severely criticize, one man they thought could have prevented its tragic outcome: Captain Stanley Lord of the *Californian*. Both Senator Smith and Lord Mersey ruled that Captain Lord could have saved the lives of those who died when the *Titanic* went down if he had only responded to the *Titanic*'s distress rockets.

Ahoy There!

The ice by which the Californian *was surrounded was loose ice extending for a distance of not more than two or three miles in the direction of the* Titanic. *The night was clear and the sea was smooth. When she first saw the rockets, the* Californian *could have pushed through the ice to the open water without any serious risk and so have come to the assistance of the* Titanic. *Had she done so she might have saved many if not all of the lives that were lost.*

—Lord Mersey at the British inquiry into the *Titanic* disaster

On the Californian, Dreaming

Lord seemed unable to account for himself on the witness stand. He said he didn't realize the rockets were distress signals, but acknowledged that he didn't bother to find out. He said he was half asleep in the *Californian*'s chart room when the ship's apprentice told him about the rockets, and doesn't remember getting the message, even though he responded to it at the time.

First Senator Smith, then Lord Mersey, found Lord's failure to take action incomprehensible and inexcusable. There was speculation that Lord must have been drunk at the time, but he claimed he never drank liquor. Many thought he was too worried about ice to want to risk helping the *Titanic*, but it seems Captain Lord never bothered to find out that the *Titanic* was in danger.

Lording it Over

Lord claimed that the *Californian* was too far away—19 miles, he claimed—to help the *Titanic* anyway. The investigators believed the two ships were only five or six miles apart.

Lord also claimed that the ship that was visible from the deck of his ship was not the *Titanic* as the investigators believed, but a third steamer. The Board of Trade looked into the possibility that a third ship was in the area, but could find no evidence of one. Investigators concluded that Lord was simply trying to cover up for himself.

As a result of the criticism he received at the inquiries, Lord was asked to resign from his job as a steamship captain with the Leyland Line. In the years that followed, he repeatedly asked the Board of Trade to review the case and change the inquiry's judgment. They refused, however, thus branding Captain Lord's reputation for life.

Sea Legs to Stand On

Fortunately for Lord, he was able to get a job with another steamship company and resume his career as a sea captain. He continued at sea for another 25 years after the *Titanic* disaster. Even so, he continued to feel wronged by the inquiries that condemned him.

He felt he had been condemned without a fair trial. In fact, he wasn't even a defendant when he took the witness stand at the two inquiries, but a witness. As a result, he felt he wasn't able to defend himself properly.

Since the inquiries, despite the fact that most people felt Lord was to blame for not doing anything as the *Titanic* went down, some experts looked at the evidence and came around to Lord's point of view. A careful look at testimony from passengers and crew on

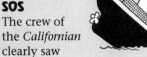

SOS
The crew of the *Californian* clearly saw another ship starting at about 11:00 in the evening. The crew of the *Titanic* did not see another ship until almost 12:30. This ship was reported to be moving, whereas the *Californian* had stopped for the night long before this time. The inquiries made no effort to account for these discrepancies.

Blow Me Down!
Captain Lord undoubtedly hurt his credibility by covering up the fact that his officers had seen rockets fired in the distance the night the *Titanic* went down. This fact was leaked by *Californian* crewman Earnest Gill, who received $500 from an American newspaper for the information.

board the *Titanic* shows that the ship they saw was moving at a time when the *Californian* had cut its engines and was staying put for the night.

It also appears that Lord may have been right when he said the two ships were too far from one another to see each other. When the wreck of the *Titanic* was discovered by Robert Ballard in 1985, it turned out that the ship went down about 10 miles from where it was supposed to have sunk. What's more, when the *Carpathia* first arrived on the scene hours later at 4:30 in the morning, the *Californian* was nowhere in sight, even though it hadn't budged since about 10:30 the previous night.

Three Ships

This evidence in support of Captain Lord has led to speculation that there might have been a third ship in the area between the *Californian* and the *Titanic*, seen by both of them. Some *Titanic* historians not only think such a ship actually existed, but have identified it as the *Samson*, a Norwegian sealing ship.

If the mysterious third ship was the *Samson*, it makes sense that it didn't stick around long enough to find out what happened to the *Titanic*. Back in 1912, it was illegal to hunt seals on Sunday, and that was just what the *Samson* was doing. The captain may have decided to keep a low profile, so the ship steamed off rather than stopping to say hello.

Lord Versus Lord

Despite their best arguments, Lord's supporters (who call themselves "Lordites") have failed to convince other *Titanic* experts of Lord's innocence. For the anti-Lord faction, the bottom line is that Lord got word of a ship firing white rockets and did not bother to find out why they were fired. It is this basic criticism that has dogged him throughout his career.

Ahoy There!

In any event, what difference does it make even if there was a third ship lying between the Californian *and the* Titanic? *Rockets are rockets. These clearly resembled distress signals, and both Stone and Gibson (crewmen on board the* Californian) *suspected some ship was in trouble.*

—Walter Lord, *The Night Lives On*, 1986

Lord felt especially bad when the best-selling *Titanic* book *A Night to Remember,* by Walter Lord (same name, no relation) came out in 1955. The book portrayed the *Californian's* captain in an unfavorable light. By then, Stanley Lord was in his 80s and—aside from the *Titanic* incident—could look back at a blameless nautical career.

Walter Lord's book evidently rankled Captain Stanley Lord a good deal. It didn't help the captain's feelings that the book was made into a motion picture three years later. Captain Lord made plans to sue Walter Lord for libel. He got help from a professional organization he belonged to for over 60 years, the Mercantile Marine Service Association, which took up his cause.

This group made public statements in defense of Lord and petitioned the British Board of Trade to review the evidence. The board refused, so that when Lord died in 1962, 50 years after the *Titanic* sank, his name had not been cleared. Since Lord's death, others have tried to persuade the Board of Trade and the public to reconsider the negative view of the *Californian*'s captain. To this day, an unresolved disagreement remains between those who support Lord and those who don't.

Who's on First?

Still more controversy surrounds the loading of the lifeboats and why some people were saved but not others. It was clear from the available statistics that a higher percentage of first-class passengers were saved than second and third class. Both inquiries noted this fact and investigated whether second- and third-class passengers were prevented from reaching the boat deck.

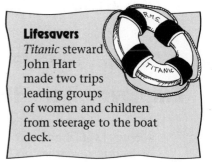

Lifesavers
Titanic steward John Hart made two trips leading groups of women and children from steerage to the boat deck.

Missing Pieces

No direct testimony was heard at either inquiry saying that any passengers were restricted from the boat deck. In fact, third-class passengers testified at the Senate inquiry that they were not kept away. Officers took the stand and made the same claim: Steerage passengers had full access to the boat deck during the time the lifeboats were being loaded and lowered.

It seems, however, that neither inquiry looked into the question very carefully. No third-class passengers were called to the stand at the British Board of Trade inquiry. No one looked into the design of the ship to see how difficult it would have been for steerage passengers to find their way to the lifeboats. No one thought to ask the officers and stewards why so few passengers were on the boat decks as the boats were being lowered.

Stacking the Deck

Archibald Gracie, a first-class passenger, gave an account that suggests steerage passengers were kept below until it was too late. He says he saw large numbers of people come up on deck after the boats had all been lowered. Like other passengers, including J. Bruce Ismay, Gracie had been under the impression that all the women and children had boarded the lifeboats. Evidently, this appeared to be the case only because a limited number of passengers made it to the boat deck in time.

Since the inquiry, numerous accounts have shown that steerage passengers were restricted. It remains a subject of debate as to why this was. It is unclear whether the ship's stewards took it upon themselves to restrict most of the steerage passengers, or whether the decision came from the captain or one of the officers.

Ahoy There!

Well, they sailed from England and were almost to the shore
As the rich refused to associate with the poor
So they put them all below
Where they were the first to go.
It was sad when the great ship went down!

—verse from the folk song, "The Titanic"

Employee Benefits

The inquiries into the disaster also noticed that a high percentage of the crew managed to survive. Even allowing for the fact that several crew members were assigned to each lifeboat to row, steer, and give directions, there was still a strangely high proportion of crew members among the survivors. Officers on the witness stand firmly denied any preference was shown to crew members.

Many of the crew, however, were pulled out of the water into collapsible "A" and "B." These boats could not be loaded properly from the boat deck because, by that time, the deck was already almost under water. Second Officer Lightoller testified that there were people in the water when the ship went down, but that they were a ways off from the collapsible.

This testimony was contradicted by Junior Wireless Operator Harold Bride. Bride was pulled out of the water onto collapsible "B," which was floating upside down in the water. This was the same boat Second Officer Lightoller made it onto. He said the collapsible was closely surrounded by dozens of people in the water wanting to get on the overturned collapsible.

Of course, there was only room for a few of them on the upside down boat. Bride said that those who were helped up out of the water were crew members. Many others were fended off for fear they would overturn and swamp the boat.

Spin Cycles

No one disagrees that the sinking of the *Titanic* was a terrible disaster. But debate over why it happened and how the people involved dealt with it has been complicated by conflicting statements people have made in response to the disaster. Much as the famous story of the sinking of the *Birkenhead* has been used to suggest that the British are especially capable of selfless, noble action (see Chapter 8), the story of the *Titanic* has been used in similar ways.

Many comments on the disaster have emphasized the selfless and resolute actions of Captain Smith, for example, or the officers, or even some passengers who seemed more concerned about the safety of others than themselves. Glorifying the behavior of the people involved suggests that, even though the *Titanic* sank, civilization still steams forward, full speed ahead.

At the time of the disaster, civilization was often thought to rest most securely in the hands of certain people. Industrialism and commerce was even more closely tied up with nationalism than it is today. Since that time, people have become increasingly aware that, for civilization to work, everyone has to be on board, regardless of how much money they have or what language they speak.

> **Blow Me Down!**
> In 1942, the German movie *Titanic* was produced with the approval of Hitler's ministry of propaganda. The film represents Captain Smith and J. Bruce Ismay as incompetent cowards while German passengers emerge as heroes. The film was heavily censored by the British before playing in England!

At the inquiries, a number of British and American witnesses testified to the noble actions of English-speaking people and disparaged other nationalities. Since then, movies about the disaster like *The Titanic* (1953) and *A Night to Remember* (1958) have implicitly glorified England and America by showing how well the officers and first-class passengers behaved in the face of crisis.

More recently, however, there has been a tendency to portray the special difficulties faced by the third-class passengers and to look to steerage for heroic behavior. Sometimes, as in the hit movie, *Titanic* (1997), third-class and first-class passengers are shown to be heroes together, just as both classes are shown to have people who act badly.

The Least You Need to Know

➤ Many *Titanic* disagreements concern whether the disaster could have been predicted and prevented.

➤ Ismay cleared himself at the inquiries, but has been suspected of interfering with Captain Smith ever since.

➤ Captain Lord of the *Californian* was condemned by the inquiries but has persuaded supporters of his innocence.

➤ The inquiries did not look deeply into the question of steerage access to the boat decks.

➤ Different generations have looked in different places for *Titanic* heroes and villains.

Charting New Courses

Sometimes bad events lead to good results. This holds true for the sinking of the *Titanic*. Precisely because it was such a shocking disaster, it woke people up to problems in the shipping industry, and supplied the motivation to do something about them.

Thanks to the *Titanic*, changes were made in almost every aspect of passenger shipping—construction, equipment, crew, navigation, communication, governance, and business practices. Suddenly it was no longer enough for a ship to be big, fast, and luxurious. Now it also had to measure up to international standards for fairness and safety.

The time was right for changes. The recent, painful memory of the *Titanic* made it difficult for shipping interests to stand in the way of reform. Many of the changes remain in effect today, having led to the formation of safety organizations that continue to keep watch over North Atlantic shipping.

Back to the Drawing Board

Blow Me Down!
Included in the hundreds of letters sent to the White House following the *Titanic* disaster were poems memorializing the event.

When the *Titanic* set sail from Southampton, England, on April 10, 1912, people had tremendous faith in the technology that had designed and built the ship. When she sank, that faith was shaken, but not completely broken. Shipbuilders, inventors, designers, and ordinary folks who had an idea or two came up with plans for keeping disasters like the *Titanic* from happening again.

Of course, governments in Europe and America got in on the act too, passing laws, signing treaties, and launching organizations to keep steamship passengers high and dry while at sea. Sweeping changes were made affecting the way ships were built, provisioned, and run.

This life ring wasn't enough to save the more than 1,500 people who lost their lives when the Titanic *went down.*
Popperfoto/Archive Photos

Keep Those Cards and Letters Coming!

During and after the U.S. Senate inquiry, hundreds of people wrote to the White House with questions, concerns, and suggestions regarding the *Titanic* disaster. Many had ideas for how to make passenger steamships safer. Some of these ideas were better than others. All of them, however, were looked over and forwarded to the Navy for further consideration.

Cabins May Be Used for Flotation

One idea was to use inflatable mattresses in all the cabins, so that everyone who had a place to sleep would also have something to float on if the ship went down. Another idea was to design the cabins themselves in such a way that they could function as lifeboats. (How these lifeboat-berths would be *lowered* was never fully worked out!) A similar suggestion that was more fully developed was for decks that could be detached from the ship and converted into lifeboats.

One of many safety measures inspired by the Titanic *that was designed but never put into practice.*

Hulton Getty/Tony Stone Images

A company that made airplanes wrote the White House to say that all the parts to a small plane could easily be stowed on deck. In the event of an emergency, the plane could be put together in a matter of about 15 minutes. The deck of a big steamship could be used as a runway, enabling the plane to take off and get help from any ship in the area. This may have been the first proposal for an aircraft carrier.

Ice Ideas

One letter proposed a rather drastic solution to the iceberg problem: Equip the bow of the steamship with a huge cannon; when the ship was in danger of running into a berg, just blast it out of the water. In fact, the Navy has looked into the possibility of destroying icebergs.

As it turns out, it would take a good deal more than a cannonball to do the job. To sufficiently blast an iceberg into pieces takes close to 2,000 tons of TNT! You could try to melt it, but you'd need to burn almost two and a half million gallons of gasoline!

A more friendly and ingenious approach to the iceberg problem was a suggestion to use grappling hooks to grab onto the berg. The idea was that the very iceberg that put the ship in danger of sinking would be able to keep the ship afloat long enough for help to arrive.

A Fish-Eye View

One suggestion for spotting icebergs sooner emerged at the British inquiry after it appeared that the lookouts in the crow's nest of the *Titanic* didn't see the iceberg soon enough because they were looking down on it. From their angle it didn't stand out against the horizon, but blended in with the sea. The suggestion was for lookouts to be stationed on a platform built down close to the water. From this platform, the lookouts would have a view straight out across the surface of the sea and might be able to pick out ice on the horizon more easily.

Lifesavers
After the *Titanic* disaster, even before it became the law, J. Bruce Ismay ordered that all White Star ships be equipped with enough lifeboats for everyone on board. His feelings matched those of the crew of *Titanic*'s sister ship, the *Olympic*, who refused to sail without more boats.

Ruling the Waves

Although these suggestions were undoubtedly well intentioned, none of them were passed into law. Many laws were passed, however, with the same goal in mind: Keep people in ships safe.

Not Rocking the Boat

Not surprisingly, most officials agreed that steamships needed to have enough lifeboat space for everyone on board. Some shipping companies were annoyed by this new rule, regarding it as "panic legislation," but, despite some complaints, the rule was successfully adopted.

It even became standard practice for a specific lifeboat seat to be assigned ahead of time to each passenger. The assignment would be printed on the ticket. Directions for the quickest way to get from the berths to the assigned boats would be provided for all passengers.

Twice a month, crews were required to conduct lifeboat drills. At least four crewmen were assigned to each boat. All boats had to be easy to get to and ready to go. The Engelhardt collapsibles that turned out to be so much trouble on the *Titanic* were considered unacceptable.

All the Extras

New laws were passed requiring other equipment as well. Ships had to have transverse (horizontal) bulk-heads in addition to the vertical ones. As we mentioned in Chapter 10, one reason the ship sank was that its vertical bulkheads didn't keep water from pouring into its watertight compartments from above. Horizontal bulkheads on top of the vertical ones would have averted this problem, enabling the ship to stay afloat. As a further precaution, in case any bulkheads get breached, ships had to have stronger pumps for bailing out water.

Still more measures were considered, including the idea of equipping ships with searchlights such as those used by Navy steamers. This feature, however, was finally considered unnecessary for passenger ships.

Sending a Clear Signal

It quickly became clear after the sinking of the *Titanic* how important wireless telegraphy could be to ship safety—both for providing ice warnings and for signaling for help in an emergency. It became clear as well that problems existed with the way wireless was used. One problem was that the main job of steamship wireless operators was to send telegraphs for passengers. Listening for warnings and relaying them to the bridge was secondary. New laws were passed to enforce the use of wireless as a safety feature:

➤ Wireless became mandatory for all steamers carrying 50 or more passengers.

SOS
According to schedule, the crew of the *Titanic* was supposed to conduct a lifeboat drill on Sunday, April 14, the day of the collision. For some un-known reason, Captain Smith didn't bother to have the drill!

SOS
There can be no doubt that legislation passed since the *Titanic* went down has significantly increased the safety of passen-ger ships in the North Atlan-tic. Even so, disastrous accidents have continued to occur. In 1959, the *Hans Hedtoft* collided with an iceberg and disappeared without a trace with some 95 passengers and crew on board. This prompted the Danish Meteorological Institute to begin "ice mapping" by radar and satellite.

➤ Wireless equipment had to include an auxiliary power supply.

➤ Two or more operators had to be available to provide 24-hour service.

➤ Direct communication between the wireless office and the bridge became mandatory, so that any warnings could be promptly posted where the officers on watch could see them.

In the United States, wireless regulation stemming from the *Titanic* disaster was extended to cover use of radio on land. Operators had to be licensed and regulated by the government. The body in charge of this eventually became the Federal Communications Commission (FCC). Amateurs were restricted from using the same radio frequencies used by licensed broadcasters. Instead, they were limited to short-wave radio.

Another safety rule was passed aimed at ships that didn't have to carry wireless. Any ship that fired rockets for any reason other than an emergency could be fined.

Ahoy There!

Any person who shall discharge or permit the discharge of any rocket or candle from any vessel on the high seas or within the jurisdiction of the United States for any purpose other than a signal of distress shall be guilty of a misdemeanor punishable by law as like offenses are now punishable.

—Smith Bill, later signed into law

Clear Sailing

Lawmakers didn't stop at making new rules for how ships had to be equipped. They also passed laws affecting navigation. For one, the standard shipping route between Europe and America was moved 60 miles to the south from February to August to avoid ice that drifts into the transatlantic lanes during these months. Steamers entering areas known to contain ice must slow down to a reasonable speed.

Lifesavers
The U.S. Coast Guard drops a wreath at the site of the sinking of the *Titanic* every year on the anniversary of the disaster.

In order to keep track of ice in the North Atlantic and to assist ships in trouble, the International Ice Patrol was organized in February 1914. The American branch of this international organization became the U.S. Coast Guard.

Many laws were designed with the aim of securing international cooperation among all countries whose ships traveled the North Atlantic. Many of these laws had to be postponed during World War I, but were put into practice afterward. Not long after the *Titanic* went down, however, on November 12,

1913, the International Conference for the Safety of Life at Sea met to agree on international rules. This group has continued to meet at various times since then.

Staying Afloat

There was still another aspect of shipping addressed by the new laws—the economic issues. In the U.S., when the *Titanic* went down, sailors generally had to put up with lousy working conditions. Not only were there long hours, low pay, and few benefits, but sailors often had to sign contracts guaranteeing that they wouldn't take another job with another shipping company. The owners, in other words, had sailors right where they wanted them.

This meant that you had to be pretty desperate for work in order to go to sea. As a result, American sailors tended to be low-skilled and poorly trained. Many of them were immigrants who couldn't speak English.

Sailor's Pay

Lawmakers came to believe that this work situation was not just bad for the sailors, it made shipping more dangerous. An untrained, overworked sailor who had a hard time understanding the captain's orders would be unlikely to respond well to an emergency.

To fix this problem, Congress passed the Seaman's Act in 1915, protecting the rights of American sailors. This act enabled them to take jobs freely with any company they wanted to work for and limited the length of their workdays to eight hours. Thanks to the Seaman's Act, sailing in America became a much more rewarding profession than it had been.

Ahoy There!

Unless the calling of the sailor can be dignified and put upon a basis which will encourage efficiency and devotion to that calling, we shall not have American sailors.

—Senator William Alden Smith

Checks and Balances

Finally, new laws were passed to discourage monopolies in the passenger-ship business that violated the Sherman Anti-Trust Act. Monopolies make businesses so powerful that they don't have to follow anyone else's rules, so to prevent this, shipping companies were made to provide information about how they are owned and organized. The idea behind this legislation was to make sure companies do not compromise on safety and fairness for the sake of profit. No matter what country they are from, companies that refuse to comply can be fined, sued, denied certification, and banned from American harbors.

The Least You Need to Know

➤ Many people wrote to the White House following the *Titanic* disaster with suggestions for improving the safety of ships.

➤ New shipping laws passed as a result of the *Titanic* sinking required more lifeboats, more bulkheads, stronger pumps, and more wireless officers.

➤ The *Titanic* disaster gave rise to the International Ice Patrol and the International Conference for the Safety of Life at Sea.

➤ The *Titanic* disaster prompted the Seaman's Act to be written into American law, improving work conditions for sailors.

Part 5
Hard to Fathom

The Titanic sank but was never forgotten. Plans to find and salvage the wreck have been proposed continually ever since the sinking. Since its discovery in 1985, expeditions to the sunken ship have served a range of purposes, including profit, entertainment, education, and historical, scientific, and technological research. Most recently, trips to the Titanic have combined all of these aims at once.

The great ship on its way to the bottom, as depicted by artist Simon W. Fisher. (©S.W. Fisher)

The once proud Titanic—*now an ominous presence on the ocean floor.*
(©Emory Kristof/National Geographic Society Image Collection)

Stacked, but not dried, are these dishes from one of the Titanic's *kitchens.*
(©Ralph White/Corbis)

This seat isn't taken…although it was once attached to the deck of the Titanic.
(©Ralph White/Corbis)

This fallen angel, which once adorned the Titanic's grand staircase, was pulled from the bottom of the sea. (©R.B. White)

This good-luck figurine from Egypt was saved from the sinking ship by the real Molly Brown. (Stanley Lehrer Collection)

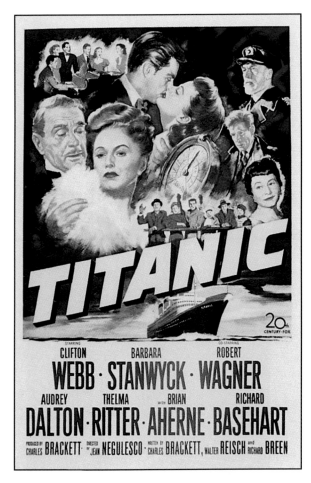

Poster for the 1953 film Titanic, in which Clifton Webb is an arrogant socialite who loses his life but finds his humanity. (©Everett Collection)

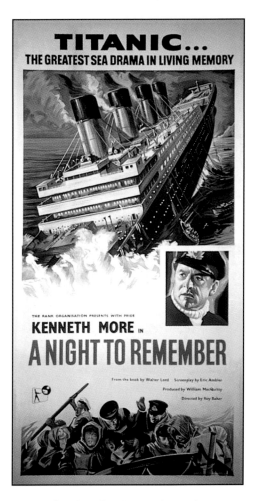

Poster for the classic 1958 semi-documentary film that surprised many with its gutsy honesty. (©Everett Collection)

A fiery Debbie Reynolds plays the title role in The Unsinkable Molly Brown, *the 1964 movie based on the Broadway musical.* (©Everett Collection)

Kathy Bates (center, just left) as the latest in a long line of movie Molly Browns. (©Photofest)

All the ship's a stage in the current hit Broadway musical Titanic. *(©Joan Marcus)*

Gloria Stewart, as present-day Rose Bukater, looks at sunken treasures from the past in the 1997 film Titanic. *(©Globe Photos)*

Superstars Kate Winslet and Leonardo DiCaprio dance divinely in the 1997 film Titanic. *(©Photofest)*

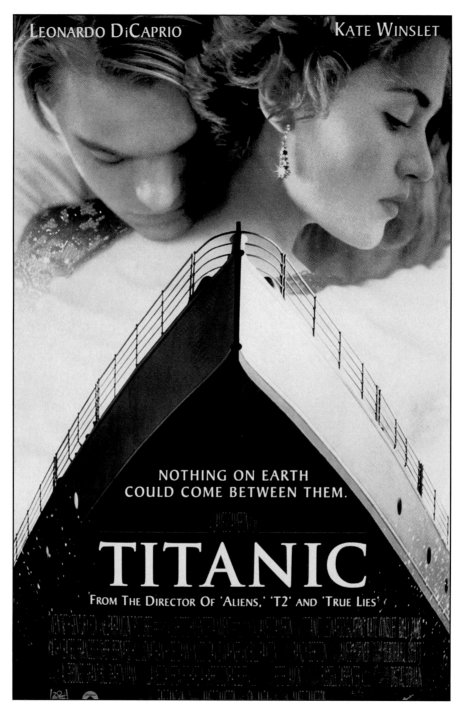

From one of the world's saddest disasters to an Academy Award® sweep 85 years later. (©Globe Photos)

Chapter 19

Salvage Schemes

In This Chapter

➤ Plans to raise the *Titanic*

➤ Expeditions in search of the wreck

➤ Jack Grimm's sonar search

➤ *Raise the Titanic*, the book and the movie

The outcome of the many plans to recover the *Titanic* shows that some things are easier said than done. A slew of imaginative ideas for getting the ship back to the surface have been proposed—most of them long before anyone even knew where the ship actually was.

Some of these ideas seem pretty far-fetched; others sound like they might have worked. Many were scrapped simply because they cost too much—stories and rumors of safes full of jewels and gold couldn't finally offset the reality of the high cost of a recovery operation working two and a half miles under water.

Simply finding the wreck proved to be a difficult feat, involving years of searching, lots of high-tech equipment, and several failed attempts. Now that what's left of the *Titanic* has been found and we know how shattered and rusted it is, it seems unlikely that anyone will ever bring it to the surface. Some prefer to leave it where it is, regarding the wreck as a gravesite.

Deep Thoughts

Not long after the *Titanic* went down, people started thinking about getting it back up again. Many of these were families of wealthy passengers who had been lost with the ship. After inquiring with the Merritt and Chapman wrecking company, they learned that the job was beyond the scope of a typical salvage team.

A Certain Magnetism

In March 1914, an architect named Charles Smith came forward with a carefully worked-out plan for getting the wreck up from the bottom. Submarines equipped with electromagnets were to locate the sunken ship and attach the magnets to the hull. More electromagnets would then be lowered on cables from a fleet of barges at the surface. The cables would then be cranked upward on winches. Smith thought that with enough magnets, cables, and barges, 162 people could do the job. He said the work could be done for $1.5 million.

Blow Me Down!
Electromagnetism was cutting-edge technology back before World War I. In fact, the *Titanic*'s watertight doors were held open by electromagnets. Shutting off power to the magnets with a flip of a switched closed the doors automatically.

Even at this high price, Smith may have underestimated the difficulty of the job. For one thing, the wreck hadn't even been located, and as it turned out was quite a ways from the location calculated by the *Titanic*'s Officer Boxhall as the ship was sinking. In any case, the plan was never attempted, so we'll never know if it would have worked. No one wanted to put up the money Smith required.

Uphill All the Way

A version of Smith's plan, also involving electromagnets attached to cables, was put forward shortly afterward. This time, the idea was to lift the wreck gradually while dragging it toward the shore. As the *Titanic* got closer to the shore and closer to the surface, it could set down to rest from time to time on the bottom, which gets less deep towards land. According to this plan, gradual progress could be made even if the cables broke or the electromagnets had to be shut off. Again, however, the idea was never put into practice.

Catch the Drift
A **pontoon** is a float, often consisting of a hollow drum, that can be used for supporting docks and bridges. A pontoon is also a kind of flat-bottomed boat or one of the floats of a sea-plane.

Still another scheme to raise the *Titanic* involving electromagnets was to attach the magnets to *pontoons* which would float the ship up to the surface. A problem with this idea is that it would take a lot of weight to get the pontoons deep enough to attach them to the ship. In fact, these ideas were never put into practice.

Blown Out of the Water

For many years, the wrecked *Titanic* was largely ignored. In the 1950s, however, people began making salvage plans once again. In July 1953, a company known as Risdon Beazley, Ltd., chartered a salvage vessel and sailed out of Southampton, England, where the *Titanic* embarked, to the site of the sinking. This vessel, the *Help*, was equipped with undersea explosives, undersea telephoto cameras, and remote-control submarines.

The idea was not to lift the hull to the surface, but to blow it open with explosives and then gather up any artifacts that looked valuable with the remote-control subs. Possibly because this operation threatened to destroy more of the *Titanic* than it promised to recover, the mission was attempted in secret. Unlike many of the *Titanic* recovery attempts to follow, there wasn't much media coverage of the Risdon Beazley enterprise.

The mission failed because the sunken wreck turned out to be more difficult to find than people thought. The undersea telephoto cameras showed nothing, so the *Help* returned to Southampton and the *Titanic* remained undisturbed.

Low on Gas

During the 1960s, a couple of Hungarian inventors got together with an energetic English factory worker named Douglas Wooley. Wooley devised a plan involving a *bathysphere* equipped with mechanical arms. The bathysphere would descend to the *Titanic* and attach nylon balloons to the hull of the wreck. Once attached, the balloons could be inflated with compressed air to drag the hull of the sunken ship back to the surface.

The Hungarians, Ambros Balas and Laszlo Szaskoe, modified Wooley's idea. Their plan was to attach hundreds of plastic containers for holding air to the hull of the sunken ship. These containers were to be filled with hydrogen generated from the seawater itself by charging the water with an electric current.

Once back on the surface, the *Titanic* would be towed back to England and fixed up as a museum. The project got attention from the press in articles that suggested the mission would soon be carried out. It never was. The idea generated some excitement, but not enough real interest to get the necessary funds, equipment, and know-how. It didn't help that an American chemistry professor published an article saying the plan to break down seawater into hydrogen gas was impractical. He claimed it would take 10 years for the process to generate enough gas to float the ship!

Catch the Drift
A **bathysphere** is a manned, deep-sea research submarine supplied with air from the surface through a hose.

Blow Me Down!
Douglas Wooley claimed to be sole legal owner of the sunken wreck of the *Titanic*, saying he had the last remaining share of stock in the ship and a signed disclaimer from the Cunard company, which inherited the ship when it bought White Star Line!

Needing a Lift

Some of the goofiest sounding ideas for recovering the *Titanic* were drawn up during the 1970s—some of which sound like they were inspired by the lava lamp! The lava-lamp principle holds that gunk can be made to rise through the water as it changes temperature.

One plan called for 180,000 tons of hot wax to be pumped into the hull of the ship. As the wax hardened, it would become lighter than seawater and float the wreck to the surface. Another version substituted petroleum jelly for the hot wax. The Vaseline would be stowed into the ship in thousands of plastic bags where it would harden, become buoyant, and lift the wreck upward. Like many appealing ideas, this one was never actually tried.

Still more outlandish is the suggestion to load the ship with millions of Ping-Pong balls, which would pop the ship up from the ocean floor. Then there's the plan to wrap the wreck in wire mesh and spray the mesh with liquid nitrogen. The nitrogen would freeze, forming a huge iceberg around the ship, which would, in a stunningly ironic reversal of events, float it to the top.

This plan was suggested by John Pierce, a British expert on salvaging ships. Earlier he had helped bring to the surface objects that were on board the sunken Cunard liner *Lusitania*.

Lifesavers
Compressed air, pontoons, and injections of buoyant foam have been used successfully to recover sunken ships—but not the *Titanic*.

Pierce proposed an alternative idea that had been used successfully in 1985 to recover the *Rainbow Warrior*, a ship belonging to the environmental activist group Greenpeace that had been sunk to the bottom of Aukland Harbor in New Zealand in an act of sabotage. This ship was filled with huge airbags that were pumped full of compressed air.

Pierce hoped not only to recover the *Titanic*, but restore it and actually sail it once more. As we know now, this would be extremely difficult, if not impossible, since the ship lies on the bottom in two big main sections and innumerable small fragments.

Grimm Determination

As with previous ideas, these suggestions were never tried. For one thing, they were just too expensive. For another, no one really new exactly where the ship was. Starting in the 1980s, an oil tycoon named Jack Grimm organized a series of searches that showed finding the wreck was no easy feat.

Jack Grimm, in the center, was an oil tycoon who set his sights on the wreck of the Titanic.
Topham/The Image Works

Long Sought and Far Fetched

Grimm had always been attracted to the challenge of making difficult discoveries. Despite many failed attempts to find oil, he finally struck the well that made him rich. He used his wealth to fund a number of expeditions in search of exotic missing things, including Noah's Ark, the Loch Ness Monster, and the Abominable Snowman!

Undaunted by past failures, he organized a search for the *Titanic*. His intention was to make the most of the opportunity to become famous by courting the media. He not only played the event up for the newspapers but helped produce a documentary on the expedition, *Search for the Titanic*, narrated by the famous actor Orson Welles.

Blow Me Down!
Grimm planned to add spice to the documentary on his expedition by bringing along Titan, a monkey trained to point to the spot on the map where Grimm believed the *Titanic* rested. The scientists were unimpressed and told Grimm to choose between them and the monkey. Grimm responded, "Fire the scientists!" (He later reconsidered and left the monkey on shore.)

Men, Money, and Machines

In addition to attracting the attention of the media, Grimm also managed to attract some noted oceanographers to the project, William Ryan of Columbia University and Fred Spiess of the Scripps Oceanographic Institute in California. It helped that Grimm donated $330,000 to Columbia's Lamont-Doherty Geological Observatory to be used toward some state-of-the-art sonar equipment. Grimm obtained the use of this equipment for his *Titanic* search, together with technicians who knew how to use it.

The plan was to locate the wreck using sonar equipment and use robot submarines to blowtorch openings in the hull. Artifacts taken out through the openings would be donated to the Smithsonian Institute.

Sonar equipment used by the Grimm search expedition.

Topham/The Image Works

Propped Up Hopes

Grimm and his team set off from Florida in July 1980 on the *F.J.W. Fay*. They spent three weeks scanning the site, during which time they identified some undersea objects that seemed possibly to belong to the *Titanic*. The objects couldn't be confirmed, however, in part because they had lost their magnetometer, an instrument used for detecting metal. The time available to the group for use of the ship ran out and they had to return to shore with inconclusive results.

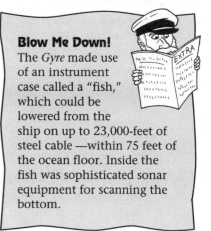

Blow Me Down!
The *Gyre* made use of an instrument case called a "fish," which could be lowered from the ship on up to 23,000-feet of steel cable —within 75 feet of the ocean floor. Inside the fish was sophisticated sonar equipment for scanning the bottom.

The following summer, Grimm and his team went back out again, this time on the *Gyre*, a research vessel. Although they had clues about where the wreck might be, they chose not to follow them, but instead checked on the possibilities they identified the previous year. Each of these turned out not to be the *Titanic*. Near the end of the nine-day run, however, the team identified what Grimm thought was one of the *Titanic*'s propellers, but the ship had to return before they could tell for certain.

A Tale About Nothing

By this time, some of the media attention Grimm's expedition was receiving started to backfire as the press made jokes about "Grimm's fairy tales." Many were doubtful that the sonar pictures Grimm brought back really represented the ship's propeller as he claimed. Two years elapsed before Grimm had the opportunity to find out for certain whether he had found what he was looking for.

In 1983, the team set out for a final run on board the *Robert Conrad*. The propeller turned out to be an oddly shaped rock. The mission called it quits after two weeks at sea and no sign of the *Titanic*. Despite the failure of the expedition, Grimm coauthored a book on the attempt called *Beyond Reach* together with William Hoffman. The documentary went ahead as planned, but failed to arouse much interest among movie-goers.

Rock Bottom

The *Titanic* was found in 1985 by oceanographer Robert Ballard. We'll talk about that story in the following chapter. The chapter after that deals with the recovery of artifacts from the wreck. The wreck itself remains on the bottom of the ocean and many doubt that it ever will—or could—be brought to the surface.

One problem is that the ship may not be strong enough to be moved. Year by year, the steel hull of the ship continues to corrode in the salt water. The fact that the ship is already badly damaged makes the enormous task of raising it that much less worthwhile. Obviously, the ship could never be restored.

A Novel Idea

The only successful attempt to raise the *Titanic* is a work of fiction. In 1976, Clive Cussler's novel *Raise the Titanic* became a best-seller. Cussler's book uses the wreck of the big ship as a centerpiece for an adventure/spy thriller during the Cold War between the U.S. and the Soviet Union.

In the story, a radioactive element called byzanium is strategically important in the arms race between the two global superpowers. By a strange twist of fate, the only known byzanium available in the world went to the bottom of the ocean on board the *Titanic* in 1912. (No, there was never any byzanium on the *Titanic* or anywhere else!) A fierce and secret contest ensues as the two nations try to get to the sunken ship first.

In 1980, the book was made into a $40 million film directed by Jerry Jameson. This prompted the film's producer, Lord Grade, to exclaim, "Raise the *Titanic*! It would be cheaper to lower the Atlantic!" In fact, the movie lost big money, making back only $7 million of the $40 million it cost.

Jason Robards stars in one of Hollywood's all-time sinkers, Raise the Titanic.
Everett Collection

Ahoy There!

Hits new depths hitherto unexplored by the worst of Lew Grade's overloaded ark melodramas.

—*Variety* on the film *Raise the Titanic*

The longer it all goes on, the more one hopes that, if they ever do raise the Titanic, *they'll heave the film overboard to replace it.*

—*The Guardian* on the film *Raise the Titanic*

One strong point of the film was its underwater special effects. Like many ship movies made prior to the beginning of computer-imaging technology, scenes were shot using a model of a ship in a tank. Often, scenes shot in this manner look like they were filmed in someone's bathtub; *Raise the Titanic* avoided this problem by building a ship model of enormous size.

The model of the Ti used in the film was 55 feet long. It was shot inside a huge tank that could hold 9 million gallons of water. Together, the model and the tank cost $8 million, more than the cost of the original ship!

The Least You Need to Know

➤ Electromagnetism inspired early plans for salvaging the wreck.

➤ Other plans involve pontoons, liquid nitrogen, inflatable plastic containers, Vaseline, and Ping-Pong balls!

➤ The most extensive and costly failed search for the *Titanic* was spearheaded by oil tycoon Jack Grimm.

➤ The *Titanic* has been raised only in fiction—Clive Cussler's 1976 novel, made into a film in 1980.

In This Chapter

➤ Discovering the *Titanic*

➤ Robert Ballard and the French-American collaboration

➤ High-tech undersea equipment

➤ Filming the wreck

As you probably know already, the wreck of the *Titanic* was finally discovered. In the course of the discovery and the exploration that followed, some new *Titanic* heroes emerged: Dr. Robert Ballard, *Alvin* the submarine, and *Jason Junior*, the tiny but intrepid undersea robot.

Most of the work involved in finding the *Titanic* was not especially exciting. It involved hours and hours of staring at sonar screens and video monitors, waiting for something to show up other than the endless stretch of mud and rock on the ocean bottom. Obviously, patience paid off as state-of-the-art equipment began sending images of scattered pieces of the *Titanic* back to the surface.

Just as technology caused much of the initial excitement surrounding the *Titanic* back in 1912, technology was a large part of the story in 1985 when the ship was found. In 1912, the technology emerged in a climate of arrogance, greed, and intense international rivalry—with famously disastrous results. In contrast, the discovery in 1985 is characterized by caution, respect, and international cooperation.

Gearing Up

The wreck of the *Titanic* was discovered in 1985 by a team of French and American scientists headed by Dr. Robert Ballard. The search took a whole summer (longer than other expeditions had been able to spend), used two research vessels and three submersible equipment sleds, cost $6 million, and drew on expertise provided by some of the best oceanographic institutions of France and America, including the U.S. Navy.

Robert Ballard with a model of the Titanic.
Topham/The Image Works

Titanic Plans

Ballard, a Ph.D. in marine geology and geophysics, served as an officer in the Navy for five years before becoming head of the Deep Submergence Lab run by the Woods Hole Oceanographic Institute on Cape Cod, Massachusetts. His combined connections in the Navy and in the world of scientific research helped him mount a successful expedition using the latest technology and know-how.

Ballard had long been interested in finding the *Titanic*, as well as in undersea exploration more generally. In 1978, he helped form Seonics International, along with William Tantum IV of the *Titanic* Historical Society, for the purpose of getting the necessary backing to locate the wreck. At this point, Ballard approached the Navy for support, but couldn't get enough help. Tantum died shortly afterward, and plans seemed to come to an end.

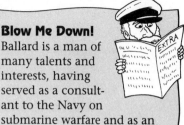

Blow Me Down!
Ballard is a man of many talents and interests, having served as a consultant to the Navy on submarine warfare and as an advisor to Walt Disney World.

All Aboard!

Since then, however, the Navy developed new undersea exploration equipment that it wanted to put to use. This equipment was designed with military purposes in mind, but Ballard's *Titanic* project provided the Navy with a good opportunity for testing. Meanwhile, the French government had also been developing new underwater sonar equipment. The French, led by scientist Jean-Louis Michel, accepted Ballard's invitation to join the project.

Additional sponsors included the National Science Foundation and the National Geographic Society. With this backing, Ballard was able to launch an expedition costing an estimated $6 million dollars, using the latest combined undersea technology of France and the U.S. and a team of 24 scientists and 25 crew.

Blow Me Down!
The Navy set aside three weeks during the summer for some of its new undersea equipment to be tested. Ballard suggested that the equipment be tried out by using it to search for the *Titanic*. The Navy okayed the idea.

All Decked Out

The mission used two ships and various manned and unmanned submersible vessels. Here's a checklist of the ships and subs used by Ballard's team.

➤ The *Knorr*   Two-thousand ton, 245-foot U.S. Navy-owned research vessel, hooked up to a satellite navigation system and equipped with special propellers that can send the ship forward, backward, and sideways.

➤ *Le Suroit*   Research vessel belonging to IFREMER, the French National Institute of Oceanography. This ship didn't find the wreck, but it helped the team zero in on the site.

➤ SAR   Unmanned French sonar vehicle suspended on a cable from *Le Suroit*, used to sweep 80 percent of a 150 square mile field.

➤ *Argo*   Towed sled equipped with five TV cameras and powerful strobe lights pulled by a cable from the *Knorr*.

➤ *ANGUS* (Acoustically Navigated Geological Underwater Survey vessel) Towed sled similar to the *Argo*, but equipped with still cameras instead of video.

➤ *Atlantis II* Research vessel used by Ballard and his team when exploring the wreck in 1986.

➤ *Alvin* Woods Hole Institute's three-person sub with a titanium hull for withstanding deep-sea pressure of over 6,000 pounds per square inch. From here, technicians control the unmanned submersible robot, *Jason Jr.*

➤ *Jason Jr. (JJ)* Small, remote-controlled submersible equipped with powerful searchlights and mechanical arms connected by a cable to *Alvin.*

Poised for Success

SOS
Ballard was afraid the wreck might be especially hard to find as a result of an undersea earthquake that occurred in the 1920s. The quake damaged some undersea cables in the region, and Ballard thought it might possibly have damaged and covered up the sunken *Titanic*.

All the equipment available gave the Ballard team a great deal of control in organizing their search, enabling them to cover a lot of territory efficiently. Even so, Ballard was aware of the amount of time that could be required for the search, having learned from the failure of his predecessor Jack Grimm not to expect immediate results.

The mission began on board the French ship, *Le Suroit*, which began searching on July 11, 1985 with its sophisticated SAR sonar equipment. This sonar was powerful enough to take readings of areas three-fifths of a mile wide. This was a big help in covering much of the 150 square mile field the team identified as their search window. The SAR was dragged back and forth across the bottom in an activity the team referred to as "mowing the lawn."

Sound and Vision

Le Suroit, with Jean-Louis Michel and Robert Ballard on board, stopped conducting the sonar search on August 7. They returned shortly afterward in the U.S. Navy ship, *Knorr*, after making a brief stop at the site of another wreck south of the Azores. This wreck was the sunken U.S. nuclear sub *Scorpion*, which had been lost in 1968 with 99 crewmen aboard. The Navy wanted Ballard to test the *Scorpion* wreck site for radiation leakage (there was none detected) and to see if he could find the cause of the disaster. (He couldn't. It seems that the sub had been singled out for a drastically reduced maintenance program as an experiment!). Ballard and his team used the *Argo* and *Jason Junior* to explore and take photos of the sub for the Navy before heading north to finish the search for the *Titanic*.

Unlike the first phase of the search on board *Le Suroit*, which relied on the sonar of SAR, phase two aboard the *Knorr* used the video capabilities provided by the *Argo*. The *Argo* represents a breakthrough in underwater exploration technology as one of the first submersibles of its kind able to stay at the job underwater for days at a time. This factor may have made a crucial difference in the success of the mission.

Bingo!

Days passed as teams took turns monitoring *Argo*'s video footage. If you think you've seen some boring TV shows, imagine having to watch round-the-clock videos of the deep ocean floor, showing only mud and an occasional rock. There weren't even any discarded beer bottles to liven up the scenery.

Finally, at about 1:00 a.m. on September 1, *Argo* swept over part of the *Titanic*'s debris field. Pieces of metal were visible on the viewing screen in the control room where Jean-Louis Michel and some of the crew were watching. Michel gave the order to notify Ballard, but no one wanted to miss what was going to appear on screen! The ship's cook eventually carried the message.

Ballard arrived in the control room shortly before one of the *Titanic*'s boilers appeared on the screen. When the ship sank, the heavy boilers broke through the hull and made their way separately to the bottom. Obviously, the rest of the ship wasn't far away.

Fearing that *Argo* might smash into, or get entangled by, a piece of the wreck, the team decided to wait until the next day to resume filming. At that point, it was close to the time of night when the *Titanic* disappeared 73 years ago. Before turning in, the crew held a 10-minute memorial service.

Blow Me Down!
The *Knorr* towed the undersea video sled, *Argo*, by a cable as it recorded footage of the ocean bottom. During the process, the ship had to cruise at a steady pace, since its speed affected the slackness of the cable. If the ship went too fast, the cable would tighten and lift the *Argo* too far from the ocean bottom for it to take good pictures. If the ship went too slow, the *Argo* risked scraping along the bottom.

Lifesavers
In keeping with his sense of reverence toward the victims of the *Titanic* disaster, Ballard cut short an interview with TV anchorman Tom Brokaw in order to pay his last respects before his ship left the site of the wreck.

Long Shots

The *Knorr* remained at the site another four days. Using *Argo* and *ANGUS*, Ballard's team took thousands of shots of the bow-half of the hull and the debris surrounding it. Among the debris, spread out across about 600 yards, were lumps of coal, pieces of luggage, bedsprings, wine bottles, and other objects.

During the final days of the mission, the sea started getting rough. Ballard decided it was too risky to use *Argo* under those conditions, so the team used the older, less delicate *ANGUS* to photograph the hull. The crew referred to this submersible affectionately as "the dope on a rope."

ANGUS was difficult to control from the ship in rough seas, but precision was necessary in order to get good pictures. Preliminary shots taken at a safe distance from the wreck were out of focus. In order to get good photos, Ballard's technicians risked damaging *ANGUS* or even losing it altogether by getting it tangled in wreckage.

Catch the Drift

A **bollard** (not to be confused with Robert Ballard) is a metal post used for tying the ship to its **moorings**. A ship is moored when it is tied to a dock.

The hull was, and is, in an upright position, resting with only a slight list. Much of the ship's gear could still be seen on deck—anchor chains, davits, cranes, and *bollards*, metal posts for securing the ship to its *moorings*, lines tied to a dock. A big hole was left in the middle of deck at the bow from where the funnel collapsed as the ship sank.

When Ballard and his team arrived back in Massachusetts, a crowd was gathered in port to welcome them home. The sky was filled with helicopters filming the *Knorr* from above. The papers and TV news were full of the story of the discovery. Ballard became a hero and was in demand for interviews with all the major networks.

Photo Op

Ballard returned to the wreck the following year on the research ship, *Atlantis II* to take more video footage and still photos. He came this time without Michel and the French, but brought with him the three-person submersible, *Alvin*. *Alvin*'s crew could descend to the wreck and, from there, control the undersea robot, *Jason Jr.* by means of a joystick. *JJ* had lights, a camera, and was ready for action, with mechanical arms for grabbing and exploring.

The research vessel Atlantis II with the submersible Alvin.
SYGMA

Drifting Down

Ballard took many dives inside *Alvin*. To save energy, the submersible floated down to the wreck at a maximum speed of 100 feet per minute, pulled by its own gravity. Each trip down took about two and a half hours. Once down, *Alvin* could scoot around or rest on the deck of the sunken ship.

Lifesavers
The U.S. Navy used a prototype of *Alvin* in 1966 to locate a hydrogen bomb that fell into the Mediterranean Sea after an airplane accident.

Swimming Downstairs

The deck provided a good base of operations for sending *JJ* down inside to explore. There was a hole left that once was covered by a glass dome skylight right above the *Titanic*'s grand staircase. Down the staircase, *JJ* transmitted pictures of oak pillars still in place. Still more surprising, one of the chandeliers was still hanging from the ceiling, only slightly bent out of shape, with a feathery growth of coral attached to it. The pictures show much of the ship is hung with festoons of rust Ballard called "rusticles." These were caused by bacteria that eat iron.

It was Ballard's policy not to disturb the wreck or take anything up from the bottom other than pictures. His curiosity got the better of him, however, as *JJ* encountered one of the ship's safes. *JJ*'s mechanical arm tested the handle to see if it could be opened, but the door stayed tightly shut. It later appeared in video footage that the bottom of the safe had rusted out, so it was probably empty.

Look But Don't Touch

Ballard tried to leave the wreck just as he had found it except for one detail. Using *JJ*'s mechanical arm, he deposited a plaque at the site, commemorating the catastrophe. Ballard supported a resolution that was passed in Congress to preserve the wreck as a grave site and to prevent salvage operations. This resolution proved impossible to enforce, however, and expeditions have followed in Ballard's footsteps and returned with artifacts from the bottom.

Ballard is known all over the world for leading the team that found the *Titanic*. He has continued to work with undersea technology, exploring the floor of the Mediterranean and sending video footage to the surface.

The Least You Need to Know

➤ The *Titanic* was discovered in 1985 by an international team spearheaded by Dr. Robert Ballard.

➤ Debris from the ship was first spotted on video footage transmitted to the surface by the deep-sea equipment sled, *Argo*.

➤ The ship is two and a half miles down and was broken into two main sections.

➤ Ballard returned to the wreck in 1986 to explore and take photos and videos, using *Alvin* and *Jason Junior*.

➤ At the end of his last dive, Ballard left a plaque at the wreck commemorating the disaster.

Coming Up with the Goods

In This Chapter

➤ Salvage and research expeditions

➤ Complaints and lawsuits over artifacts

➤ Hype and media coverage of the expeditions

➤ Science and technology

In the process of exploring the wreck and recovering artifacts, *Titanic* expeditions have stirred up silt from the ocean floor that has gone undisturbed for decades. They've stirred up resentment and controversy as well. Yet despite complaints, criticism, and law suits, missions to the *Titanic* have flourished ever since the discovery of the wreck. Their success has had a lot to do with their ability to unite various goals and purposes.

Expeditions have included boatloads of scientists, technicians, and other experts, including geologists, archaeologists, microbiologists, historians, engineers, restoration experts, journalists, TV and movie producers, and promoters. Still more people on shore are also involved, including investors, more producers, museum directors, and advertisers. In short, practically everyone is going along for the ride.

All these people are accomplishing various objectives: scientific and historical discoveries are being made, high-tech equipment is being tested and developed, entertainment and educational features are being produced, objects are being recovered and restored for sale and display, and products are being endorsed. In the face of this kind of enthusiasm, complaints that *Titanic* expeditions are desecrating a gravesite are dead in the water.

Hard Feelings Surface

The expedition to discover the *Titanic*, led by Dr. Ballard in 1985, included the assistance of IFREMER, the French National Institute of Oceanography run by the French Government. IFREMER did not participate in Ballard's return expedition in 1986 to explore and photograph the wreck. The following year, however, IFREMER mounted an expedition of its own. Unlike the Ballard-led missions, an important goal of this trip was to bring artifacts up from the bottom.

Auctioneer Patrick Boque shows off artifacts recovered in 1987 from the wreck of the Titanic. *The goods were sold at the Kew Bridge Engines Museum in Brentford in Middlesex, England, in 1988.*

Topham/The Image Works

Objects of Controversy

In 1987, some 1,800 artifacts were recovered from the wreck with the help of the manned submersible *Nautile*, equipped with sonar, video, communications gear, and mechanical arms. The expedition was launched with the support of international investors. In the process, it triggered some intense controversy.

One issue was the moral question of whether it was acceptable to disturb what many regarded as a grave-site. Some, including survivors and descendants of *Titanic* passengers, felt that the ship and its contents should remain undisturbed.

Another question involved whether artifacts that were recovered should be sold to the public or preserved in museums. The expedition's investors wanted to sell the artifacts (naturally). In an attempt to appease survivors and descendants who objected, the salvors offered them first choice in buying certain artifacts, but, in general, this proposal did not go over well.

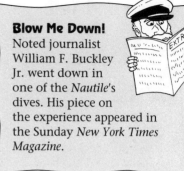

Blow Me Down!
Noted journalist William F. Buckley Jr. went down in one of the *Nautile*'s dives. His piece on the experience appeared in the Sunday *New York Times Magazine*.

Still another touchy issue concerned the archeological aspects of the expedition. Many complained that due care was not taken in recovering artifacts. For one thing, the crow's nest was destroyed in the process of bringing up a major trophy, one of the ship's bells. What's more, the team didn't bother to map out the site and record where the objects were before taking them. Some feared this lack of archeological rigor could hamper future attempts to study the wreck.

This German doll, recovered from the wreck of the Titanic, *isn't saying how she feels about the recovery expeditions.*
Popperfoto/Archive Photo

Show and Tell

Many of the artifacts recovered by the 1987 IFREMER mission were featured in a TV special hosted by Telly Savalas called "Return to the *Titanic ... Live!*" Publicized as a news event, the show provided historical background on the *Titanic* while glamorizing the recovery of artifacts. The focus throughout the show was a safe brought up from the bottom that was to be opened "live" at the show's climax.

Inside the safe were some bank notes and collectibles. Some observers felt these contents were anticlimactic, given the importance of the big sinking. "Return to the *Titanic ... Live!*" was criticized for weeks afterward in the press for staging a variety show and calling it a news event.

The IFREMER research vessel Nadir *with the submersible* Nautile *aboard, out on the 1987 expedition.*
SYGMA

Something for Everyone

Just as the passenger shipping industry learned valuable lessons from the sinking of the *Titanic*, exploration and salvage missions have learned valuable lessons from the way the hype and controversy surrounding the sunken ship were mishandled in 1987. *Titanic* expeditions have continued to court the undersea limelight, but in doing so, emphasize scientific and historical aspects of artifact recovery.

Low Down on the Titanic

In 1991, an international expedition to the *Titanic* was launched for research and filming as well as artifact recovery. A key figure in this expedition was Canadian filmmaker Stephen Low. Low wanted to make a documentary on exploring the sunken *Titanic*. He had hoped to cover Robert Ballard's 1986 expedition, but did not have the necessary funds and equipment. Later he was able to organize a mission with the help of Russia's Shirov Institute of Oceanography.

The Shirov Institute provided the research vessel *Akademic Keldysh* and two Mir submersibles, one of which carried a powerful lighting system, capable of generating 150,000 watts, for the sake of the filming. The lights were also useful to the geological and biological researches involved in the expedition.

Stephen Low's IMAX film Titanica *served up some fresh images of the wreck such as this on-site shot of an artifact.*
SYGMA

The following year, 1992, Stephen Low produced his movie, *Titanica*, chronicling the event, using the IMAX/OMNIMAX format of 3-D projection, which is especially effective for panoramic footage. The film is shown in special dome-shaped theaters, so the action fills the audience's entire field of vision. *Titanica* proved to be a successful film, bringing large audiences to IMAX theaters.

Lifesavers
Among the interesting bits of information revealed by Stephen Low's film *Titanica* is that the *Titanic*'s class hierarchy was reflected in its toilets. Third-class toilets were iron, second-class were porcelain, and first-class were marble.

Blow Me Down!
Lumps of coal supposed to have been recovered from the *Titanic* have been advertised for sale over the Internet for $25 each.

Salvage Rights

IFREMER, the French group who went to the wreck in 1987, returned with the *Nautile* years later, in 1993, to collect more artifacts. This time they were working for a New York Company called R.M.S. Titanic, a group led by George Tulloch. Tulloch and R.M.S. Titanic secured legal rights to *Titanic* salvage after a court battle with a group from Memphis, Tennessee, called Marex-Titanic. A prominent member of this group was Jack Grimm, who, as you may remember from Chapter 19, led several failed searches for the wreck in the 1980s.

Winning its court case, R.M.S. Titanic agreed to limit sales of the artifacts it salvaged in order to keep most of the collection together for public display. Among the items it retained permission to sell were lumps of coal. The 15-day expedition recovered 800 artifacts that were put on display at the National Maritime Museum in England before the exhibit traveled to other parts of the world.

Deep Sea TV

Since then, IFREMER and R.M.S. Titanic have continued their partnership, salvaging artifacts and studying the wreck. Some of their expeditions have been accompanied by TV crews that recorded and produced footage for educational programming, complete with added special effects and interviews with scientists, historians, and other experts. Among the prominent experts who have accompanied IFREMER/R.M.S. Titanic expeditions are *Titanic* historians John Eaton and Charles Haas.

Well-Equipped Ships

Expedition leader George Tulloch and his team conduct their mission from the IFREMER research vessel, *Nadir*. The *Nadir* can carry 40 passengers and crew, as well as the deep-sea submersible, *Nautile*. The *Nadir* has a crane for lifting the *Nautile* in and out of the water. It also has sonar and computers that show sonar images in 3-D. Also aboard are labs for cleaning and restoring objects brought up from below.

Nautile, the IFREMER submarine, is made of four-inch titanium. It holds three people and can go as deep as 20,000 feet—even deeper than *Titanic*'s grave—carried down by its own gravity at a rate of about 100 feet per minute. The crew controls depth by releasing sacks of ballast to make it stop sinking. When it's time to return to the surface, they release even more ballast to make it rise again. The yellow submarine cost about $20 million to build.

Blow Me Down!
Divers typically go without eating overnight in preparation for a 12-hour round trip to the bottom on board the *Nautile*.

Some expeditions have been accompanied by video camera and production crews from cable TV's Discovery Channel. The TV people bring along their own floating studio, the ship *Ocean Voyager*. The *Ocean Voyager* was an ice breaker owned by the Canadian Coast Guard before it was purchased by a French television company and converted into a TV-production ship. Both the *Nadir* and the *Ocean Voyager* have video monitors aboard for watching dive footage as it is shot under water.

Not all the high-tech undersea equipment is carried aboard the *Nadir*. The *Ocean Voyager* and its TV crew have brought a powerful lighting system to the site, consisting of four separate towers that can illuminate large portions of the wreck. Prior to the use of these towers, light for exploration and filming was supplied by beams from submersibles. The lighting towers cast a wider glow. They can shine for about an hour at a stretch; afterwards they need to be floated back to the surface to be recharged.

Getting a Good Image

In addition to collecting artifacts and providing material for TV programs, Tulloch's expeditions have contributed to the continually growing body of knowledge surrounding the disaster. One especially interesting piece of research was conducted by team member Paul Matthias of Polaris Imaging Company. Matthias used high-tech sonar equipment to inspect for hull damage in a critical portion of the wreck that was buried deep in the silt of the ocean floor.

The part of the ship that collided with the iceberg is buried in the ocean floor. As a result, it's been impossible to see just what the berg did to the ship. Using special sonar equipment known as a seismic profiler, Matthias collected data on the damage in the *Titanic*'s hull.

The *Nautile* carried the seismic profiler down to the wreck and buried the sonar equipment in the silt as

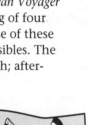

SOS
As scientists continue to study the wreck, the question of why the stern section suffered so much damage remains a mystery. Pieces of steel that made up the stern are bent in such strange ways that scientists have yet to discern a pattern or provide a reliable explanation. Most of the damage was caused when the ship was still near the surface and the hull broke in two. Additional damage occurred as the ship sank.

close as possible to the damaged portions of the hull. A three-hour sonar reading produced information on what the damage was like. The data showed that the hull was not breached in a long, continuous gash as had been generally believed. Instead, several of the ship's steel plates were bent, causing them to separate from the ship in a number of places, opening seams in the hull and dooming the ship.

Matthias has used his imaging equipment in other ways as part of the IFREMER/R.M.S. Titanic team. From high above the wreck, he has produced a map of the entire debris field, showing the relationship of the positions of the bow, the shattered stern, and the scattered objects and pieces of metal spread out around them. The field of debris covers approximately one square mile. The bow and stern sections of the ship rest about 2,000 feet apart.

Raising a Little Hull

IFREMER and R.M.S. Titanic joined forces again in 1996 to mount an ambitious expedition to recover a section of the *Titanic*'s hull. The expedition was accompanied by a video crew from cable TV's Discovery Channel, who captured the event on film. The expedition set off in the IFREMER research vessel, *Nadir*. The TV crew sailed alongside in the *Ocean Voyager*. The idea was to get the largest *Titanic* trophy yet recovered.

Blow Me Down! Closely observing the 1996 IFREMER/R.M.S. Titanic expedition were 12 winners of a promotion sponsored by Bass Ale, aboard the yacht *Ballymena* nearby. They watched footage of the expedition and had dinner with R.M.S. Titanic leader George Tulloch and historian Jack Eaton. The promotion centered on the belief that Bass Ale bottles from 1912 were among the objects to be salvaged by the expedition. In fact, bottles identified as Bass Ale bottles were recovered.

Heavy Duty

In addition to the video cameras aboard the *Nautile*, filming was also done by two other subs named *Jules* and *Jim*. These subs can only dive a short way down—about 3,000 feet—and were not used to film the wreck itself. Instead, they took footage of the *Nautile* on its way from the bottom.

The plan was to use huge plastic bags filled with diesel fuel to float a 15-ton chunk of the *Titanic*'s hull to the surface. Diesel is lighter than seawater, so it floats. The bags were attached to weights and sunk to the bottom. Several bags were tied to the piece of hull—enough to float it to within 76 meters of the surface, where the supply ship, *Jim Kilabuk* waited to take the salvaged steel aboard. The *Jim Kilabuk* ordinarily carried anchors for oil rigs, so its crew knew how to handle large, heavy chunks of metal.

A Hand On Deck

Thousands of spectators watched from nearby cruise ships, having sailed to the site especially for the event. Many expected to be disappointed, but eventually the bags full of diesel fuel floated to the surface with the big chunk of steel attached. The crowd cheered and chanted.

The tricky job of getting the chunk of hull the rest of the way up to the surface was made difficult by rough seas stirred up by Hurricane Edward. Much to everybody's disappointment, the section of hull broke free from some of the diesel floats before it could be secured by the salvage team. It sank to the bottom once more, some 10 miles from the site of the wreck.

Other, smaller sections of hull have been successfully salvaged from the *Titanic*, as have some 5,000 other artifacts as of 1997. Some have been sold at auction, but many have been exhibited around the world.

The Least You Need to Know

➤ Expeditions to the *Titanic* have combined many purposes including profit, research, education, and entertainment.

➤ The French Oceanographic Institute, IFREMER, has participated in expeditions, including cooperative efforts with the salvage organization, R.M.S. Titanic.

➤ The TV special, "Return to the *Titanic* … Live!," drew criticism for sensationalizing a recovery expedition and calling it news.

➤ Some 5,000 objects have been recovered from the wreck as of 1997. Many of these have been exhibited around the world.

Part 6
Titanimania

When the facts have been sifted, the witnesses heard, the wreck found and the artifacts recovered, there's still one more question: What does it all mean? To this one question there are hundreds of answers. It's getting so you can tell a lot about people just based on how they feel about the Titanic. It seems impossible to leave the thing alone—as deep as it's sunk under water, it's sunk even deeper under our skin. The 20th century is filled with myths, stories, beliefs, songs, novels, movies, and shows all harkening back to the ill-fated big ship.

Hello?
Get me
J.P. Morgan...

Chapter 22

Deep Prophecies

In This Chapter

➤ Premonitions and prophecies

➤ Strange coincidences

➤ W.T. Stead and the spiritualists

➤ Morgan Robertson's *Futility*

To many, the *Titanic* disaster was not simply a tragedy, but a spooky occurrence. Since the ship went down, dozens have claimed they felt something bad was going to happen, even before it did. Some had dreams and strange experiences, which they interpreted as warnings of disaster. Others were warned by psychics and fortune-tellers that danger awaited at sea. Still others just didn't feel comfortable sailing on the big ship.

The sinking of the *Titanic* looms large, not only in the history of shipping disasters, but in the quirky body of writings on "paranormal" occurrences in the 20th century. Perhaps the irony and coincidence of the grand, "unsinkable" ship sinking to a watery grave on its very first voyage demanded more explanation than simple happenstance could provide. Many who have searched for evidence of psychic and supernatural phenomena believe they have found it in uncanny circumstances surrounding the *Titanic*. They point to a pile of stories and incidents connected with the event that suggest it was not just your run-of-the-mill disaster.

Many of these stories and incidents are known to be hoaxes. Others are truly remarkable coincidences. Whatever the case, the legends have been kept alive by the combined efforts of occultists and *Titanic* fans.

The Missed-the-Boat Bandwagon

After the sinking, thousands of people claimed to have just missed the *Titanic*'s disastrous maiden voyage. Most regarded this simply as a matter of good luck. Many, however, felt that supernatural forces kept them off the ship.

Some believe the
Titanic *tragedy was*
in the cards even
before she sailed.
Todd Gipstein/Corbis

All Psyched-Out

Several of these psychic experiences were described and analyzed in academic journals in the 1960s by psychiatry professor Ian Stevenson. Stevenson regarded the examples he studied as powerful evidence of paranormal phenomena. Stevenson wrote two papers on strange experiences pertaining to the *Titanic*.

Stevenson describes, for example, the experience of a Mr. Middleton, who was planning to take the *Titanic* to the U.S. for business reasons. Since making his plans, however, the *Titanic* appeared in two dreams, sinking. The dreams made such an impression on Middleton that he changed his travel plans.

Dozens of similar accounts have been collected over the decades. Many are dreams and premonitions of people who never intended to take the ship in the first place. Others tell of funny feelings experienced by people who actually got on board—both those who survived and those who didn't. Other "psychic experiences" have taken place since the disaster.

Reliving the Wreck

One famous example of a post-sinking psychic experience was that of Doris Williams. Although she was born in Ohio and later moved to California, she had always been afraid of ships and the ocean. In 1960, Doris consulted a spiritual advisor, Reverend Young, about her strange phobia. Young hypnotized her in order to see if he could discover any repressed childhood memories that would explain it.

He was unable to find any pertinent childhood memories, so he thought he'd check back further—into her previous life! Sure enough, hypnosis revealed that Doris had been reincarnated. In her previous life she was a man named Blackwell, a passenger who perished on board the *Titanic*!

Later research showed that there was, in fact, a Stephen Weart Blackwell who was lost with the *Titanic*. Supposedly, Doris even revealed Blackwell's address while under hypnosis. Doris's case created a stir among *Titanic* fans as well as among psychic phenomena buffs. She even (amazingly enough) became the subject of an article in the *National Enquirer*.

Through a Glass Darkly

A number of legends have sprung up telling of mysterious *Titanic*-related happenings. It seems that a White Star executive named Frank Bustard acquired a dressing cabinet that

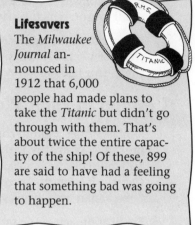

Lifesavers
The *Milwaukee Journal* announced in 1912 that 6,000 people had made plans to take the *Titanic* but didn't go through with them. That's about twice the entire capacity of the ship! Of these, 899 are said to have had a feeling that something bad was going to happen.

SOS
In 1936, London shortwave radio operator Gordon Cosgrave picked up, on several occasions, Morse code distress signals supposedly from the *Titanic* to the *Carpathia* … over 14 years after the *Titanic* sank. A response that help was on the way followed, "signed" with the identification signals of the *Carpathia*. Repeated *Titanic* messages were verified days later by wireless experts whom Cosgrave had contacted. Apparently, however, the signals were sent as a joke.

once belonged to J. Bruce Ismay before Ismay left the company. Inside the cabinet was a small mirror, which Ismay undoubtedly used while waxing his mustache.

Bustard took the mirror out of the cabinet and hung it in his office. Years later, on October 17, 1937, Ismay died. Bustard entered his office the next morning and found that the mirror had fallen on the floor *and was smashed to pieces.*

A Friend in High Places

Similar stories abound concerning crockery, watches, and other personal effects that were broken in sympathy with the *Titanic* disaster or the death of someone involved with it. Still more bizarre is a claim made by Captain Peter Pryall, an acquaintance of *Titanic* Captain E.J. Smith. Three months after Smith went down with his ship, Pryall encountered a man who, he was sure, was Smith himself.

Pryall approached the man and said, "Captain Smith, how are you?" The man answered Pryall by name and said he was well, but could not stop to talk. Pryall followed "Smith" to the railroad station and watched him buy a ticket to Washington. As he went to board his train, "Smith" turned to Pryall and said, "Be good, shipmate, until we meet again."

SOS

Two sisters made plans to sail to America on April 5, 1912, aboard the *Empress of Ireland*. Realizing the ship was scheduled to depart on Good Friday, and thinking that this was bad luck, one sister canceled and booked a passage for the following week. She sailed on the *Titanic* and was lost! The other sister made a safe trip on the *Empress of Ireland*!

Buoyed by Faith

Some *Titanic* mysteries have religious significance. One famous legend concerns a number printed on the ship below its name: 3909 04. When looked at in a mirror, the numbers appear to spell out the words, "NO POPE." Some have felt this anti-Catholic sentiment has something to do with the disaster. This view is reinforced by the fact that White Star didn't follow the tradition of christening ships.

More religious significance stems from the widespread use of ships and sailing as metaphors for religious situations. Apparently, two sermons by different ministers on the *Titanic* the day it collided with the iceberg (a Sunday, you'll recall) referred to religion as a "lifeboat" that could save people who had been "spiritually shipwrecked." Unfortunately, it soon turned out there were not enough physical lifeboats to save people from the physical shipwreck!

English Channeling

Much of the excitement concerning paranormal circumstances around the *Titanic* has been fueled by amateur and professional spiritualists. These people actively seek out psychic experiences through ESP, seances, telepathy, automatic writing, and other techniques for contacting the spirit world. Many spiritualists have been especially drawn to the *Titanic* because of its fame and deep emotional significance.

An additional source of paranormal interest in the ship is the fact that one of the victims of the disaster, W.T. Stead (1849–1912), was a noted spiritualist. Stead was a British journalist with a fascination with spirituality. He believed strongly in the possibility of communicating with spirits of the dead. In 1893, he started up a spiritualist journal called *Borderland*. The title refers to the boundary between the world of the living and the spirit world.

Spiritualist W.T. Stead, who perished during the Titanic *disaster.*

Mariners' Museum

Among the pieces published in *Borderland* were messages that supposedly came from Julia Ames, a friend of Stead's who had died. Stead claimed he was able to receive these messages through automatic writing—by freeing his mind, he enabled the spirit of Julia to control his body and write whatever she wanted to. Stead later started up a circle of spiritualist friends known as "Julia's Bureau," which met frequently to conduct seances.

Stead supposedly consulted with seers and fortune tellers who warned him not to sail on the *Titanic*. He refused to take these warnings seriously, however, since he believed that he would meet his end by being trampled or beaten by a mob of people. Nevertheless,

spiritualists point to events in Stead's life as strange foreshadowings of the *Titanic* disaster.

One of these concerned a crucifix belonging to Stead that was thought to have belonged to Catherine the Great. The cross was decorated with a skull and crossbones and was supposed to bring bad luck. Despite this supposition, Stead kept it with him. Although he was a spiritualist, he appeared unconcerned about portents of bad luck. Fellow spiritualists later said he was tempting fate.

Tempting Fate

Stead tempted spiritual fate in other ways. While on board the *Titanic*, he told of an Egyptian mummy with a mysterious inscription written on the case. Included in the inscription was a warning that anyone who uttered the message out loud would suffer a violent death. Stead went on to utter the message.

To emphasize his defiance of superstition, he even pointed out that he began his story on Friday before midnight, and ended it on the 13th of the month. Apparently, the mummy's curse took effect, since he died two nights later. According to one *Titanic* legend, Stead actually owned the mummy, which was present in the hold of the ship when it sank.

Spiritualists point to another strange foreshadowing of Stead's death. Stead was giving a lecture on spiritualism and used a shipwreck metaphor to explain the nature of communicating with the dead. His point was that living people tended to be overly concerned with verifying unimportant facts about spirits and not attentive enough to what the spirits had to say.

To illustrate this point, he imagined himself as a shipwreck victim in danger of drowning and crying for help—the supposed predicament of spirits trying to contact living people. Rather than rescuing him, the people on a nearby ship—the skeptical people who want more proof that spirits actually exist—want more facts and ask him who he is and what was his grandmother's name. Since the *Titanic* disaster, spiritualists have regarded Stead's shipwreck analogy as a premonition of his death.

Present in Spirit

Since the *Titanic* disaster, a number of spiritualists and mediums have claimed to be in contact with the spirit of W.T. Stead. In fact, if reports are true, Stead has made a number of appearances in spirit form at seances. One seance held shortly after the disaster, on May 6, 1912, was attended by Stead's daughter, Estelle. On this occasion, Estelle was seen and heard having a conversation with her departed father. They spoke about taking care of some of his unfinished business as well as about personal matters.

Those present were able to hear Stead's spirit speaking through a specially designed "trumpet" set up in the room ahead of time, which amplified the voices of the dead. At the end of the spirit's talk with Estelle, he was heard to shout, "Oh my God!" Estelle was visibly upset throughout much of the conversation.

Rewriting History

Mediums in contact with Stead's spirit have put forth interesting information about Stead's behavior on board the *Titanic* as the ship sank. One reports that President Taft's advisor, Major Archibald Butt, was threatening to shoot some men who were trying to force their way into one of the lifeboats. According to his spirit, Stead interposed and prevented Butt from shooting.

Another spiritual report has it that the band played "Nearer My God to Thee" as its final selection because Stead suggested it. Still another report holds that Stead's spirit became good friends with the spirit of Captain Smith! Smith's spirit has also appeared at seances where he revealed that Captain Lord of the *Californian* was not to blame for the death of the *Titanic* passengers.

SOS
One technique employed by mediums to contact spirits following the *Titanic* disaster was "spirit photography," photographs taken at seances showing mysterious apparitions on film. One such photo depicts Stead in a swirl of white mist. In the mist appears a statement to the photographer, signed "W.T. Stead," saying that he will "keep you posted" on events in the spirit world! Close examination strongly suggests the photographic plates were doctored.

A Tale of Two Ships

One further indication of paranormal circumstances connecting Stead to the sinking of the *Titanic* is a short story Stead wrote about a ship that hit an iceberg. "From the Old World to the New" tells of an English doctor who travels from England to America on the White Star ship *Majestic*. This ship actually existed. In Stead's story, the captain of the ship was none other than E.J. Smith!

Two passengers aboard the *Majestic* are psychics and receive telepathic distress calls from survivors of another ship, some ways ahead, that had collided with an iceberg and sunk, leaving the survivors stranded on the berg. The psychics warn Captain Smith, who is skeptical, but agrees to keep a sharp eye out for people marooned on ice. Sure enough, the *Majestic* encounters the survivors on the iceberg and rescues them before arriving safely in America.

Truth is sometimes stranger than fiction, but fiction sometimes comes sooner than truth. Morgan Robertson's novel, Futility *anticipated the* Titanic *disaster by 14 years.*

Mary Evans Picture Library

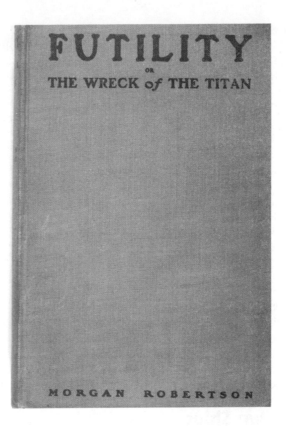

Rehearsing the Tragedy

Stead's tale was only one of a number of literary works that eerily foreshadowed the sinking of the *Titanic*. The most astonishing of these is a novel by American writer Morgan Robertson (1861–1915) called *Futility, or the Wreck of the Titan*, published in a magazine in 1898. Robertson was the son of a sea captain who sailed on America's Great Lakes. He wrote numerous sea stories, many of which were popular during his lifetime.

Separated at Berth

The story of Robertson's fictional ship, the *Titan*, has numerous features in common with the history of the *Titanic*—not to mention the name. Like the *Titanic*, the *Titan* was the

Blow Me Down!
A number of stories and poems were written about steamships hitting icebergs before the *Titanic* went down. These include Mayn Garnett's story, "The White Ghost of Disaster," which was actually being printed for publication when the disaster occurred. Another is Celia Thaxter's poem, "A Tryst," written in the 1870s.

largest ship ever built, and struck an iceberg in the North Atlantic between England and America.

Unlike the *Titanic*, the *Titan* sank on her third round trip while heading toward Europe. The fictional ship was filled to capacity, leaving only 13 survivors. Here are some stats comparing the two ships:

	The *Titan*	The *Titanic*
Length	800 feet	882.5 feet
Capacity	3,000 people	3,000 people
Gross tonnage	45,000 tons	46,328 tons
Watertight compartments	19	16
Lifeboats	24	20
Propellers	3	3
Speed before collision	25 knots	21.5 knots
Location of collision	Starboard side	Starboard side
Month of accident	April	April
Time of accident	Near midnight	11:40 p.m.
Weather conditions	Foggy but calm	Clear and calm

Ahoy There!

Amid the roar of escaping steam, and the bee-like buzzing of nearly three thousand human voices, raised in agonized screams and callings from within the enclosing walls, and the whistling of air through hundreds of open dead-lights as the water, entering the holes of the crushed and riven starboard side, expelled it, the Titan *moved slowly backward and launched herself into the sea, where she floated low on her side—a dying monster, groaning with her death-wound.*

—from Morgan Robertson's novel, *Futility*, 1898

Supernatural or Super-Careless?

Occult enthusiasts have argued that mere coincidence could not account for so many close similarities between Robertson's novel and the *Titanic* disaster. Robertson wrote his tale years before steamship technology made such large ships possible. Non-occultists argue that Robertson could easily have imagined where the steamship industry was headed without supernatural assistance. They say that *Futility* is just one of dozens of instances that show ordinary people of the time were often more concerned about the safety of big ocean liners than industry officials themselves.

One striking instance is the case of Emil Taussig, an executive from New York who was interested in steamship travel and concerned that ships were not required to carry enough lifeboats for everyone on board. He wrote a number of letters to the U.S. Steamship Inspection Service in 1908 and 1909, expressing his concerns. Years later, Taussig and his wife and daughter were passengers on board the *Titanic*. The females made it into a lifeboat, but Taussig remained on deck since, of course, there were not enough lifeboats for everyone.

Occultists and non-occultists can agree that the sinking of the *Titanic* was indeed a creepy occurrence. For the occultists, the spooky thing is that so many people seem to have been forewarned through psychic or spiritual means. For the non-occultists, the creepy thing is that even though so many sensible people could see the potential for tragedy posed by big steamships, industry officials didn't do enough to prevent it.

The Least You Need to Know

➤ Thousands of people claimed to have "just missed" sailing on the *Titanic*.

➤ Premonitions of the disaster have taken the form of dreams, prophecies, stories, and poetry.

➤ W.T. Stead was a noted spiritualist who perished with the *Titanic*. He is supposed to have appeared in spirit form at numerous seances since the disaster.

➤ Morgan Robertson's novel *Futility, or the Wreck of the Titan*, written in 1898, exhibits astonishing parallels with the sinking of the *Titanic*.

Myth Making

Few disasters have been so attention-getting as the sinking of the *Titanic*. People took notice and immediately began asking themselves what the whole thing meant. The sinking was clearly important; it was too spectacular to ignore. There were lessons to be learned, and thousands of commentators set themselves up as teachers.

Many felt the *Titanic* was symbolic of what was wrong with society. They felt the forces responsible for the disaster were still at work and had to be stopped. Others felt that the *Titanic* showed how nobly people could act in the face of disaster. There was a redemptive aspect to the catastrophe that could be kept alive.

The disaster was important because people made it important. In fact, different groups of people have made the event important in different ways. People from all walks of life throughout America, Britain, and Europe interpreted the sinking according to their ideals and beliefs. In general, these interpretations reinforced particular world views. Different takes on why the disaster occurred and who was to blame and who acted bravely suggested different orientations toward the problems of society and what should be done about them.

Ship of State

As people used the *Titanic* disaster to trumpet their own causes, many of their views conflicted with one another. An especially clear indication of this is the way the disaster was used as a metaphor by both sides of the Republican presidential primary campaign underway at the time between William Howard Taft and Theodore Roosevelt. Taft supporters said that it was the same over-confident, thoughtless style of leadership that Roosevelt exhibited that caused the ship to sink.

Similarly, Roosevelt supporters felt that Taft was guilty of the kind of indecisive leadership that led to the sinking of the *Titanic*. They underscored the comparison by pointing out that Taft, who weighed over 300 pounds, was, like the ship, too big for his own good! The *Titanic* was also used as a metaphor for the Republican Party's leadership in general. The comparison proved apt, since the 1912 presidential election was won by the Democratic candidate, Woodrow Wilson.

The *Titanic* was used not only in party politics, but as a moral lesson to support a variety of social agendas. Observers and commentators often used the disaster to argue for nationalist and racist causes, sexual chauvinism, and class snobbery. The sinking was also used to illustrate the dangers of wealth and luxury, big business, and selfishness in general.

A Few Good Men

SOS
Soon after the disaster, the Travelers Insurance Company used the slogan, "Women and Children First" to advertise insurance. Just as the men on the *Titanic* protected women and children by escorting them to the lifeboats, men on land can protect their families by taking out insurance policies!

In the wake of the sinking, one of the most popular myths stemming directly from the disaster was the idea that the wealthy Anglo-Americans in first class, together with the British officers of the ship, acted with exceptional bravery, nobility, and self-sacrifice. Hundreds of newspaper editorials, speeches, sermons, and poems praised the wealthy and powerful men on the ship who had guided women and children to the lifeboats only to perish themselves. These men were widely regarded as heroes: John Jacob Astor, Benjamin Guggenheim, Captain Smith, Major Archibald Butt, John Thayer, George Widener, and others.

Praising the heroism of these leaders of society reassured people that society was, in fact, in good hands. Often, the particular heroic acts attributed to these heroes reinforced conservative Anglo-American values.

An illustration dedicated to the Titanic's *"brave men."*
Topham/The Image Works

A Woman's Place

Central to these values was the sanctity of the family. By following the "women and children first" rule, the first-class heroes suggested that the leaders of society were working, not just to make money, but to protect the family. According to the dominant traditional and conservative model of the Anglo-American family, the men went out and took care of business while the women stayed home and took care of the kids. For people who believed in these traditional ideals, the *Titanic* disaster showed that the leaders of society were doing their jobs.

This myth of male heroism on board the *Titanic* was sometimes used directly to combat women's rights. The "women and children first" rule as practiced on the *Titanic* was used to illustrate the supposed folly of feminists and *suffragettes*—women who believed women should have the right to vote. According to the traditional, anti-suffragette view, women were better off without political rights, because men were already looking out for their interests.

Many who held this view felt that the *Titanic* story bore out their beliefs. A poem published in the *St. Louis Post-Dispatch* condemned women's suffrage by making fun of the slogan "Votes for Women!" and substituting "Boats for Women!" in its place. Suffragettes had an effective comeback for the male-heroism myth: They said that if women had the vote, they would have elected leaders who would have made sure there were enough lifeboats on board for everybody!

Steerage Stigmas

Some versions of the myth of Anglo-American male heroism were told in such a way as to support racial, nationalistic, and class prejudice. Heroic first-class Anglo-Americans were occasionally contrasted with cowardly male passengers from steerage who supposedly tried to sneak in or force their way into lifeboats ahead of women. Criticism of steerage passengers obviously ignored the fact that many were denied access to the Boat Deck, and were poorly informed of what was going on. What's more, stories of steerage cowardice are clearly exaggerated, if not made up altogether.

According to one popular myth, presidential aide Major Archibald Butt heroically fended off male steerage passengers who tried to rush the lifeboats, brandishing a gun and refusing to let them save themselves ahead of the women. A number of stories have been told of "cowardly" steerage men who dressed up as women in order to save themselves.

Sometimes the "cowardly" steerage passengers were identified as immigrants of a particular nationality. Among the groups singled out for criticism were Italians, Chinese, Armenians, Filipinos, Japanese, and others. While testifying at the U.S. Senate inquiry, Officer Lowe complained specifically about members of the "Latin races."

A clear indication of the tendency to make up racist stories is the fact that some of them portray blacks in a negative

Catch the Drift
Politically active women who supported women's voting rights were known as **suffragettes** ("suffrage" is the right to vote). Conservatives pointed to the "women and children first" rule on the *Titanic* to suggest that women's suffrage was unnecessary. The suffragettes finally prevailed, however, when the 19th Constitutional Amendment was passed in the 1920s, guaranteeing women the right to vote.

Blow Me Down!
One of the three survivors Officer Lowe's boat rescued from the water was an Asian man who had tied himself to a door. Before taking him on board. Lowe complained that there were others he'd rather save than a "Jap." The Asian quickly recovered, stamped his feet to warm up, and took over one of the oars. This made Lowe revise his opinion, and he said, "I'd save the likes of him six times over!"

light—even though there were no black people on board! Wireless Officer Harold Bride recounted the story of how a stoker tried to steal Jack Phillips' life jacket while he was busy sending for help. Bride hit the man on the head with something heavy. In subsequent versions of this story, the stoker was turned into a "negro."

All in the Same Boat

Other myths tried to undo the stigmas put forward by the racist and elitist stories, emphasizing that people of different nationalities and social classes went down together. Although these myths were not directly racist, nationalist, or elitist, they still tended to uphold the ideal of male heroism. They depict male millionaires going down with the ship side by side with heroic male steerage passengers while their widows lay aside their class differences to grieve for their husbands together.

Down to Earth

Of course, not everyone subscribed to the myths that idealized the behavior of those on board the *Titanic*. Socialists in America and England objected to depictions of the first-class male passengers as heroes, saying they were sugarcoating the disaster. Among the most outspoken critics of *Titanic* myth-making was the famous Irish socialist playwright George Bernard Shaw.

On May 14, 1912, Shaw published an essay called "Unmentionable Morals" in London's *Daily News and Leader*, criticizing what he called the outpouring of "romantic lying" in response to the disaster. Shaw argued that there was nothing to be proud of about the tragedy. He said the glorification of heroes among the passengers and crew were actually attempts to disguise the fact that the disaster was caused by negligence.

In particular, Shaw complained of idealized characterizations of Captain Smith. Shaw said that Smith helped cause the accident and was no hero. He also pointed out that the "women and children first" rule was often ignored. He even claimed that sentimental accounts of the band playing "Nearer My God to Thee" were a distortion: that they actually went down playing ragtime tunes to prevent passengers from panicking.

Shaw's essay was answered the following week by an essay in the same paper by novelist Sir Arthur Conan Doyle, best known as the creator of Sherlock Holmes. Doyle defended the idealistic conception of Captain Smith, the ship's officers, and the band, and said that Shaw's complaints ignored the more uplifting facts of the incident and only aggravated the tragedy.

> **Blow Me Down!**
> As Shaw and Doyle bickered in the press, another British literary giant, *Heart of Darkness* author Joseph Conrad, published an essay called "Reflections on the Loss of the *Titanic*," in which he criticized the U.S. Senate inquiry and the shipping industry while defending British seamanship.

Luxury Cruise

The myth of *Titanic* heroism was not the only popular take on the tragedy. Many referred to the disaster to draw a different set of conclusions, namely, that the ship sank as a result of the evils of greed and luxury. This theme was developed in the religious sermons of puritan ministers, as well as in the American press.

A number of commentators pointed out that the reason the *Titanic* was not equipped with enough lifeboats was to leave more room on deck, yet while the designers of the ship sacrificed lifeboat space, they made room for luxuries such as the gym, the swimming pool, and the Turkish baths. This supposedly exemplifies the moral lesson that materialism and luxury lead to destruction.

Ship of Fools

In general, complaints about greed and materialism on board the *Titanic* did not involve criticism of the first-class passengers who were in the best position to enjoy the luxuries on board. An exception to this rule was a diatribe launched by the Episcopal minister George Richmond, who claimed that the sinking of the *Titanic* represented divine retribution for sins committed by John Jacob Astor and his circle of friends.

Richmond had previously criticized Astor for his divorce and subsequent remarriage, and now he evidently felt that Astor got what he deserved. Richmond was rebuked for his opinions in the *Washington Post*, which claimed Astor died a hero and deserved respect. Years later, Richmond was suspended from the Episcopal clergy for his extreme views.

Better Safe Than Sorry

Another response to the *Titanic* that was critical of the wealth and luxury of the passengers on board came from rural African-American observers who commented on the disaster through story-songs known as "toasts." *Titanic* toasts told versions of a story about a black man named Shine who was on board the doomed ship and managed to escape and swim to New York, leaving the wealthy whites to sink along with their luxuries.

Blow Me Down! Musical responses to the *Titanic* disaster by African Americans inspired songwriter Bob Dylan to write "Desolation Row," which uses the ship as a metaphor for the harshness of a heavily policed and mechanized society.

As the ship goes down, the rich passengers plead with Shine to come back and help them. Some offer him money. Prostitutes on board offer him sex. In some versions, the captain's daughter is on board and begs Shine to save her. She turns out to be pregnant by another man. Refusing all that he is offered, Shine swims away and returns to his friends on land.

Another African-American account of the disaster is a song by the blues singer-songwriter Huddie Ledbetter, better known as Leadbelly. In the song, the prize fighter Jack

Johnson tries to book passage on the *Titanic*, but is refused because he is black. When he learns later of the disaster he dances the "Eagle Rock" to celebrate his safety.

Song and Story

Just as the *Titanic* has inspired a plethora of popular mythology, it has figured prominently in literary efforts throughout the century. Novels, stories, and poems intended to appeal to every kind of audience have dealt with the *Titanic*, whether treating it directly, as a metaphor, or as an evocative background.

Deep Ditties

Soon after the disaster, British novelist and poet Thomas Hardy wrote the probing poem, "The Convergence of the Twain," about the fateful meeting of the ship and the iceberg. The poem is deep in more ways than one as it describes the wreck on the bottom of the sea as it is seen through the eyes of "moon-eyed fishes."

In 1935, Canadian poet E.J. Pratt wrote another of the most notable poems on the ship, called simply "The *Titanic*." Unlike Hardy's lyric treatment, Pratt's work is an epic, and draws on the poet's knowledge of ships, seamanship, and the sea. More recently, in 1978, the German poet, Hans Magnus Enzensberger wrote a series of 33 poems narrating the disaster, "The Sinking of the *Titanic*," relating the event to student radicalism of the 1960s, communism, welfare, and the decline of literature. Enzensberger has returned to the *Titanic* theme in more recent poems as well.

Ahoy There!

Whisper mutter blather mumble
Whistle purr murmur mibble

. . .

Rumble clash clatter bang

. . .

Sob squeal whine groan

. . .

Roar roar roar roar

—from the poem, "Audio Signal of May 15, 1912"
by Hans Magnus Enzensberger, 1995

Good Yarns

Titanic novels and stories abound, running the gamut from pulp fiction to magnum opus. Robert Prechtl's dense *Titanic*, published first in Germany in 1938 and later translated for American readers, is a painstaking and tortuous book, juxtaposing facts about the disaster and fictional vignettes with long stretches of philosophizing. Much of the book focuses on John Jacob Astor, who is portrayed attempting to buy White Star Line from J. Bruce Ismay. The book's somewhat negative portrayal of Captain Smith and the other British officers was picked up and grossly exaggerated in Herbert Selpin's 1942 Nazi propaganda film *Titanic*.

More popular and less intellectually challenging is the short story "You're Dead!" by Wilson Mizner, published in 1936, about a couple of con men who survived the shipwreck—one after being pulled out of the water and the other by dressing up as a woman and entering a lifeboat.

A more recent popular *Titanic* book is Danielle Steel's 1991 romance novel, *No Greater Love*. Steel's heroine, Edwina Winfield, is full of lust for her fiancé, but vows to hold off until their marriage, tempted though she is by their romantic cruise on the *Titanic*. Tragically, the young couple never taste the forbidden fruits of love together, as he is lost with the ship and she carries on to fend for herself and her younger siblings.

Blow Me Down!
In 1955, the year Walter Lord's *A Night to Remember* was published, the TV show *You Are There* ran an episode based on the *Titanic*. In the show, Walter Cronkite interviews actors portraying passengers on the ship.

By far the most popular *Titanic* book of all time is Walter Lord's *A Night to Remember*. Meticulously researched, the non-fiction book strings fact after fact together into a gripping narration of the disaster. Lord provides background and recreates dialogue based on eyewitness accounts, so the book reads like a cross between a novel and a documentary. It quickly became a best-seller when it came out in 1955. It returned to the best-seller list in 1998 on the coattails of James Cameron's blockbuster movie—the only book to become a best-seller twice in non-sequential decades.

Figures of Speech

The *Titanic* continues to serve as a powerful symbol in the politics and culture of our time. Anything that seems potentially disastrous may be likened to the *Titanic*, especially if human greed, arrogance, or incompetence is at fault. Recently, an official with the New York Stock Exchange warned investors that the stock market could turn out to be "another *Titanic*." In Germany a political candidate with the environmentalist Green party compared the public's attitude toward the environment to "dancing on the *Titanic*."

In America, numerous politicians who have ventured into the icy waters of public office have been accused of launching a *Titanic*. Zell Miller, the governor of Georgia, quipped that Republicans who wanted to relive the Reagan-Bush years were "like the captain of the *Titanic* calling for more icebergs!" Dubious business enterprises are also labeled *Titanic*s.

Poster for a Titanic *attraction at Coney Island, New York.*
Mariners' Museum

Beneath the trivial references, the disaster continues to have a powerful hold on people. Perhaps this is because it reminds of the ever-present possibility of unexpected disaster. Or perhaps because it makes us feel like we've been through the disaster already.

The Least You Need to Know

➤ Popular mythology glorified the courage of first-class male passengers who were lost with the *Titanic.*

➤ Many *Titanic* myths were elitist, sexist, or racist in character.

➤ The *Titanic* has symbolized, greed, pride, incompetence, and luxury.

➤ The disaster has worked its way into our everyday vocabulary.

Chapter 24

TITANIC II:
The Revenge

Classic Catastrophes

In This Chapter

➤ *Titanic* movies, 1912–1979

➤ *Saved From the Titanic* (1912)

➤ *Titanic* (1942, German)

➤ *Titanic* (1953)

➤ *A Night to Remember* (1958, British)

➤ *Unsinkable Molly Brown* (1964)

➤ *S.O.S. Titanic* (1979, MFTV)

As it turns out, the *Titanic* happens to be a good subject to make movies about. *Titanic* flics go back almost to the very start of movie-making itself. Since that time, the ship has come a long way, changing as successive generations of movie-goers look to learn new lessons from the old disaster.

Titanic film genres include melodrama, docudrama, propaganda film, spy thriller, and even musical comedy. And of course there's the disaster movie.

From production to production, despite the various spins different directors put on the sinking, the historical subject matter adds an element of drama to the action. And it helps

Blow Me Down!
The original footage of the *Titanic* being launched still looks impressive. It shows a huge crowd gathered as the huge ship slides into the water, dragging big chains. This footage is spliced into the opening scenes of two *Titanic* films: *A Night to Remember*, where it's hard to tell apart from the staged action, and the made-for-TV *S.O.S. Titanic*, where it stands out despite being colorized.

that the time the ship took to sink after hitting the iceberg is about the same amount of time it takes to watch a feature film!

First Runs

In the weeks immediately following the disaster, movie theaters scrambled to show *Titanic*-related footage. Of course, very little *Titanic* footage actually existed. The only existing film of the *Titanic* shows the ship being launched. Theaters also showed slides depicting *Titanic*-related scenes, including the *Titanic* before it sailed and the *Carpathia* as it arrived in New York.

Quick Flics

Many movie houses showed films of other ships, such as the *Mauretania* or the Ti's sister ship, *Olympic*, implying they were the *Titanic*. Of course, the sinking itself wasn't captured on film, although a number of theaters advertised just that.

In the absence of documentary footage, it took almost no time at all for a silent-screen dramatization to be produced called *Saved From the Titanic*. The 10-minute film was released in May 1912, the very next month after the sinking, and it starred Dorothy Gibson, an actress who survived the real event.

Half Hitched

The film is a love story in which Dorothy, who has survived the *Titanic* disaster, is reunited with Jack, her fiancé in the U.S. Jack happens to be an officer in the Navy. Dorothy describes the harrowing shipwreck to Jack and her family with the help of primitive special effects that leave a great deal to the imagination. Dorothy then an-

Lifesavers
Dorothy Gibson starred in *Saved From the Titanic* of 1912 wearing a dress that she wore aboard the actual ship.

nounces that she is no longer willing to go through with the marriage unless Jack agrees to change careers. She is so upset by her experience at sea that she can't bear the thought of marrying a sailor!

Although Jack is torn, he feels it is his duty to carry on with the Navy. Giving up Dorothy is a noble sacrifice he is willing to make for his country. Dorothy's father, who witnesses Jack's decision, refuses to let such a manly son-in-law slip away and informs Dorothy that the wedding will take place. Presumably what's good for the Navy is good for Dorothy, so the movie ends on a positive note.

Getting All Choked Up

Producer David Selznick made plans to put out a *Titanic* movie in the 1930s, but legal and logistical problems got in the way. As a result, no *Titanic* films were made in America until 1953. In 1943, a Nazi propaganda film set on board the *Titanic* was produced. The lead in this film is a fictional German first officer, the one good man among a slew of cowardly and incompetent Brits.

This film was directed by Herbert Selpin, whose work was closely supervised by Nazi Minister of Propaganda Joseph Goebbels. Apparently, Selpin was not as interested as Goebbels in using his film to glorify Germany and vilify the British and resisted Goebbels' influence. Goebbels responded by having Selpin strangled!

Timeless Tragedy, Dated Drama

The first Hollywood *Titanic* feature, *Titanic* of 1953, subtitled *Nearer My God to Thee*, stars Clifton Webb as Richard Sturges and Barbara Stanwyck as wife Julia. Richard is a sharp and snobby high-society type who wants his daughter Annette and son Norman to circulate among the European upper crust. Julia, however, yearns for the simple life in a small town in the Midwest. She books passage aboard the *Titanic* for herself and the kids in order to rescue them from the shallow, pretentious existence favored by her husband.

Richard gets wise to her and signs aboard at the last minute, planning to take the youngsters back to Europe with him. Julia takes the wind out of his sails by telling him he's not really Norman's father. The family looks as doomed as the ship as Richard disowns his stepson (without telling him) and plans to return to Europe with his daughter, Annette. Meanwhile, Annette develops a crush on clean-cut, wholesome, Purdue University tennis player Giff Rogers, who gradually cures her of the snobbish attitude she picked up from her father.

Blow Me Down!
Titanic's Giff Rogers was played by the young Robert Wagner early in his career. Wagner later starred in an even campier disaster flic: the fourth and final Airport movie, *Airport '79—the Concorde.*

As tangled up as things seem, it all comes out in the wash when the ship starts sinking. The young, illegitimate Norman acts like a real man in the face of danger, making his stepfather proud. Father and stepson go down together on the ship. Julia and Richard patch up their differences just in time to say good-bye as she steps into a lifeboat with daughter Annette. Giff, the tennis player, makes it into a lifeboat after heroically cutting it free from the falls.

When you have a family like the Sturges' in Titanic *(1953), disaster is all just part of the boat ride.*

Everett Collection

Other lives get turned around at the last minute too, notably that of an ex-priest who was defrocked for alcoholism. He rediscovers his spiritual calling in time to comfort anguished souls on the ship.

Although the film sketches an outline of *Titanic* history, it fails to evoke 1912 convincingly. It's worth seeing, though, if you like 1950s Hollywood. The script won an Oscar and the art direction got an Oscar nomination.

A Good Night

In a class by itself among *Titanic* films is the 1958 British movie *A Night to Remember*, based on Walter Lord's non-fiction best-seller. The carefully scripted docudrama is an admirably plausible interpretation of its subject. Although not without its idealistic and sentimental moments, it succeeds in providing balanced views of the many undecided and controversial questions that still surround the disaster.

Only the main character, Officer Lightoller, played by Kenneth More, is a little too perfect, repeatedly stepping in to quell outbreaks of red-blooded panic. Otherwise, although sundry heroes and heroines play out their special scenes—Guggenheim, the Strauses, Molly Brown, and the orchestra—the response the film attempts to produce in its viewers is not admiration but understanding.

Blow Me Down!
Despite having less glamour and fewer big stars, the British *A Night to Remember* did better at the American box office than Hollywood's *Titanic* with Clifton Webb and Barbara Stanwyck.

Despite bathtub-quality special effects, A Night to Remember *remains one of the best* Titanic *films of all time.*
Everett Collection

259

Nobody's Perfect

The movie opens as the *Titanic* is christened and God's blessing is invoked on the ship, its passengers, and crew. The scene is not ironic, as you might expect (especially since the real ship was never christened), but instead announces the attitude of the production itself, which, in effect, blesses the passengers and crew by presenting human weakness in a sympathetic light, despite the tragedy.

The film made some tough choices in bringing the disaster to the screen. There is no villain, the heroes are upstaged by the disaster itself, and almost everyone, including Captain Smith, has their faults but is likable. Critics have complained the film is too long and lacks pizzazz, but it remains a thorough and effective study of behavior in response to the disaster.

Ismay's Dismay

Even Ismay is likable in scenes prior to the sinking. In his first scene, he good-naturedly refers to himself as "the office boy" in order to defer to Thomas Andrews' knowledge of the ship. The script acquits him of pressuring the captain to make a fast crossing. Although many doubted the real Ismay when he denied interfering at the Senate Inquiry, it's hard not to believe the modest and affable film Ismay as he claims to have no say in navigational matters.

Later, when he learns of the danger the ship is in, Ismay is understandably upset and exhibits a lack of control that seems entirely appropriate under the circumstances. Although at this point he seems weak in comparison with the calm, firm, and efficient officers and the resigned and philosophical Andrews, he also seems more believable. What's more, he seems shaken not simply by the threat to his personal safety; he is thrown for a loop by the impossible idea that the whole ship is sinking.

Two Sides to the Sinking

The film's generosity in depicting Ismay's foibles extends toward other passengers as well. Some first-class passengers are shown to be priggish and sheltered, but they aren't cold or arrogant. Some steerage passengers are boisterous and reckless, but they aren't mean or stupid. A few first-class passengers are heroic, but in several cases, their heroism consists of pretending things aren't as bad as they are. They are to be admired because they realize what a mess they are in, but do their best to help prevent panic.

Ahoy There!

Clinch Smith and myself noticed a list on the floor of the companionway. We kept our own counsel about it, not wishing to frighten anyone or cause any unnecessary alarm, especially among the ladies, who then appeared upon the scene. We did not consider it our duty to express our individual opinion upon the serious character of the accident which now appealed to us with the greatest force.

—first-class passenger Colonel Archibald Gracie

If this refusal to admit how bad things are seems heroic on the Boat Deck, it is an injustice in steerage. The stewards who keep the steerage passengers below seem unaware of how serious the danger is, and unaware of the injustice. They are simply following the rules. On the other side of the coin, when some steerage men rush a lifeboat and another wraps himself in a shawl, they are not presented as object lessons in cowardice. Instead, it seems a shame that they are dragged out of the boat.

Even Captain Lord is given his due as someone who has at least taken care of his own ship. When "iceberg ahead" is first shouted from a ship's crow's nest, it turns out not to be the *Titanic*, but Captain Lord's *Californian*. It's a relief when the ship stops in time with no harm done. In contrast to Captain Rostron of the *Carpathia*, who is initially outraged when the ship's wireless operator barges in and wakes him up with the news of the *Titanic*, Lord responds patiently when repeatedly awakened with reports about the ship.

Ahoy There!

The principal fact that stands out is the almost entire absence of fear or alarm on the part of passengers, and the conformity to the normal on the part of almost everyone. I think it is no exaggeration to say that those who read of the disaster quietly at home, and pictured to themselves the scene as the Titanic *was sinking, had more of the sense of horror than those who stood on the deck and watched her go down inch by inch. The fact is that the sense of fear came to the passengers very slowly—a result of the absence of any signs of danger and the peaceful night.*

—second-class passenger Lawrence Beesley

Soft Soap

The film isn't sanctimonious about its forgiving attitude. After all, in choosing not to re-enact the standard, popular *Titanic* myths, the movie risks appearing subversive and disrespectful of traditional values. Since it doesn't make a big deal about the noble men on board who lost their lives, you might think that the film intends to criticize society—to turn the *Titanic* into a ship of fools.

Blow Me Down!
The *Titanic* was a cargo ship as well as a passenger ship. The cargo manifests lists eight cases of soap, three cases of perfumed soap, and 490 bundles of cheese!

The script actually confronts this problem head-on in an early scene that introduces Lightoller. He is shown laughing at an advertisement for "Vinolia Otto toilet soap" provided in first-class on the *Titanic*. (These ads really existed. You can see one in Chapter 1 of this book.) A stodgy gentlemen next to him takes offense and asks him if he is a "foreigner or a radical." Obviously, the hero of the film is no radical. The point is, even though the movie leaves out the soft soap in looking back at the *Titanic*, it's not trying to tear down the fabric of society.

Practical Matters

At fault, finally, for the disaster in the eyes of the film, is simply the out-dated Board of Trade regulations that failed to require enough lifeboats. In a delightful bit of tactful understatement, as Captain Smith and Thomas Andrews are facing up to the grim facts of their predicament, Smith says, "I don't think the Board of Trade regulations visualized this situation, do you?" In this scene, the navigator and the shipbuilder are let off the hook, but the Board of Trade isn't evil, either; it just has some catching up to do.

As the film ends with footage of debris floating on the water, a caption scrolls up the screen announcing the disaster has resulted in "lifeboats for all, unceasing radio vigil," and "the International Ice Patrol." This may seem like a prosaic way to redeem such a spectacular catastrophe, especially in light of the tendency to glorify heroes and demon-ize villains that has played such a large part in responses to the *Titanic* before and since the film. Even so, it makes for a sensible conclusion.

More poignant, however, is Lightoller's famous line uttered a few scenes prior to the end: "I don't think I'll ever be sure again. About anything."

Stealing the Show

Among *Titanic*'s most glorified passengers is "Unsinkable Molly" Brown, whose life was depicted in the 1960 Broadway musical named for her with Tammy Grimes in the title role. The musical was made into a movie starring Debbie Reynolds in 1964. The action traces Molly's progress from rough-and-tumble Wild West orphan to European socialite.

The *Titanic* is only one episode in an eventful musical comedy, but it helps Molly decide the key question of who she is and how she wants to live. Thanks to her experiences during the disaster, she is able to straighten out her priorities before returning to her mansion in Denver and patching things up with her estranged husband, J.J.

Although she finally turns her back on high-falutin' society and rejoins her husband in the show and movie, the Browns remained separated in real life as Molly took up residence in fashionable Newport, Rhode Island, before moving to a hotel where she lived the rest of her life. The feisty Molly Brown of stage and screen is perhaps best remembered for the lifeboat scene, in which she gives her clothes away to other passengers and pulls a gun on a cowardly copassenger, threatening to "color the Atlantic" with his "yellow guts."

Lifesavers
One bit of Molly Brown mythology portrayed in the musical is that after J.J. struck it rich, Molly hid $300,000 of J.J.'s money in a stove for safe-keeping. You guessed it! J.J. lit the stove and burned up the money. J.J. takes the conflagration in stride, though, by going out the same day and striking it rich again!

Stripping to her undies doesn't take the edge off Debbie Reynolds' take-charge attitude in Unsinkable Molly Brown *(1964).*
Photofest

263

Here are some memorable Molly Browns:

➤ Tucker McGwire plays a salty and lovable Molly in *A Night to Remember* (1958). She persuades a persnickety fellow passenger to put on her life jacket by saying "Everyone's wearin' 'em this season, they're the latest thing."

➤ Tammy Grimes starred in Broadway's *Unsinkable Molly Brown* of 1960.

➤ Debbie Reynolds takes the role from innocent yokel to international socialite to wise yokel in the screen version of the musical filmed in 1964.

➤ Cloris Leachman is hot to trot with wealthy men as she spices up the 1979 made-for-TV movie, *S.O.S. Titanic*.

➤ Kathy Bates is the most recent Unsinkable Molly of the 1997 blockbuster, *Titanic*.

Cloris Leachman knows which end of an oar is which as Molly "Don't Call Her Maggie" Brown in S.O.S. Titanic *(1979).*
Everett Collection

Molly Brown proves she's one tough cookie and has picked up a lot of admirers over the years. An even tougher cookie is the secret agent hero of Clive Cussler's best selling novel, *Raise the Titanic,* which was made into one of the most financially disastrous movies of all time. We talk about this film briefly in Chapter 19. And let's see, wasn't there another *Titanic* movie worth mentioning...?

The Least You Need to Know

➤ The first *Titanic* movie, *Saved From the Titanic*, was released a month after the disaster and starred survivor Dorothy Gibson.

➤ Hollywood's *Titanic* (1953) is a melodrama pitting family values against social climbing.

➤ *A Night to Remember* (1958) is a docudrama based on Walter Lord's non-fiction best-seller.

➤ Molly Brown is the subject of her own musical comedy featuring the *Titanic* in Broadway's *Unsinkable Molly Brown* (1960), made into a Hollywood movie in 1964.

➤ Other *Titanic* films include the Nazi propaganda effort of 1943 and the made-for-TV soap opera, *S.O.S. Titanic*.

More Big Splashes

Titanic in the '90s is bigger than ever, thanks to technical wizardry and some new spins on its significance. Thanks also to millions of people who sense the importance of the disaster even after all this time. It says a lot about where we've come from and how far. Not that we've found a way to entirely prevent disasters from occurring, but perhaps we're better prepared to deal with them emotionally when they do.

Although fascination with the *Titanic* remains as strong as ever, few people feel that they have something to prove on account of the disaster. Today it seems easier to accept. We know that bad things happen to people all the time, both as a result of floods, tornadoes, and hurricanes, and due to human mistakes and miscalculations, such as the space shuttle *Challenger* explosion and the explosion of TWA Flight 800 over Rhode Island.

Still, jaded though we may be, the success of *Titanic*, the new Broadway musical, and *Titanic*, the new movie, shows that nothing looms so large for so many reasons in the history of the century as the big ship that sank. As the end of the century looms, we're ready to take one more good, hard look at the disaster and think about it in new ways.

All the Ship's a Stage

Titanic, the Broadway show written by Peter Stone with music by Maury Yeston, pulled off the unprecedented feat of sinking a ship on stage. In the process, they put together the hottest musical in a long time. The show has been breaking box office records and reeled in five Tony awards: Best Musical, Best Book (by Peter Stone), Best Original Score (by Maury Yeston), Best Scenic Design (by Stewart Laing), and Best Orchestrations (by Jonathan Tunick).

Stewart Laing's staging is an engineering feat to rival the *Titanic* itself. The stage is divided into several decks that can be illuminated one at a time or in groups to depict the "floating city." The crow's nest hangs out over the audience, and throughout most of Act II after the collision with the iceberg, the stage tilts further and further until the end.

Blow Me Down!
The original cast recording of *Titanic*, the musical, made it to number 158 during its first week. It was nominated for a Grammy for Best Musical Show Recording.

Dinner and a show really hit the spot if it's the new musical, Titanic.
©Joan Marcus

Ships Are Us

The show emphasizes the theme of human enterprise. As in many works on the *Titanic*, the ship embodies society itself, but the musical explores this idea by showing how different people are actively working to become a part of the "ship of dreams." Although the ship is driven largely by greed and ambition, everyone feels the excitement and wants to participate.

Frederick Barrett, the stoker; Frederick Fleet, the lookout; and Harold Bride, the wireless operator are as excited about the possibilities the ship holds as Andrews, Ismay, and Captain Smith. But these ordinary working men are actually part of the ship in a way the big cheeses aren't—they represent the eyes, ears, and power of the *Titanic*. Their fascination with the ship thus has to do with their futures and their fate.

> **Blow Me Down!**
> The musical's J. Bruce Ismay is played by David Garrison, formerly of the hit comedy sitcom *Married With Children*.

Big Plans

Similarly, the passengers play their part on the big liner by carrying out various projects—planning a new life in America, looking for a husband, fantasizing about the wealthy. All these different plans and dreams are finally versions of the plans that built the *Titanic* itself. Designer Thomas Andrews reminds us how important plans are by carrying around his blueprints of the ship.

Finally, the show says that we can't help making big plans, despite the painful lessons of history. The show brings out the poetic and dramatic potential of the *Titanic* as only a musical could do. Though it seems amazing how well the ambitious project worked, it also seems surprising someone hadn't tried it long before.

> **Ahoy There!**
> *Composer-lyricist Maury Yeston and I had worked together before…. During that happy time we discovered, by total coincidence, that both of us had been harboring magnificent dreams of turning the enduring myth of the* Titanic *into a musical drama. We gladly pooled resources and set to work almost immediately…. A lot of our early work was done over lunch in a small Chinese restaurant on Second Avenue.*
>
> —*Titanic* story and book writer Peter Stone

We may not all be officers, but everyone plays a part on the ship of dreams.
©Joan Marcus

A Reel Whopper

Titanic fever had to happen one way or another. As Peter Stone and Maury Yeston were thinking up their Broadway show, film director James Cameron was shooting the biggest movie ever brought to the screen. *Titanic* is the biggest box-office success ever, the first movie to gross over $1 billion dollars world wide.

Statuesque Figures

Titanic fans are everywhere. Some claim to have seen the film 50 times and more. The film's stars, Kate Winslet and Leonardo DiCaprio, have become household names, and the movie has prompted a surge of interest in the history of the disaster. Hollywood has recognized the movie's success by awarding it 11 Oscars at the 70th annual Academy Awards. Only the historical epic *Ben Hur* (1959) has won as many.

Here's who picked up the 11 little brass statues:

➤ **Best Picture**   It's actually the second Hollywood movie to go by the name of *Titanic* (the first was released in 1953). During filming, the cast and crew referred to it jokingly as "Planet Ice."

➤ **Best Director**   They laughed at James Cameron for spending twice the $100 million budgeted for the film, but it turned out to be well worth every penny.

➤ **Best Film Editing**   Cameron had snipping and splicing help from Conrad Buff and Richard Harris.

➤ **Best Special Effects**   Donald Pennington supervised a crack team of movie magicians.

➤ **Best Art Direction**   You better believe Charles Dwight Lee has heard of Picasso.

➤ **Best Cinematography**   Russell Carpenter knows how to shoot a big ship for the big screen.

➤ **Best Original Dramatic Score**   James Horner made a big sound out of little black dots.

➤ **Best Original Song**   "My Heart Will Go On," was sung by Celine Dion and written by James Horner and Will Jennings.

➤ **Best Soundtrack**   James Horner and Don Davis did the orchestrations, Randy Gerston did music supervision, Tom Bellfort supervised the sound editing, and that hot Irish band playing jigs and reels down in steerage was Gaelic Storm.

➤ **Best Sound Effects Editing**   Tom Bellfort supervised a gang that knows how to rumble.

➤ **Best Costumes**   Deborah Scott made sure the cast was well-suited to their parts.

Despite going over budget $100 million, no one has to rescue James Cameron's film, Titanic.
Photofest

Shining Stars

There were no Oscars for the cast, although there were nominations, including Best Actress for Kate Winslet and Best Supporting Actress for Gloria Stuart. Possibly more important, though, is male lead Leonardo DiCaprio's newfound status as teenage heartthrob. His devoted fans all over the world agree: He's so hot the iceberg doesn't stand a chance!

Here's one special effect that wasn't produced with computers—dreamboat Leonardo DiCaprio as winsome Jack Dawson.
Photofest

Here are the film's stars and their roles.

- ➤ **Leonardo DiCaprio** Jack Dawson, the plucky young steerage passenger who rescues Rose from suicide.

- ➤ **Kate Winslet** Rose DeWitt Bukater, the big-hearted society belle, trapped in a stifling engagement with the arrogant Cal Hockley.

- ➤ **Gloria Stuart** Rose, 85 years later, who tells her story to the crew of a *Titanic* salvage expedition.

- ➤ **Billy Zane** Cal Hockley, the proud, rich, spiteful, and controlling man who plans to marry Rose. He can't bear to see Rose fall for Jack.

- ➤ **Frances Fisher** Ruth DeWitt Bukater, Rose's prim yet anxious mother who can't bear the thought of missing out on Cal's money.

- ➤ **Kathy Bates** Molly Brown who, in this film, is less of a "rich hick" caricature than in other *Titanic* films.

- ➤ **Bernard Hill** The avuncular Captain E.J. Smith who breaks the bad news about the sinking ship.

- ➤ **Jonathan Hyde** The oily J. Bruce Ismay, who wants to make a splash in the papers by making a faster crossing than the *Olympic*.

> **Blow Me Down!**
> One of cast members now has two *Titanic* films to list on his resume. David Warner appeared in *S.O.S. Titanic* as schoolteacher Lawrence Beesley and in Cameron's film as Cal's menacing bodyguard, Spicer Lovejoy.

Fact Meets Fiction

Cameron sweated the historic details in order to make his story as faithful as possible to the actual events. He even commissioned the Welin Davit Company of Sweden to make davits exactly like the ones the company made for the original ship.

Even so, the film is daring in the way it integrates fictional characters into history. It shows Rose, her mother, and Cal hob-nobbing with famous passengers and crew, including Captain Smith, Thomas Andrews, and J. Bruce Ismay. In fact, because of her acquaintance with these historical figures, Rose (and, therefore, the audience) is able to learn first-hand and early on that the ship is doomed, before most of the other passengers know what's going on.

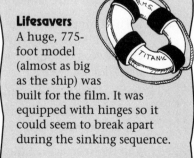

> **Lifesavers**
> A huge, 775-foot model (almost as big as the ship) was built for the film. It was equipped with hinges so it could seem to break apart during the sinking sequence.

More daring still is the film's depiction of the fatal moment when the iceberg was finally spotted by the lookouts. They spotted it too late because they were busy watching the young lovers, Rose and Jack, having fun together on deck! Leave it to a movie director to come up with a theory like this to explain the disaster.

Impressive Resume

James Cameron brought a lot of experience with him into the making of *Titanic*, but it's a major departure from his previous sci-fi, horror, spy-thriller flics. Here are Cameron's movies:

- ➤ *Piranha II: The Spawning* (1982)   There's nowhere to go but up from this horror-laugher about flying fish that terrorize a tropical resort.
- ➤ *The Terminator* (1984)   Cameron clicked with action lead Arnold Schwarzenegger in this sci-fi thriller. The two worked together on two other films as well.
- ➤ *Aliens* (1986)   This was the second of many popular space-horror films starring Sigourney Weaver.
- ➤ *The Abyss* (1989)   Cameron got his feet wet with this sci-fi submarine rescue drama.
- ➤ *Terminator II: Judgement Day* (1991)   Arnie's back in *T-2* as a kind, big-brotherly Terminator.
- ➤ *True Lies* (1994)   Schwarzenegger is a spy who solves his marital problems while bringing terrorists to justice.
- ➤ *Titanic* (1997)   Cameron traded Schwarzenegger for a male lead with much smaller muscles.

Action!

Titanic stands out among Cameron's movies as the only epic romance. Though a new-comer to this genre of film, Cameron is able to use the social attitudes of the Edwardian period to complicate his 1990s love story, managing to appeal to throngs of movie-goers who might have stayed home.

Even so, important elements from his earlier movies help account for the success of *Titanic*. Like most of his films, *Titanic* is suspenseful, has lots of action, and great special effects. As a result, movie-goers who liked Cameron's other movies have every reason to like *Titanic* as well.

These people—action film fans—can appreciate the growing suspense as Jack is trapped in the sinking ship while the icy water slowly rises. Meanwhile, Kate is searching for him, her search hampered by the fact that everyone else on board is starting to panic.

And the spectacle of the huge ship taking a nose-dive into the sea with hundreds of struggling passengers on board is quite exciting. It takes expensive and sophisticated technology to sink the *Titanic* on screen like this. Even if you're a heavy-metal type who hates mushy love scenes, it's still worth the admission—and the two-and-a-half hour wait—to watch the ship go under. (The whole show is 3 hours and 14 minutes, but everyone says it doesn't seem that long.)

There are other cool hi-tech effects, too. The famous one is where the camera shows Jack standing on the prow of the ship with his arms spread out as if he's flying (Rose does this later). Then the camera pans back and up somehow (is it done with computers?) to reveal the entire ship speeding along, with people walking around on deck. Even though the ship is going nice and fast, the shot from bow to stern takes a long time. The scene really lets you see how big the ship is.

More technical wizardry goes into the undersea salvaging scene near the beginning as a submersible explores the wreck. And when old Rose arrives on the salvage vessel, she's treated (along with the audience) to a computer simulation that shows the mechanics involved in the sinking of the ship. "That's not how it felt," she says afterward, but it's a spiffy way of showing how it happened.

SOS
Cameron organized his own expedition to the wreck of the *Titanic* to film the exploration sequences. He chartered the Russian research vessel, *Akademic Kealdysh* and two Mir submersibles to do the filming. On one of his dives, the sub's batteries failed, leaving him trapped at the bottom of the sea. Fortunately, after a wait of some five hours, the other sub arrived with replacement batteries.

A New Twist

As all the *Titanic* hoopla clearly shows, however, there's more to the movie than action, suspense, and special effects, although these things certainly help. In addition, there's the history and the love story, working together in unusual ways. The history stands behind the film, adding grandeur to the story, but the story itself is something new.

Blow Me Down!
The film's stars, Kate Winslet and Leonardo DiCaprio, took etiquette lessons to prepare for their roles.

Buddies and Lovers

Some critics have complained that Rose and Jack are typical, predictable characters, but millions of movie fans disagree with this view. Not every historical epic action disaster movie takes the time necessary to let the main characters become friends before falling in love. And the friendship seems special because it extends across old fashioned social barriers.

Like Romeo and Juliet, Jack and Rose completely lay aside their different backgrounds, which, according to society's standards, should keep them apart. Unlike Romeo and

Juliet, though, they're willing to do more than just die for one another. Instead, they rescue one another. The scenes in which Rose and Jack struggle to get each other out of trouble makes *Titanic* not only a love story, but a buddy film.

The fact that Rose and Jack are friends is an important and appealing aspect of the movie that sets it apart from other films. This fact has even spilled out into the media attention paid to the two young stars. Everyone wants to know if there's anything going on between them. The answer is always no, they're just friends.

Letting Go and Going On

The film lovers are good role models for the '90s because they don't commit to one another for life, unlike the more tragic Romeo and Juliet and unlike the old and old-fashioned Ida and Isidor Straus. They both know that anything could happen in the future, so the important thing is to have fun and be friends in the present.

Rose and Jack are lovers getting their feet wet.
Photofest

The movie emphasizes this point in many ways. Rose is willing to enter a lifeboat without Jack—at least until she learns he's trapped down on the ship and wouldn't have a chance without her help. Later, when Jack dies, it's not the end of the world for her. She has to let him sink because she has her whole life ahead of her. This idea—the heart will go on—is the lesson of the movie. We can get past tragedy—whether it's the break-up of a first love, or the *Titanic* disaster—keep the memories, and go on with life.

For many young movie fans, Leo the movie star is a kind of first love they will soon get over. They'll let go of his bloodless hand and he'll sink out of their lives forever. Hopefully, though, he'll make them a little better prepared for whoever or whatever comes next.

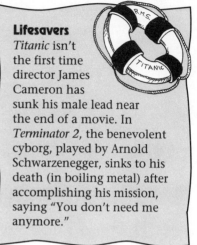

Lifesavers
Titanic isn't the first time director James Cameron has sunk his male lead near the end of a movie. In *Terminator 2*, the benevolent cyborg, played by Arnold Schwarzenegger, sinks to his death (in boiling metal) after accomplishing his mission, saying "You don't need me anymore."

Watch Your Step as You Disembark!

Well, that's about it; at least until they come out with *Titanic II*! This won't be easy, since there was only one *Titanic*, but if it can be done, someone will find a way! In the mean time, *Titanic*, the film, has done the world a favor in reminding us what an amazing event the *Titanic* disaster was.

We hope this book has helped you understand and appreciate this event a little better. To help you continue your search for the meaning of the disaster, you'll find six appendices in the following pages, including a glossary, an annotated list of ships and subs mentioned in this book, a list of important people involved with the ship, a passenger list, a list of cargo, and resources for further reading and viewing.

The Least You Need to Know

- ➤ *Titanic* the musical won five Tony Awards.
- ➤ *Titanic* the film won 11 Academy Awards.
- ➤ Prior to the *Titanic*, James Cameron directed many sci-fi action-adventure films.
- ➤ The film was the first to reach the box-office mark of $1 billion.

Titanic Terms

bathysphere   A manned diving chamber used for deep-sea research, supplied with air from the surface through a hose.

berth   A bunk on a ship or train; it is also a place where a ship may be docked or the space at sea a ship occupies.

black berg   Sometimes used as another name for a blue berg. Black bergs can also be icebergs that are partially covered by rock or dirt, making them appear dark in color.

blue berg   An iceberg that appears blue as a result of having recently rolled over in the sea. Some experts doubt they actually exist.

bollard   A metal post on the deck of a ship used for tying it to its moorings.

bow   The front part of the ship.

bridge   The section of a ship, elevated from the main deck, where steering, communication, and other ship's functions are controlled.

bulkhead   A partition dividing up a ship. Bulkheads are often water and fire resistant.

calved   When an iceberg breaks off into the water from the end of a glacier. This usually happens in spring as the weather warms up.

commutator   An instrument that measures the degree of list of a ship (see *list*).

cost-plus contract   Means the manufacturer will be paid for whatever the work costs plus an agreed on amount as profit. This is advantageous to the manufacturer, who doesn't have to bid on a job or worry about cutting corners in production.

crow's nest   The elevated part of the ship where the lookout stands. In sailing ships, the crow's nest may be attached to one of the masts. On the *Titanic*, the crow's nest was a high platform.

davit   A kind of crane operated by a pulley used for lowering lifeboats into the water from the deck of a ship.

falls   The ropes and pulleys used for raising and lowering boats and cargo to and from the deck of a ship.

field ice   An especially large, field-sized expanse of ice extending at least five miles across. Any smaller expanse of ice is an ice floe (see *floe*).

firemen   Crewmen who had the job of keeping the steam engines moving by shoveling coal into the boiler furnaces.

floe   A large, flat body of ice less than five miles across.

frigate   Traditionally a medium-sized sailing ship used for war from the 1600s through the 1800s.

funnel   The part of a steamship that serves the purpose of a smokestack in a factory building. The *Titanic*, like other major ships of the time, had four funnels, but one of them was a dummy, put there in order to make the ship look more symmetrical as well as more powerful.

gantry   A bridge-like scaffolding used in shipbuilding that enables work to be done on the inside and outside of the hull.

growler   An iceberg that is less than 15 feet high and 50 feet long.

hypothermia   Potentially fatal malady caused by exposure to cold, resulting in reduced blood flow to the extremities and finally, the brain.

iceberg   A large, floating piece of ice broken off from a glacier. "Berg" is Scandinavian for "mountain."

keel   The bottom-most part running the length of the ship in the very center.

knot   A unit of speed used at sea, roughly equivalent to 1.15 miles per hour.

list   A tilting of a ship in relation to the surface of the water.

moorings   The ties attaching a ship to a dock or pier. The term also applies to the place the ship is docked.

Morse code   A system of dots and dashes, used to represent the letters of the alphabet, developed by Samuel F.B. Morse in the early part of the 19th century. These signals can be communicated audibly by telegraph, or visually at night with a blinking lamp. By daylight, Morse signals can be sent with flags through a process called "wig-wagging."

pontoon   A float, often consisting of a hollow drum, that can be used for supporting docks and bridges. A pontoon is also a kind of flat-bottomed boat or one of the floats of a seaplane.

populist   Political views that favor the interests of ordinary people as opposed to industry, trade, or specialized interests.

port   The left-hand side of a ship.

rigging   Consists of the ropes, chains, and other equipment that are used for maneuvering the masts and sails of a sailing ship.

slip   An enclosure in which a ship is built. Ships are built differently than cars. At the time, Henry Ford was perfecting the assembly line as a way of making lots of cars in a single space. In contrast, each ship is built in its own slip.

starboard   The right-hand side of a ship.

steerage   The section of cheapest berths on a passenger ship. This section was originally located in the rear of the ship near the rudder, which steers it. There were two steerage sections on the *Titanic*, one at the stern, or rudder-end of the ship, the other all the forward at the bow.

stern   The rear of a ship.

suffragettes   Politically active women who supported women's voting rights ("suffrage" is the right to vote). Conservatives pointed to the "women and children first" rule on the *Titanic* to suggest that women's suffrage was a bad idea.

swamp   To overturn, or partially overturn, a boat, causing it to fill with water and making it essentially useless.

swell   A small, rolling that wave that doesn't break unless it runs into something, such as a ship or an iceberg.

trimmers   Kept the firemen supplied with coal which they distributed in wheelbarrows. Firemen and trimmers were known as "the black gang."

wireless telegraphy   The communication equipment used by steamships. It was invented by Guglielmo Marconi.

Historic Ships

Adriatic   The *Titanic* crew members who testified at the U.S. Senate inquiry returned to England on this White Star ship on April 29, 1912. Officer Boxhall served on board the ship for a short time prior to World War I.

Akademic Keldysh   Research vessel provided by Russia's Shirov Institute of Oceanography to help with the 1991 filming expedition to the wreck of the *Titanic* headed by Stephen Low.

Alvin   Woods Hole Institute's three-person sub used by the Ballard-led discovery and exploration expeditions of 1985 and 1986. It has a titanium hull capable of withstanding deep-sea pressure of over 6,000 pounds per square inch and equipment to control the unmanned submersible robot, *Jason Jr.*

Amerika   The German liner that transmitted the sixth wireless ice warning received by the *Titanic* on April 14 at 1:45 p.m. This message was intended for the U.S. Hydrographic Office, but the *Amerika* didn't have the sending power to get the message through, so the *Titanic* relayed it. We don't know whether any of the *Titanic*'s officers saw this message.

ANGUS (Acoustically Navigated Geological Underwater Survey vessel)   Towed sled used by the Ballard discovery expedition of 1985. It is similar to the *Argo*, but equipped with still cameras instead of video.

Antonia   Cunard liner on which Officer Boxhall served during the 1930s.

Argo   U.S. towed sled used by the Ballard discovery expedition of 1985. Equipped with five TV cameras and powerful strobe lights, it was pulled by a cable from the *Knorr*.

Arizona   The largest liner in 1879, when she hit an iceberg head-on off the coast of Newfoundland. Fortunately, the ship didn't sink and no one was killed.

Atlantic   Early White Star steamer equipped with sails built by Harland and Wolff in 1871. She left Liverpool on March 20, 1873, with passengers—mostly emigrants. At 3:00 in the morning of April 1st on a dark night, she hit some rocks near Meagher Island off the Nova Scotia coast; 481 out of 942 people on board were lost.

Atlantis II   Research vessel used by Ballard and his team when exploring the *Titanic* wreck in 1986.

Ausonia   Cunard liner on which Officer Boxhall served during the 1930s.

Austria   German HAPAG liner built in 1857 that was lost loaded with immigrants on the way to America when the ship caught fire during a failed delousing procedure.

Ballymena   Yacht from which 12 prize winners observed the efforts of a 1997 Tulloch-led salvage expedition. The contest was sponsored by Bass Ale.

Baltic   White Star liner that transmitted the fifth ice warning received by the *Titanic* at 1:42 p.m., April 14.

Birkenhead   Paddle steamer, built in 1845, used for troop transport during the colonial Kaffir wars in South Africa; 445 were lost and 193 were saved when the ship sank after hitting a rock. The captain, crew, and soldiers on board set the precedent for loading lifeboats "women and children first."

Bluebell   Trawler that helped rescue survivors after the *Lusitania* was sunk by a torpedo on May 7, 1915.

Britannic   Last of the three great White Star sister ships (the first two were the *Olympic* and the *Titanic*). It was launched in 1914, and quickly converted to a hospital ship for war duty. It was sunk by a mine or a torpedo.

Californian   Freighter drifting in the vicinity of the *Titanic* as it sank. Mysteriously, its captain didn't respond to distress rockets sighted by his officers.

Caronia   Cunard liner that sent the third ice warning received by the *Titanic* on the 14th of April at 9:00 in the morning. Captain Smith gave the message to Officer Lightoller early that afternoon.

Carpathia   Passenger steamer under Captain Arthur Rostron that rescued *Titanic* survivors from lifeboats. The ship was headed to the Mediterranean from New York and was 58 miles to the southeast of the *Titanic* when Rostron answered the distress signal.

Carroll A. Deering   Schooner found off Cape Hatteras, North Carolina, in 1922, with no one aboard except two cats.

Columbia   Passenger steamer that ran into an iceberg near Cape Race, Nova Scotia, in 1911. The crash injured a passenger and several crew, and seriously crushed the bow of the ship.

Empress of Ireland   Passenger steamer that embarked for America on April 5, 1912, on Good Friday prior to the *Titanic*'s maiden voyage.

F.J.W. Fay   Vessel used by the Grimm-led search expedition, which set off from Florida in July of 1980.

Great Britain   In 1843 this ship was the first transatlantic steamer to have an iron hull and use a screw propeller.

Gyre   Research vessel used in the summer of 1981 by the Grimm-led search expedition.

Hans Hedtoft   Passenger ship that collided with an iceberg in 1959 and disappeared without a trace with some 95 passengers and crew on board.

Hawke   Cruiser that was sucked into the wake of the *Olympic*, resulting in damage to the big liner.

Help   Salvage vessel chartered by Risdon Beazley, Ltd., in July 1953 to find and salvage artifacts from the *Titanic*. It was equipped with undersea explosives, undersea telephoto cameras, and remote-control submarines.

Imo   Norwegian steamer that ran into the cargo ship *Mont Blanc* in Halifax Harbor, resulting in an explosion that destroyed much of the harbor and surrounding town.

Jason Jr. (JJ)   Small, remote-controlled submersible robot equipped with powerful searchlights and mechanical arms connected by a cable to *Alvin*. It was used in the Ballard exploration of 1986.

Jim Kilabuk   Supply ship used in the failed Tulloch-led mission to salvage a section of the *Titanic*'s hull. The ship was to receive the section and carry it back to port.

Jules and *Jim*   IFREMER submersibles used for filming during Tulloch-led salvage expeditions.

Kaiser Wilhelm der Grosse   This North German Lloyd liner was the first ship to cross the Atlantic with wireless. It won the Blue Riband for the fastest Atlantic crossing yet made.

Knorr   2,000-ton, 245-foot, U.S. Navy-owned research vessel, used in the Ballard-led discovery expedition of 1985. It was hooked up to a satellite navigation system and equipped with special propellers that can send the ship forward, backward, and sideways.

Kronprinz Wilhelm   North German Lloyd liner that dented its bow on an iceberg at night in 1907.

Lapland   White Star ship on which surviving *Titanic* crew members returned to England.

Lusitania   Speedy Cunard passenger liner that was torpedoed by a German U-boat on May 7, 1915. Almost 1,200 were lost.

Mackay-Bennett   Vessel equipped with embalming equipment, tons of ice, and 100 coffins used to recover the bodies of *Titanic* victims. Recovery began April 20, 1912.

Majestic   White Star ship that figured into a story by W. T. Stead. In Stead's story, the captain of the ship was E.J. Smith, who later took the helm of the *Titanic*.

Mary Celeste   Brigantine found off the coast of Gibraltar in 1872. She was completely seaworthy, but not a soul was on board.

Mauretania   Cunard liner that set a speed record in 1907, crossing the Atlantic in four days, 10 hours, and 42 minutes. The record held until 1929.

Medusa   French frigate that ran aground while bound for colonies in Africa in 1816, resulting in one of the most pitiable disasters in seagoing history.

Mesaba   Ship that sent the last ice warning received by the *Titanic* at 9:40 p.m., Sunday, April 14, exactly two hours before the *Titanic* ran into an iceberg. The warning supplied coordinates locating ice in an area that included the *Titanic*'s position at the time.

Minia   The second of three ships that recovered bodies of *Titanic* victims. Starting on Friday, April 26, the *Minia* found 17 bodies.

Mont Blanc   French freighter loaded with explosives that collided with the Norwegian steamer, *Imo* on December 6, 1917, in Halifax Harbor, resulting in catastrophe.

Montmagny   The last of three ships that recovered bodies of *Titanic* victims. The ship recovered three bodies.

Nadir   IFREMER research vessel used on numerous salvage and exploration missions. The *Nadir* can carry 40 passengers and crew, as well as the deep-sea submersible, *Nautile*.

Nautile   IFREMER manned submersible equipped with sonar, video, communications gear, and mechanical arms. It is made of four-inch-thick titanium. It is built to hold three people and go as deep as 20,000 feet.

New York   Liner pulled loose from its moorings by suction from the wake of the *Titanic*.

Noordan   Dutch liner that sent the fourth ice warning received by the *Titanic* at 11:40 a.m.

Oceanic   In 1871, White Star moved into the North Atlantic with the ship. Although this ship was slower than the Cunard ships, it was larger and more luxurious, setting a White Star precedent.

Ocean Voyager   Converted ice breaker once owned by the Canadian Coast Guard before it was purchased by a French television company and used as a TV production ship for filming *Titanic* expeditions.

Olympic   *Titanic*'s sister ship launched on October 20, 1910.

Pacific   Early steamer that crossed the Atlantic in under 10 days in 1852.

Philadelphia   A liner that supplied coal to the *Titanic* during the coal strike.

Rainbow Warrior   Ship used by the environmental activist group Greenpeace, sunk in Aukland Harbor, New Zealand, in an act of sabotage.

Rappahannock   Ship that sent the second ice warning received by the *Titanic*. The warning was sent on the night of the 13th by Morse blinker. This ship had actually run into ice and got a dent in her bow and a bend in her rudder.

Republic   Ship that sank in 1909 on which Wireless Operator Jack Binns successfully sent out last minute distress calls.

Robert Conrad   Ship used by the third Grimm-led search expedition of 1983.

Royal Standard   Passenger ship that was badly damaged by a berg on the way back to Europe from Melbourne, Australia, in April 1864.

Samson   Norwegian sealing ship thought by some to be in the vicinity of the *Titanic* as it sank.

Savannah   This American steamer was the first ship to cross the Atlantic with the help of steam in 1819.

Scythia   Cunard liner on which Officer Boxhall served during the 1930s.

Le Suroit   IFREMER research vessel used in the Ballard discovery expedition in 1985.

Titan   Fictional ship of Morgan Robertson's 1898 novel *Futility*, which eerily anticipates the wreck of the *Titanic*.

Titanic   The largest man-made moving object ever at the time of its launching in 1912. It collided with an iceberg on April 14 on its maiden voyage, resulting in the loss of some 1,500 people.

Touraine   French ship that sent the first ice warning received by the *Titanic* on Friday, April 12.

Turbinia   Among the first ships to use a turbine engine in the 1890s, capable of going 34 knots.

Virginian   Steamship wrongly reported as towing the *Titanic* was being towed into Halifax after its brush with the iceberg.

Names to Know

This appendix lists people associated with the *Titanic*, including famous passengers, officers, business people, historians, explorers, and artists.

Thomas Andrews   Chief designer of the *Titanic* for Harland and Wolff shipbuilders. He was the first to realize the *Titanic* was doomed, and went down with the ship.

Colonel John Jacob Astor   Real-estate mogul reputed to have been worth $100 million; his market bottomed out when he went down along with his Airedale, Kitty.

Dr. Robert Ballard   Led the expedition that finally discovered the wreck of the *Titanic* in 1985.

Lawrence Beesley   Second-class passenger who survived to write an account of the disaster.

Fourth Officer Joseph Boxhall   Survived the disaster and later served as a technical consultant for the 1958 *Titanic* film, *A Night to Remember*. Boxhall's ashes were scattered at the site of *Titanic*'s sinking upon his death in 1967.

Junior Wireless Operator Harold Bride   He survived the *Titanic* disaster and sold his story to *The New York Times*.

"Unsinkable" Molly Brown   Outspoken "new money" refugee from a Western gold mine. When her estranged husband heard she survived, he said, "She's too mean to sink"!

Major Archibald Butt   Military aide to President Taft and erstwhile news reporter and diplomat. He attended the dinner for Captain Smith hosted by the Wideners the night of the wreck.

James Cameron   Director of the 1997 blockbuster film *Titanic*.

Helen Churchill Candee   Progressive American author of *How Women May Earn a Living* and other books. She gave fellow passenger Edward Kent a miniature photo of her mother as the ship sank. When Kent's body was recovered shortly after the disaster, the picture was found with it and returned to Candee, who survived.

Mrs. Charlotte Drake Cardeza   Famous for traveling on board with three baggage crates, four suitcases, and 14 trunks. She later valued her luggage at over $175 thousand.

Wireless Operator Harold Cottam   Received the *Titanic*'s distress signal while working on board the *Carpathia*.

Clive Cussler   Author of the 1976 best-selling spy thriller, *Raise the Titanic*.

Sir Cosmo and Lady Lucile Duff-Gordon   She was a cutting-edge dress designer and he was an English baronet. They signed on board the *Titanic* under the assumed name, "Mr. and Mrs. Morgan."

Jack Eaton   Noted *Titanic* historian.

Lookout Frederick Fleet   The first to spot the iceberg that sunk the *Titanic*. He survived the disaster and testified at the inquiries.

Jacques Futrelle   French mystery writer whose work has been compared to that of Arthur Conan Doyle, the inventor of Sherlock Holmes. Futrelle had just turned 37 when he went down with the *Titanic*.

Colonel Archibald Gracie   First-class passenger who survived to write an account of the disaster.

Jack Grimm   Led three failed search expeditions for the wreck of the *Titanic* in 1980, '81, and '82.

Benjamin Guggenheim   Swiss-American sultan of smelting who became immortalized for preparing for his final hours by changing into his formal evening wear, in order to go down like a gentlemen. Guggenheim's valet also decided to go down with him.

Charles Haas   Noted *Titanic* historian.

Henry Harris   Theater producer who had a number of plays showing in New York at the time of the disaster. He was returning from England where he had just found another play he planned to produce.

Bandleader Wallace Hartley   Led the *Titanic* orchestra as the ship sank. Thousands attended his funeral.

J. Bruce Ismay   White Star director who drew severe criticism for saving himself in a lifeboat from the sinking *Titanic*.

Second Officer Charles Lightoller   Was the highest ranking officer to survive. He supervised the loading of a number of lifeboats and was a stickler for "women and children first."

Captain Stanley Lord   He failed to take action when his crew reported sighting the *Titanic*'s distress rockets.

Walter Lord   *Titanic* historian and author of *A Night to Remember* (1955).

Fifth Officer Harold Lowe   Was in charge of the only lifeboat to return for survivors after the *Titanic* sank. Lowe is also reported to have yelled "get the hell out of the way!" to White Star exec Ismay for interfering in the lowering of the lifeboats.

Guglielmo Marconi   Inventor of wireless telegraphy used on steamships. He denied cutting an exclusive deal with *The New York Times* for the story of the *Titanic* sinking.

Lord Mersey   He conducted the British inquiry into the disaster for the Board of Trade.

Francis (Frank) Millet   American artist living in England. In his younger days he was a war correspondent in the Spanish-American War and the Russian-Turkish War.

Sixth Officer James Moody   Relayed the message from the lookout to Officer Murdoch that the iceberg had been sighted. He went down with the ship.

John Pierpont Morgan   American steel tycoon and owner of International Mercantile Marine, which bought out the British White Star Line.

First Officer William Murdoch   In command on the bridge when the iceberg was sighted by the lookouts. He gave the order "hard a-starboard!" in time to avoid a direct collision, but too late avoid a long, fatal scrape. Murdoch did not survive the disaster and may have shot himself after using his gun on a passenger rushing to enter a lifeboat.

Senior Wireless Operator Jack Phillips   Contacted the *Carpathia* by wireless the night of the disaster. He was lost with the ship.

Third Officer John Pittman   Was ordered to take charge of a lifeboat by Officer Murdoch after he had supervised its loading. Also present in this lifeboat was White Star Director J. Bruce Ismay.

Morgan Robertson   Author of the 1898 novel *Futility, or the Wreck of the Titan*, which eerily anticipates the sinking of the *Titanic*.

Captain Arthur Rostron   Brought his ship, the *Carpathia*, to the rescue of the *Titanic*, saving survivors in the lifeboats.

Captain Edward J. Smith   Served as captain with White Star Line for 25 years before going down with what was to be his last ship at the age of 59.

Senator William Alden Smith   Conducted the U.S. Senate inquiry into the disaster.

Samuel Ward Stanton   Illustrator and editor of marine publications. He had been on a trip to Spain to gather inspiration for a mural he was designing for an American ship.

William T. Stead   Influential editor of *Review of Reviews* during the early days of British political journalism who later developed a fascination for psychic phenomena and spiritualism. His novel, *From the Old World to the New*, has been cited as evidence that Stead anticipated his own fate through psychic means.

Isidor and Ida Straus   Elderly owners of Macy's department stores; the story of Ida refusing a seat on a lifeboat to stay with her husband has been lumping up throats for over 85 years.

Mr. and Mrs. John B. Thayer   He was the self-made president of Pennsylvania Railroad. He died, but she and her son went on to provide poignant commentary on the disaster.

George Tulloch   Chief of the salvage organization R.M.S. Titanic and leader of artifact recovery and exploration expeditions.

Carr Van Anda   Editor of *The New York Times*, the first paper to report the sinking of the *Titanic*.

Mr. and Mrs. George Widener and son Harry   Hosts of *Titanic*'s swanky last supper. George and Harry were lost, but she survived and later endowed Harvard's Widener Library in Harry's name with the provisos that all students learn to swim and that ice cream be served at every meal.

Chief Officer Henry Wilde   Was assigned to the *Titanic* as an afterthought as a result of his experience on the *Olympic*, the *Titanic*'s sister ship. He died the night of the collision.

Ship's Registry

1st class	2nd class	Ice-bergs

Titanic Passengers

This is a complete list of passengers who signed on aboard the *Titanic* according to White Star Line. Passengers are grouped according to class, nationality and, in the case of third-class passengers, where they embarked. Survivor's names are italicized.

First-Class Passengers

Allen, Miss Elizabeth Walton
Allison, Mr. H. J.
Allison, Mrs. H. J. and Maid
Allison, Miss L.
Allison, Master T. and Nurse
Anderson, Mr. Harry
Andrews, Miss Cornelia I.
Andrews, Mr. Thomas
Appleton, Mrs. E. D.
Artagaveytia, Mr. Ramon
Astor, Colonel J. J.
    and Manservant
Astor, Mrs. J. J. and Maid
Aubert, Mrs. N. and Maid
Barkworth, Mr. A. H.
Baumann, Mr. J.
Baxter, Mrs. James
Baxter, Mr. Quigg
Beattie, Mr. T.
Beckwith, Mr. R. L.
Beckwith, Mrs. R. L.
Behr, Mr. K. H.
Bishop, Mr. D. H.
Bishop, Mrs. D. H.
Bjornstrom, Mr. H.
Blackwell, Mr. Stephen Weart
Blank, Mr. Henry
Bonnell, Miss Caroline

Bonnell, Miss Lily
Borebank, Mr. J. J.
Bowen, Miss
Bowerman, Miss Elsie
Brady, Mr. John B.
Brandeis, Mr. E.
Brayton, Mr. George
Brewe, Dr. Arthur Jackson
Brown, Mrs. J. J.
Brown, Mrs. J. M.
Bucknell, Mrs. W. and Maid
Butt, Major Archibald W.
Calderhead, Mr. E. P.
Candee, Mrs. Churchill
Cardoza, Mrs. J. W. M.
    and Maid
Cardoza, Mr. T. D. M and
    Manservant
Carlson, Mr. Frank
Carran, Mr. F. M.
Carran, Mr. J. P.
Carter, Mr. William E.
Carter, Mrs. William E.
    and Maid
Carter, Miss Lucile
Carter, Master William T.
    and Manservant
Case, Mr. Howard B.

Cassebeer, Mrs. H. A.
Cavendish, Mr. T. W.
Cavendish, Mrs. T. W. and Maid
Chaffee, Mr. Herbert F.
Chaffee, Mrs. Herbert F.
Chambers, Mr. N. C.
Chambers, Mrs. N. C.
Cherry, Miss Gladys
Chevre, Mr. Paul
Chibnafl, Mrs. E. M. Bowerman
Chisholm, Mr. Robert
Clark, Mr. Walter M.
Clark, Mrs. Walter M.
Clifford, Mr. George Quincy
Colley, Mr. E. P.
Compton, Mrs. A. T.
Compton, Miss S. P.
Compton, Mr. A. T., Jr.
Cornell, Mrs. R. G.
Crafton, Mr. John B.
Crosby, Mr. Edward G.
Crosby, Mrs. Edward G.
Crosby, Miss Harriet
Cummings, Mr. John Bradley
Cummings, Mrs. John Bradley
Daly, Mr. P. D.
Daniel, Mr. Robert W.
Davidson, Mr. Thornton

Davidson, Mrs. Thornton
de Villiers, Mrs. B.
Dick, Mr. A. A.
Dick, Mrs. A. A.
Dodge, Dr. Washington
Dodge, Mrs. Washington
Dodge, Master Washington
Douglas, Mrs. F. C.
Douglas, Mr. W. D.
Douglas, Mrs. W. D. and Maid
Dulles, Mr. William C.
Earnshew, Mrs. Boulton
Endres, Miss Caroline
Eustis, Miss E. M.
Evans, Miss E.
Flegenheim, Mrs. A.
Flynn, Mr. J. I.
Foreman, Mr. B. L.
Fortune, Mr. Mark
Fortune, Mrs. Mark
Fortune, Miss Ethel
Fortune, Miss Alice
Fortune, Miss Mabel
Fortune, Mr. Charles
Franklin, Mr. T. P.
Frauenthal Mr. T. G.
Frauenthal, Dr. Henry W.
Frauenthal, Mrs. Henry W.
Frolicher, Miss Marguerite
Futrelle, Mr. J.
Futrelle, Mrs. J.
Gee, Mr. Arthur
Gibson, Mrs. L.
Gibson, Miss D.
Giglio, Mr. Victor
Goldenberg, Mr. S. L.
Goldenberg, Mrs. S. L.
Goldschmidt, Mrs. George B.
Gordon, Sir Cosmo Duff
Gordon, Lady Duff and Maid
Gracie, Colonel Archibald
Graham, Mr.
Graham, Mrs. William G
Graha, Miss Margaret
Greenfield, Mrs. L. D.
Greenfield, Mrs. W. B.
Guggenheim, Mr. Benjamin
Harder, Mr. George A.
Harder, Mrs. George A.
Harper, Mr. Henry Sleeper
  and Manservant
Harper, Mrs. Henry Sleeper
Harris, Mr. Henry B.

Harris, Mrs. Henry B.
Harrison, Mr. W. H.
Haven, Mr. H.
Hawksford, Mr. W. J.
Hays, Mr. Charles M.
Hays, Mrs. Charles M. and Maid
Hays, Miss Margaret
Head, Mr. Christopher
Hilliard, Mr. Herbert Henry
Hipkins, Mr. W. E.
Hippach, Mrs. Ida S.
Hippach, Miss Jean
Hogeboom, Mrs. John C.
Holverson, Mr. A. O.
Holverson, Mrs. A. O.
Hoyt, Mr. Frederick M.
Hoyt, Mrs. Frederick M.
Holt, Mr. W. F.
Isham, Mrs. A. E.
Ismay, Mr. J. Bruce
  and Manservant
Jakob, Mr. Birnbaum
Jones, Mr. C. C
Julian, Mr. H. F.
Kent, Mr. Edward A.
Kenyon, Mr. F. R.
Kenyon, Mrs. F. R.
Kimball, Mr. E. N.
Kimball, Mrs. E. N.
Klaber, Mr. Herman
Lambert-Williams, Mr. Fletcher
  Fellows
Leader, Mrs. F. A.
Lewy, Mr. E. G.
Lindstroem, Mrs. J.
Lines, Mrs. Ernest H.
Lines, Miss Mary C.
Lingrey, Mr. Edward
Long, Mr. Milton C.
Langley, Miss Gretchen F.
Loring, Mr. J. H.
Madill, Miss Georgette Alexandra
Maguire, Mr. J. E.
Marechal, Mr. Pierre
Marvin, Mr. D. W.
Marvin, Mrs. D. W.
McCaffry. Mr. T.
McCarthy, Mr. Timothy J.
  Rohan
McGough, Mr. J. R.
Meyer, Mr. Edgar J.
Meyer, Mrs. Edgar J.
Millet, Mr. Frank D.

Minahan, Dr. W. E.
Minahan, Mrs. W. B.
Minahan, Miss Daisy
Moch, Mr. Pkdtp E.
Moch, Mr. Phillip E.
Molson, Mr. H. Markland
Moore, Mr. Clarence and
  Manservant
Natsch, Mr. Charles
Newell, Mr. A. W.
Newell, Miss Alice
Newell, Miss Madeline
Newsom, Miss Helen
Nicholson, Mr. A. S.
Omont, Mr. F.
Ostby, Mr. E. C
Ostby, Miss Helen R.
Ovies, Mr. S.
Parr, Mr. M. H. W.
Partner, Mr. Austin
Payne, Mr. V.
Pears, Mr. Thomas
Pears, Mrs. Thomas
Penasco, Mr. Victor
Penasco, Mrs. Victor and Maid
Peuchen, Major Arthur
Porter, Mr. Walter
  Chamberlain
Potter, Mrs. Thomas, Jr.
Reuchlin, Mr. Jonkheer, J. G.
Rheims, Mr. George
Robert, Mrs. Edward S. and Maid
Roebling, Mr. Washington
  A., 2nd
Rolmane, Mr. C.
Rood, Mr. Hugh R.
Rosenbaum, Miss
Ross, Mr. J. Hugo
Rothes, the Countess of and Maid
Rothschild, Mr. M.
Rothschild, Mrs. M.
Rowe, Mr. Alfred
Ryerson, Mr. Arthur
Ryerson, Mrs. Arthur and Maid
Ryerson, Miss Emily
Ryerson, Miss Susan
Ryerson, Master Jack
Saalfeld, Mr. Adolphe
Schabert, Mrs. Paul
Seward, Mr. Frederick K.
Shutes, Miss E. W.
Silverthorne, Mr. S. V.
Silvey, Mr. William B.

Silvey, Mrs. William B.
Simonius, Mr. Oberst Altons
Sloper, Mr. William T.
Smart, Mr. John M.
Smith, Mr. J. Clinch
Smith, Mr. R. W.
Smith, Mr. L. P.
Smith, Mrs. L. P.
Snyder, Mr. John
Snyder, Mrs. John
Soloman, Mr. A. L.
Spedden, Mr. Frederick O.
Spedden, Mrs. Frederick O.
and Maid
Spedden, Master R. Douglas
and Nurse
Spencer, Mr. W. A.
Spencer, Mrs. W. A. and Maid
Stahelin, Dr. Max
Stead, Mr. W. T.
Steffanson, B. B.
Steffanon, H. B.
Stehli, Mr. Max Frolicher

Stehli, Mrs. Max Frolicher
Stengel, Mr. C. E. H.
Stengel, Mrs. C. E. H.
Stewart, Mr. A. A.
Stone, Mrs. George M. and Maid
Straus, Mr. Isador
and Manservant
Straus, Mrs. Isador
and Maid Ellen Bird
Sutton, Mr. Frederick
Swift, Mrs. Frederick Joel
Taussig, Mr. Emil
Taussig, Mrs. Emil
Taussig, Miss Ruth
Taylor, Mr. E. Z
Taylor, Mrs. E. Z.
Thayer, Mr. J. B.
Thayer, Mrs. J. B. and Maid
Thayer, Mr. J. B., Jr.
Thorne, Mr. G.
Thorne, Mrs. G.
Tucker, Mr. G. M., Jr.
Uruchurtu, Mr. M. R.

Van der Hoef, Mr. Wyckoff
Walker, Mr. W. Anderson
Warren, Mr. F. M.
Warren, Mrs. F. M.
Weir, Mr. J.
White, Mr. Percival W.
White, Mr. Richard F.
White, Mrs. J. Stuart and Maid
and Manservant
Wick, Mr. George D.
Wick, Mrs. George D.
Wick, Miss Mary
Widener, Mr. George D.
and Manservant
Widener, Mrs. George D.
and Maid
Widener, Mr. Harry
Willard, Miss Constance
Williams, Mr. Duane
Williams, Mr. R. N., Jr.
Woolner, Mr. Hugh
Wright, Mr. George
Young, Miss Marie

Second-Class Passengers

Abelson, Mr. Samson
Abelson, Mrs. Hanna
Aldworth, Mr. C.
Andrew, Mr. Edgar
Andrew, Mr. Frank
Angle, Mr. William
Angle, Mrs.
Ashby, Mr. John
Baily, Mr. Percy
Baimbridge, Mr. Chas. R.
Balls, Mrs. Ada E.
Banfield, Mr. Frederick J.
Bateman, Mr. Robert J.
Beane, Mr. Edward
Beane, Mrs. Ethel
Beauchamp, Mr. H. J.
Becker, Mrs. A. O.
and three children
Beesley, Mr. Lawrence
Bentham, Miss Lilian W.
Berriman, Mr. William
Botsford, Mr. W. Hull
Bowenur, Mr. Solomon
Bracken, Mr. Jas. H.
Brito, Mr. Jose de
Brown, Miss Mildred

Brown, Mr. S.
Brown, Mrs.
Brown, Miss E.
Bryhl, Mr. Curt
Bryhl, Miss Dagmar
Buss, Miss Kate
Butler, Mr. Reginald
Byles, Rev. nomas R. D.
Bystrom, Miss Karolina
Caldwell, Mr. Albert F.
Caldwell, Mrs. Sylvia
Caldwell, Master Alden G.
Cameron, Miss Clear
Carbines, Mr. William
Carter, Rev. Ernest C.
Carter, Mrs. Lillian
Chapman, Mr. John H.
Chapman, Mrs. Elizabeth
Chapman, Mr. Charles
Christy, Mrs. Alice
Christy, Miss Juli
Clarke, Mr. Charles V.
Clarke, Mrs. Ada Maria
Coleridge, Mr. R. C.
Collander, Mr. Erik
Collett, Mr. Stuart

Collyer, Mr. Harvey
Collyer, Mrs. Charlotte
Collyer, Miss Marjorie
Corbett, Mrs. Irene
Corey, Mrs. C. P.
Cotterill, Mr. Harry
Davies, Mr. Charles
Davis, Mrs. Agnes
Davis, Master John M.
Davis, Miss Mary
Deacon, Mr. Percy
del Carlo, Mr. Sebastian
del Carlo, Mrs.
Denbou, Mr. Herbert
Dibden, Mr. William
Doling, Mrs. Ada
Doling, Miss Elsie
Downton, Mr. William J.
Drachstedt, Baron von
Drew, Mr. James V.
Drew, Mrs. Lulu
Drew, Master Marshall
Duran, Miss Florentina
Duran, Miss Asimcion
Eitemiller, Mr. G. F.
Enander, Mr. Ingvar

Fahlstrom Mr. Arne J.
Faunthorpe, Mr. Harry
Faunthorpe, Mrs. Lizzie
Fillbrook, Mr. Charles
Fox, Mr. Stanley H.
Funk, Miss Annie
Fynney, Mr. Jos.
Gale, Mr. Harry
Gale, Mr. Shadrach
Garside, Miss Ethel
Gaskell, Mr. Alfred
Gavey, Mr. Lawrence
Gilbert, Mr. William
Giles, Mr. Edgar
Giles, Mr. Fred
Giles, Mr. Ralph
Gill, Mr. John
Gillespie, Mr. William
Givard, Mr. Hans K.
Greenberg, Mr. Samuel
Hale, Mr. Reginald
Hamalainer, Mrs. Anna
    and Infant
Harbeck, Mr. Wm. H.
Harper, Mr. John
Harper, Miss Nina
Harris, Mr. George
Harris, Mr. Walter
Hart, Mr. Benjamin
Hart, Mrs. Esther
Hart, Miss Eva
Herman, Miss Alice
Herman, Mrs. Jane
Herman, Miss Kate
Herman, Mr. Samuel
Hewlett, Mrs. Mary D.
Hickman, Mr. Leonard
Hickman, Mr. Lewis
Hickman, Mr. Stanley
Hiltunen, Miss Martha
Hocking, Mr. George
Hocking, Mrs. Elizabeth
Hocking, Miss Nellie
Hocking, Mr. Samuel J.
Hodges, Mr. Henry P.
Hoffman, Mr. and *two children*
    (Loto and Louis)
Hold, Mrs. Annie
Hold, Mr. Stephen
Hood, Mr. Ambrose
Hosono, Mr. Masabumi
Howard, Mr. Benjamin
Howard, Mrs. Ellen T.

Hunt, Mr. George
Ilett, Miss Bertha
Jacobsohn, Mrs. Amy P.
Jacobsohn Mr. Sidney S.
Jarvis, Mr. John D.
Jefferys, Mr. Clifford
Jefferys, Mr. Ernest
Jenkin, Mr. Stephen
Jervan, Mrs. A. T.
Kantor, Mrs. Miriam
Kantor, Mr. Sehua
Karnes, Mrs. J. F.
Keane, Mr. Daniel
Keane, Miss Nora A.
Kelly, Mrs. F.
Kirkland, Rev. Charles L
Kvillner, Mr. John Henrik
Lahtinen, Mrs. Anna
Lahtinen, Mr. William
Lamb, Mr. J. J.
Lamore, Mrs. Ameliar
Laroche, Mr. Joseph
Laroche, Mrs. Juliet
Laroche, Miss Louise
Laroche, Miss Simonne
Lehman, Miss Bertha
Leitch, Miss Jessie
Levy, Mr. R. J.
Leyson, Mr. Robert W. N.
Lingan, Mr. John
Louch, Mr. Charles
Louch, Mrs. Alice Adela
Mack, Mrs. Mary
Malachard, Mr. Noel
Mallet, Mr. A.
Mallet, Mrs.
Mallet, Master A.
Mangiavacchi, Mr. Emilio
Mantvila, Mr. Joseph
Marshall, Mr.
Marshall, Mrs. Kate
Matthews, Mr. W. J.
Maybery, Mr. Frank H.
McCrae, Mr. Arthur G.
McCrie, Mr. James
McKane, Mr. Peter D.
Mellers, Mr. William
Mellinger, Mrs. Elizabeth and
    Child
Meyer, Mr. August
Milling, Mr. Jacob C.
Mitchell, Mr. Henry
Morawick, Dr. Ernest

Mudd, Mr. Thomas C.
Myles, Mr. Thomas F.
Nasser, Mr. Nicolas
Nasser, Mrs.
Nesson, Mr. Israel
Nicholls, Mr. Joseph C.
Norman, Mr. Robert D.
Nye, Mrs. Elizabeth
Otter, Mr. Richard
Oxenham, Mr. P. Thomas
Padro, Mr. Julian
Pain, Dr. Alfred
Pallas, Mr. Emilio
Parker, Mr. Clifford R.
Parrish, Mrs. L. Davis
Pengelly, Mr. Frederick
Pernot, Mr. Rene
Peruschitz, Rev. Jos. M.
Phillips, Mr. Robert
Phillips, Miss Alice
Pinsky, Miss Rosa
Ponesell, Mr. Martin
Portaluppi, Mr. Emilio
Pulbaun, Mr. Frank
Quick, Mrs. Jane
Quick, Miss Vera W.
Quick, Miss Phyllis
Reeves, Mr. David
Renouf, Mr. Peter H.
Renouf, Miss Lillie
Reynolds, Miss E.
Richard, Mr. Emile
Richards, Mrs. Emily
Richards, Master William
Richards, Master George
Ridsdale, Miss Lucy
Rogers, Mr. Harry
Rogers, Miss Selina
Rugg, Miss Emily
Sedgwick, Mr. C. F. W.
Sharp, Mr. Percival
Shelley, Mrs. Imanita
Silven, Miss Lyyli
Sincook, Miss Maude
Sinkkenen, Miss Anna
Sjostedt, Mr. Ernest A.
Slayter, Miss H. M.
Slemen, Mr. Richard J.
Smith, Mr. Augustus
Smith, Miss Marion
Sobey, Mr. Hayden
Stanton, Mr. S. Ward
Stokes, Mr. Phillip J.

Swane, Mr. George
Sweet, Mr. George
Toomey, Miss Ellen
Trant, Miss Jessie
Tronpiansky, Mr. Moses A.
Troutt, Miss E. Celia
Tupin, M. Dorothy
Turpin, Mr. William J.
Veale, Mr. James
Walcroft, Miss Nellie
Ware, Mrs. Florence L.

Ware, Mr. John James
Ware, Mr. William J.
Watt, Miss Bertha
Watt, Mrs. Bessie
Webber, Miss Susiev
Weisz, Mr. Leopold
Weisz, Mrs. Matilda
Wells, Mrs. Addie
Wells, Miss J.
Wells, Master Ralph
West, Mr. E. Arthur

West, Mrs. Ada
West, Miss Barbara
West, Miss Constance
Wheadon, Mr. Edward
Wheeler, Mr. Edwin
Wilhelms, Mr. Charles
Williams, Mr. C.
Wright, Miss Marion
Yrois, Miss H.

Third-Class Passengers—British/Southampton Embarkment

Abbott, Eugene
Abbott, Rosa
Abbott, Rossmore
Abbing, Anthony
Adams. J.
Aks, Filly
Aks, Leah
Alexander, William
Allen, William
Allum, Owen G.
Badman, Emily
Barton David
Beavan, W. T.
Billiard, A. van
Billiard, James (child)
Billiard, Walter (child)
Bing, Lee
Bowen, David
Braund, Lewis
Braund, Owen
Brocklebank, William
Cann, Erenst
Carver, A.
Celotti, Francesco
Chip, Chang
Christmann, Emil
Cohen, Gurshon
Cook, Jacob
Corn, Harry
Coutts, Winnie
Coutts, William (child)
Coutts, Leslie (child)
Coxon, Daniel
Crease, Ernest James
Cribb, John Hatfield
Cribb, Alice
Dahl, Charles
Davies, Evan

Davies, Alfred
Davies, John
Davies, Joseph
Davison, Thomas H.
Davison, Mary
Dean, Mr. Bertram F.
Dean, Mrs. Hetty
Dean, Bertran (child)
Dean, Vera (infant)
Dennis, Samuel
Dennis, William
Derkings, Edward
Dowdell, Elizabeth
Drapkin, Jenie
Dugemin, Joseph
Elsbury, James
Emanuel, Ethet (child)
Everett, Thomas J.
Foo, Choong
Ford, Arthur
Ford, Margaret
Ford, Mrs. D. M.
Ford, Mr. E. W.
Ford, M. W. T. N.
Ford, Maggie (child)
Franklin, Charles
Garthfirth, John
Gilinski, Leslie
Godwin, Frederick
Goldsmith, Frank J.
Goldsmith, Emily A.
Goldsmith, Frank J. W.
Goodwin, Augusta
Goodwin, Lillian A.
Goodwin, Charles E.
Goodwin, William F. (child)
Goodwin, Jessie (child)
Goodwin, Harold (child)

Goodwin, Sidney (child)
Green, George
Guest, Robert
Harknett, Alice
Harmer, Abraham
Hee, Ling
Howard, May
Hyman, Abraham
Johnston, A. G.
Johnston, Mrs.
Johnston, William (child)
Johnston, Mrs. C. H. (child)
Johnson, Mr. A.
Johnson, Mr. W.
Keefe, Arthur
Kelly, James
Lam, Ali
Lam, Len
Lang, Fang
Leonard, Mr. L
Lester, J.
Ling, Lee
Lithman, Simon
Lobb, Cordelia
Lobb, William A.
Lockyer, Edward
Lovell, John
MacKay, George W.
Maisner, Simon
McNamee, Eileen
McNamee, Neal
Meanwell, Marian O.
Meek, Annie L.
Meo, Alfonso
Miles, Frank
Moor, Beile
Moor, Meier
Moore, Leonard C.

Morley, William
Moutal, Rahamin
Murdlin, Joseph
Nancarrow, W. H.
Niklasen, Sander
Nosworthy, Richard C.
Peacock, Alfred
Peacodc., Treasteall
Peacock, Treasteall (child)
Pearce, Ernest
Peduzzi, Joseph
Perkin, John Henry
Peterson, Marius
Potchett, George
Rath, Sarah
Reed, James George
Reynolds, Harold
Risien, Emma
Risien, Samuel
Robins, Alexander
Robins, Charity
Rogers, William John
Rouse, Richard H.

Rush, Alfred George J.
Sadowitz, Harry
Sage, John
Sage, Annie
Sage, Stella
Sage, George
Sage, Douglas
Sage, Frederick
Sage, Dorothy
Sage, William (child)
Sage, Ada (child)
Sage, Constance (child)
Sage, Thomas (child)
Sather, Sinon
Saundercock, W. H.
Sawyer, Frederick
Scrota, Maurice
Shellard, Frederick
Shorney, Charles
Simmons, John
Slocovski, Selman
Somerton, Francis W.
Spector, Woolf

Spinner, Henry
Stanley, Amy
Stanley, E. R. Mr.
Storey, T. Mr.
Sunderland, Victor
Sutehall, Henry
Theobald, Thomas
Thomas, Alex
Thorneycrolt, Florence
Thorneycroft, Percival
Tomlin, Ernest P.
Torber, Ernest
Trembisky, Berk
Tunquist, W.
Ware, Frederick
Warren, Charles W.
Webber, James
Wilkes, Ellen
Willey, Edward
Williams, Harry
Williams, Leslie
Windelov, Einar
Wiseman, Philip

Third-Class Passengers—Non-British/Southampton Embarkment

Abelseth, Karen
Abelseth, Olaus
Abramson, August
Adahl, Mauritz
Adolf, Humblin
Ahlin, Johanna
Ahmed, Ali
Alhomaki, Ilmari
Ali, William
Anderson, Alfreda
Anderson, Erna
Anderson, Albert
Anderson, Anders
Anderson, Samuel
Anderson, Sigrid (child)
Anderson, Thor
Anderson, Carla
Anderson, Ingeborg (child)
Anderson, Ebba (child)
Anderson, Sigvard (child)
Anderson, Ellis
Anderson, Ida Augusta
Anderson, Paul Edvin
Angheloff, Minko
Asplund, Carl (child)
Asplund, Charles

Asplund, Felix (child)
Asplund, Gustaf (child)
Asplund, Johan
Asplund, Lillian (child)
Asplund, Oscar (child)
Asplund, Selma
Arnold, Joseph
Arnold, Josephine
Aronsson, Ernest Axel A.
Asim, Adola
Assam, Ali
Augustsan, Albert
Backstrom, Karl
Backstrom, Marie
Balkic, Cerin
Benson, John Viktor
Berglund. Ivar
Berkeland, Hans
Bjorklund, Ernst
Bostandyeff, Guentcho
Braf, Elin Ester
Brobek, Carl R.
Cacic, Grego
Cacic, Luka
Cacic, Maria
Cacic, Manda

Calie, Peter
Carlson, Carl R.
Carlsson, Julius
Carlsson, August Sigfrid
Coelho, Domingos Fernardeo
Coleff, Fotio
Coleff, Peyo
Cor, Bartol
Cor, Ivan
Cor, Ludovik
Dahl, Mauritz
Dahlberg, Gerda
Dakic, Branko
Danbom, Ernest
Danbom, Gillber (infant)
Danoff, Sigrid
Danoff, Yoto
Dantchoff, Khristo
Delalic, Regyo
Denkoff, Mito
Dimic, Jovan
Dintcheff, Valtcho
Dyker, Adoff
Dyker, Elizabeth
Ecimovic, Joso
Edwardsson, Gustaf

Eklunz, Hans
Ekstrom, Johan
Finote, Luigi
Fischer, Eberhard
Goldsmith, Nathan
Goncalves, Manoel E.
Gronnestad, Daniel D.
Gustafson, Alfred
Gustafson, Anders
Gustafson, Johan
Gustafsson, Gideon
Haas, Aloisia
Hadman, Oscar
Hagland, Ingvald O.
Hagland, Konrad R.
Hakkarainen, Pekko
Hakkarainen, Elin
Hampe, Leon
Hankonen, Eluna
Hansen, Claus
Hansen, Janny
Hansen, Henry Damgavd
Heininen, Wendla
Hendekevoic, Ignaz
Henriksson, Jenny
Hervonen, Helga
Hervonen, Hildwe (child)
Hickkinen, Laina
Hillstrom, Hilda
Holm, John F. A.
Holten, Johan
Humblin, Adolf
Ilieff, Ylio
Ilmakangas, Ida
Ilmakangas, Pista
Ivanoff, Konio
Jansen, Carl
Jardin, Jose Netto
Jensen, Carl
Jensen, Hans Peter
Jensen, Svenst L.
Jensen, Nilho R.
Johannessen, Bernt
Johannessen, Elias
Johansen, Nils
Johanson, Oscar
Johanson, Oscal L.
Johansson, Erik
Johansson, Gustaf
Johnson, Jakob A.
Johnson, Alice
Johnson, Harold
Johnson, Eleanora (infant)

Johnsson, Carl
Johnsson, Malkolm
Jonkoff, Lazor
Jonsson, Nielo H.
Jusila, Katrina
Jusila, Mari
Jusila, Erik
Jutel, Henrik Hansen
Kallio, Nikolai
Kalvig Johannes H.
Karajic, Milan
Karlson, Einar
Karlson, Nils August
Kekic, Tido
Kink, Anton
Kink, Louise
Kink, Louise (child)
Kink, Maria
Kink, Vincenz
Klasen, Klas A.
Klasen, Hilda
Klasen, Gertrud (child)
Laitinen, Sofia
Laleff, Kristo
Landegren, Aurora
Larson, Viktor
Larsson, Bengt Edvin
Larsson, Edvard
Lefebre, Frances
Lefebre, Henry (child)
Lefebre, Ida (child)
Lefebre, Ida (child)
Lefebre, Mathilde (child)
Leinonen, Antti
Lindablom, August
Lindell, Edvard B.
Lindell, Elin
Lindahl, Agda
Lindqvist, Einar
Lulic, Nicola
Lundahl, John
Lundin, Olga
Lundstripm, Jan
Madsen, Fridjof
Maenpaa, Matti
Makinen, Kalle
Mampe, Leon
Marinko, Dmitri
Markoff, Marin
Melkebuk, Philemon
Messemacker, Guillaume
Messemacker, Emma
Midtsjo, Carl

Mikanen, John
Misseff, Ivan
Minkoff, Lazar
Mirko, Dika
Mitkoff, Mito
Moen, Sigurd H.
Mona, Mae A.
Moss, Albert
Mulder, Theo
Myhrman, Oliver
Naidenoff, Penko
Nankoff, Minko
Nedeco, Petroff
Nenkoff, Christo
Nieminen, Manta
Nilsson, August F.
Nilson, Berta
Nilson, Helmina
Nirva, Isak
Nyoven, Johan
Nyston, Anna
Odahl, Martin
Orman, Velin
Olsen, Arthur
Olsen, Carl
Olsen, Henry
Olsen, Ole M.
Olson, Elon
Olsson, John
Olsson, Elida
Oreskovic, Luka
Oreskovic, Maria
Oreskovic, Jeko
Osman, Mara
Pacruic, Mate
Pacruic, Tome
Panula, Eino
Panula, Ernesti
Panula, Juho
Panula, Maria
Panula, Sanni
Panula, Urhu (child)
Panula, William (infant)
Pasic, Jakob
Pentcho, Petroff
Paulsson, Alma C
Paulsson, Gosta (child)
Paulsson, Paul (child)
Paulsson, Stina(child)
Paulsson, Torborg (child)
Pavlovic, Stefo
Pekonemi, E.
Pelsmaker, Alfons de

Peltomaki, Nikolai
Person, Ernest
Peterson, Johan
Peterson, Ellen
Petranec, Matilda
Petterson, Olaf
Plotcharsky, Vasil
Radeff, Alexander
Rintamaki, Matti
Rosblom, Helene
Rosblom, Salfi (child)
Rosblom, Viktor
Rummstvedt, Kristian
Salander, Carl
Saljilsvik, Anna
Salonen, Werner
Sandman, Johan
Sandstrom, Agnes
Sandstrom, Beatrice (child)
Sandstrom, Margretha (child)
Sdycoff, Todor
Sheerlinck, Jean
Sihvola, Antti
Sivic, Husen
Sjoblom, Anna
Skoog, Anna

Skoog, Carl (child)
Skoog, Harald (child)
Skoog, Mabel (child)
Skoog, Margret (child)
Skoog, William
Slabenoff, Petco
Smiljanic, Mile
Sohole, Peter
Solvang, Lena Jacobsen
Sop, Jules
Staneff, Ivan
Stoytcho, Mihoff
Stoyehoff, Ilia
Strandberg, Ida
Stranden, Jules
Strilic, Ivan
Strom, Selma (child)
Svensen, Olaf
Svensson, Johan
Svensson, Coverin
Syntakoff, Stanko
Tikkanen, Juho
Todoroff, Lalio
Tonglin, Gunner
Turcin, Stefan
Turgo, Anna

Twekula, Hedwig
Uzelas, Jovo
Waelens, Achille
Van Impe, Catharine (child)
Van Impe, Jacob
Van Impe, Rosalie
Van der Planke, Augusta Vander
Van der Planke, Emilie Vander
Van der Planke, Jules Vander
Van der Planke, Leon Vander
Van der Steen, Leo
Van de Velde, Joseph
Van de Walle, Nestor
Vereruysse, Victor
Vook, Janko
Wende, Olof Edvin
Wennerstrom, August
Wenzel, Zinhart
Vestrom, Huld A. A.
Widegrin, Charles
Wiklund, Karl F.
Wiklund, Jacob A.
Wirz, Albert
Wittenrongel, Camille
Zievens, Renee
Zimmermann, Leo

Third-Class Passengers—Non-British/Cherbourg Embarkment

Assaf, Marian
Attala, Malake
Baclini, Latila
Baclini, Maria
Baclini, Eugene
Baclini, Helene
Badt, Mohamed
Banoura, Ayout
Barbara, Catherine
Barbara, Saude
Betros, Tannous
Boulos, Hanna
Boulos, Sultani
Boulos, Nourelain
Boulos, Akar (child)
Banous, Elias
Caram, Joseph
Caram, Maria
Shabini, Georges
Chehab, Emir Farres
Chronopoulos, Apostolos
Cbronopoulos, Demetrios
Dibo, Elias

Drazenovie, Josip
Elias, Joseph
Elias, Joseph
Fabini, Leeni
Fat-ma, Mustmani
Gerios, Assaf
Gerios, Youssef
Gerios, Youssef
Gheorgheff, Stanio
Hanna, Mansour
Jean Nassr, Saade
Johann, Markim
Joseph, Mary
Karun, Franz
Karun, Anna (child)
Kassan, M. Housseing
Kassem, Fared
Kassein, Hassef
Kalil, Betros
Khalil, Zahie
Kraeff, Thodor
Lemberopoulos, Peter
Malinoff, Nicola

Meme, Hanna
Monbarek, Hanna
Moncarek, Omine
Moncarek, Gonios (child)
Moncarek, Halim (child)
Moussa, Mantoura
Naked, Said
Naked, Waika
Naked, Maria
Nasr, Mustafa
Nichan, Krikorian
Nicola, Jamila
Nicola, Elias (child)
Novel, Mansouer
Orsen, Sirayanian
Ortin, Zakarian
Peter, Catherine Joseph
Peter, Mike
Peter, Anna
Rafoul, Baccos
Raibid, Razi
Saad, Amin
Saad, Khalil

Samaan, Hanna
Samaan, Elias
Samaan, Youssef
Sarkis, Mardirosian
Sarkis, Lahowd
Seman Betros (child)
Shedid, Daher
Sleiman, Attalla
Stankovic, Jovan
Tannous, Thomas
Tannous, Daler

Thomas, Charles P.
Thomas, Tamin
Thomas, Assad (infant)
Thomas, John
Tonfik, Nahli
Torfa, Assad
Useher, Paulner
Vagil, Adele Jane
Vartunian, David
Vassilios, Catavelas
Wazli, Yousif

Weller, Abi
Yalsevae, Ivan
Yazbeck, Antoni
Yazbeck, Salini
Youssef, Brahim
Youssef, Hanne
Youssef, Maria (child)
Youssef Georges (child)
Zabour, Tamini
Zabour, Hileni
Zakarian, Maprieder

Third-Class Passengers—Queenstown Embarkment

Barry, Julia
Bourke, Catherine
Bourke, John
Bradley, Bridget
Buckley, Daniel
Buckley, Katherine
Burke, Jeremiak
Burke, Mary
Burns, Mary
Canavan, Mary
Carr, Ellen
Car, Jeannie
Chartens, David
Cannavan, Pat
Colbert, Patrick
Conlin, Thos. H.
Connaghton, Michel
Connors, Pat
Conolly, Kate
Conolly, Kate
Daly, Marcella
Daly, Eugene
Devanoy, Margaret
Dewan, Frank
Dooley, Patrick
Doyle, Elin
Driscoll, Bridget
Emmeth, Thomas
Farrell, James
Foley, Joseph
Foley, William
Flynn, James
Flynn, John
Fox, Patrick
Gallagher, Martin
Gilnagh, Katie
Glynn, Mary
Hagardon, Kate

Hagarty, Nora
Hart, Henry
Healy, Nora
Horgan, John
Hemming, Norah
Henery, Delia
Jenymin, Annie
Kelly, James
Kelly, Annie K.
Kelly, Mary
Kerane, Andy
Kennedy, John
Kilgannon, Thomas
Kiernan, John
Kiernan, Phillip
Lane, Patrick
Lemom, Denis
Lemon, Mary
Linehan, Michel
Madigan, Maggie
Mahon, Delia
Mannion, Margareth
Mangan, Mary
McCarthy, Katie
McCoy, Agnes
McCoy, Alice
McCoy, Bernard
McCormack, Thomas
McDermott, Delia
McElroy, Michel
McGovern, Mary
McGowan, Katherine
McGowan, Annie
McMahon, Martin
Mechan, John
Meeklave, Ellie
Moran, James
Moran, Bertha

Morgan, Daniel J.
Morrow, Thomas
Mullens, Katie
Mulvihill, Bertha
Murphy, Norah
Murphy, Mary
Murphy, Kate
Naughton, Hannah
Nemagh, Robert
O'Brien, Denis
O'Brien, Thomas
O'Brien, Hannah
O'Connell, Pat D.
O'Connor, Maurice
O'Connor, Pat
O'Donaghue, Bert
O'Dwyer, Nellie
O'Keefe, Pat
O'Leary, Norah
O'Neill, Bridget
O'Sullivan, Bridget
Peters, Katie
Rice, Margaret
Rice, Albert (child)
Rice, George (child)
Rice, Eric (child)
Rice, Arthur (child)
Rice, Eugene (child)
Riordan, Hannah
Ryan, Patrick
Ryan, Edw.
Sadlier, Matt
Scanlan, James
Shaughnesay, Pat
Shine, Ellen
Smyth, Julian
Tobin, Roger

Cargo Hold

This appendix is a list of goods signed on aboard the *Titanic*, based on the original manifest, which was saved from the sinking ship and later printed in American newspapers. The value of the entire load was estimated at $420,000.

Manifest Destiny

Net worth of total cargo: $420,000

Wakem & McLaughlin
1 case wine
25 case biscuits
42 case wines

Thorer & Praetorius
1 bl skins

Carter, W.E.
1 case auto (parts?)

Fuchs & Lang Manufacturing
4 case printers blank.

Spaulding & Brothers
34 case athletic goods

Park & Tilford
1 case toothpaste
5 case drug sundries
1 case brushware

Maltus & Ware
8 case orchids

Spencerian Pen Company
4 case pens

Sherman Sons & Company
7 case cotton

Claflin, H.B. & Company
12 case cott. lace

Muser Brothers
3 case tissues

Isler & Guve
4 bales straw

Rydeman & Lassner
1 case veil and scarve
  netting (tulle)

Petry, P.H. & Company
1 case veil and scarve
  netting (tulle)

Metzger, A.S.
2 case veil and scarve
  netting (tulle)

Mills & Gibb
20 case cottons

Marshall Field & Company
1 case gloves

NY Motion Pic.Co.
1 case film

Thorburn, J.M. & Company
3 case bulbs

Rawstick Trading Company
28 bags sticks

Dujardin & Ladnick
10 Box melons

American Express Company
25 case merchandise

Tiffany & Company
1 cask china

Lustig Bros
4 case straw hats

Kuyper, P.C. & Company
1 case elastic cords
1 case leather

Cohen, M. Bros
5 package skins

Gross, Engle Co
61 case tulle veil and scarves
   netting

Gallia Textile Company
1 case lace goods

Calhoun, Robbins & Company
1 case cotton laces
1/2 case brushware

Victor & Achiles
1 case brushware

Baumgarten, Wm & Co
3 case furniture

Spielman Company
3 case silk crepe

Nottingham Lace Works
2 case cotton

Naday & Fleisher
1 case laces

Rosenthal, Leo J. & Company
4 case cotton

Leeming, T. & Company
7 case biscuits

Crown Perfume Company
3 case soap perfume

Meadows, T. & Company
5 case books
3 Box samples
1 case parchment

Thomas & Pierson
2 case hardware
2 case books
2 case furniture

American Express Company
1 case elastics
1 case Edison gramophones

4 case hosiery
5 case books
1 case canvas
1 case rubber goods
3 case prints
6 case film
1 case tweed
1 case (?syringe) fittings
oak beams
1 case plants
1 case speedometers
1 package effects
2 case samples
8 case paste
3 case cameras & stands
4 case books

Sheldon, G.W. & Company
1 case machinery

Maltus & Ware
15 case alarm apparatus
11 case orchids

Hempstead & Sons
30 case plants

Brasch & Rothenstein
2 case lace collars
2 case books

Isler & Guve
53 package straw

Baring Bros. & Company
63 case rubber
100 bgd gutta (percha)

Altman, B. & Company
1 case cotton

Stern, S.
60 case salt powders

Arnold, F.R. & Company
6 case soap

Shieffelin & Company
17 package wool fat

American Motor Company
1 package candels

Strohmeyer & Arpe
75 bales fish

**National City Bank of
   New York**
11 bales rubber

**Kronfeld, Saunders &
   Company**
5 case shells

Richard, C.B.
1 case films

Corbett, M.J. & Company
2 case hat leather

Snow's Express Company
3 case books

Van Engen E.H. & Company
1 case woolens

Lippincott, J.B. & Company
10 case books

Lazard Freses
1 bale skins

Aero Club of America
1 case machinery
1 case printed matter

**Witcombe, McGrachlin &
   Company**
856 rolls linoleum

Wright & Grahm Company
437 casks tea

Gillman J.
4 bales skins

Arnold & Zeiss
134 case rubber

Brown Brothers & Company
76 case dragon's blood
3 case gum

American Shipping Company
5 case books

Adams Express
35 case books

Lasker & Bernstein
117 case sponges

Oelrichs & Company
2 case pictures

Stechert, G.E. & Company
12 package periodicals

Milbank, Leaman & Company
2 case woolens

Vandegrift, F.B. & Company
63 case champagne

Downing, R.F. & Company
1 case felt
1 case metal
2 case tennis balls
1 case engine packing

Dublin, Morris & Kornbluth
2 package skins

International Trading Company
1 case surgical instruments
1 case ironware

Pitt & Scott
4 case printed matter
1 case machinery
1 case pictures
1 case books
1 case merchandise
1 case notions
1 case photos

Sheldon, G.W. & Company
1 case elastics
2 case books
1 box golf balls
5 case instruments

American Express Company
2 parcels merchandise

Vandegrift, F.B.
1 case merchandise

Budd, S.
1 parcel merchandise

Lemke & Buechner
1 parcel merchandise

Nicholas, G.S. & Company
1 case merchandise

Adams Express Company
4 rolls linoleum
3 bales leather
1 case hats
6 case confectionery
5 case books
1 case tin tubes
2 case soap
2 case boots

Wells Fargo & Company
3 case books
2 case furniture
1 case pamphlets
1 case plants
1 case eggs
1 case whiskey

International News Company
10 package periodicals

Van Ingen, E.H. & Company
1 parcel

Sterns, R.H. & Company
1 case cretonne (silk)

Downing, R.F. & Company
1 case iron jacks
1 case bulbs
1 case hosiery

Carbon Machinery Equip. Company
1 case clothing

Sanger, R. & Company
3 case hair nets

Flietman & Company
1 case silk goods

Rush & Company
1 case hair nets

Blum, J.A.
3 case silk goods

Tiedeman, T. & Sons
2 case silk goods

Costa, F.
1 case silk goods

Tolson, A.M. & Company
1 case gloves

Mathews, G.T. & Company
2 case books and lace

Tice & Lynch
5 case books
1 bag frames
1 case cotton
2 case stationery

US Export Company
1 case scientific instruments
1 case sundries
3 case test cords
1 case briar pipes
1 case sundries
2 case printed matter

Pape, Chas. & Company
1,196 bags potatoes

Sauer, J.P. & Company
318 bags potatoes

Rusch & Company
1 case velvets

Mallouk, H.
1 case laces

Bardwill Bros
8 case laces

Heyliger, A.V.
1 case velvet

Peabody, H.W. & Company
13 bales straw goods

Simon, A.I. & Company
1 case raw feathers

Wilson, P.K. & Sons
2 case linens

Manhattan Shirt Company
3 case tissues

Broadway Trust Company
3 case coney skins (rabbit)

Prost. G.
1 case auto parts

Young Bros.
1 case feathers

Wimpfheimer, A. & Company
3 case leather

Brown Bros. & Company
15 case rabbit hair

Goldster, Morris
11 case feathers

Cobb. G.H.
1 case lace tissue

Anderson Refridg, Mach. Company
11 case refrigeration apparatus

Suter, Alfred
18 case machinery

American Express Company
1 case packed packages
3 case tissues
2 barrels mercury
1 barrel earth
2 barrels glassware
3 case printed matter
1 case straw braids
3 case straw hats
1 case cheese

Meadows, Thomas & Company
3 case hosiery

Uchs & Hegnoer
3 case silk goods

Cauvigny Brush Company
1 case brushware

Johnson, J.G. Company
2 case ribbons

Judkins & McCormick
2 case flowers

Spielman Company
1 case gloves

American Express Company
18 case merchandise

Wakem & McLaughlin
6 bales cork

Acker, Merrall & Condit
75 case anchovies
225 case mussels
1 case liquor

Engs. P.W. & Sons
190 case liquor
25 case syrups

Schall & Company
25 case preserves

NY & Cuba SS Company
12 case butter
18 case oil
2 hogsheads vinegar
19 case vinegar
6 case preserves
8 case dried fruit
10 bundles of 2 case wine

Du Bois, Geo. C.
16 hogshead wine

Hollander, H.
185 case wine
110 case brandy

Van Renssaller, C.A.
10 hogshead wine
15 case cognac

Brown Brothers & Company
100 case shelled walnuts

Bernard, Judas & Company
70 bundles cheese

American Express Company
30 bundles cheese
2 case cognac

Moquin Wine Company
1 case liquor
38 case oil

Knauth, Nachod & Kuhne
107 case mushrooms
1 case pamphlets

Lazard Freres
25 case sardines
3 case preserves

Acker, Merrall & Condit
50 case wine

Dubois, Geo. F.
6 case vermouth
4 case wine

Heidelbach, Ickelheimer & Company
11 case shelled walnuts

Brown Brothers & Company
100 bales shelled Walnuts

First National Bank of Chicago
300 case shelled walnuts

Blechoff, H. & Company
35 bags rough wood

Baumert, F.X. & Company
50 bundles cheese

Rathenberger & Company
190 bundles cheese

Haupt & Burgi
50 bundles cheese

Sheldon & Company
40 bundles cheese

Percival, C.
50 bundles cheese

Stone, C.D. & Company
50 bundles cheese

Phoenix Cheese Company
30 bundles cheese

Petry, P.H. & Company
10 bundles cheese

Reynolds & Dronig
15 bundles cheese

Fouger, E.
41 case filter paper

Munro, J. & Company
22 case mushrooms
15 case peas
3 case beans
10 case mixed vegetables
10 case peas
25 case olives
12 bundles capers
10 bundles fish
20 bundles merchandise

Austin, Nichols
25 case olive oil
14 case mushrooms

<u>On Order</u>
14 case factice
13 case gum
14 cask gum
285 cask tea
8 bales skins
4 case opium
3 case window frames
8 bales skins
8 package skins
1 case skins
2 case horsehair
2 case silk
8 bales raw silk
4 package hair nets
200 package tea
246 case sardines
30 rolls jute bagging
1.963 bags potatoes
7 case raw feathers
10 case hatters fur
3 case tissues
1 case rabbit hair
31 package crude rubber
7 case vegetables
5 case fish
10 case syrups
2 case liquors
150 case shelled walnuts

15 bundles cheese
8 bales buchu
2 case grandfather clocks
2 case leather

<u>Holders of original bills of lading</u>
79 goats skins
16 case calabashes
5 bales buchu
4 case embroidery
3 barrels wine
12 case ostrich feathers
4 case feathers
3 bales skins
33 bags argols
3 bales sheep skins

Titanic Reading and Viewing

This appendix includes books, movies, shows, and Web sites on the *Titanic* and related subjects.

Books

Archibold, Rick and Dana McCauley. *Last Dinner on the Titanic: Menus and Recipes From the Legendary Liner*. New York: Hyperion, 1997.

Ballard, Robert and Rick Archibold. *The Discovery of the Titanic*. New York: Warner, 1987.

Biel, Stephen. *Down With the Old Canoe: A Cultural History of the Titanic Disaster*. New York: Norton, 1996.

Davie, Michael. *Titanic: The Death and Life of a Legend*. New York: Henry Holt, 1986.

Eaton, John and Charles Haas. *Titanic, Destination Disaster: The Legends and the Reality*. New York: Norton, 1987.

Gardner, Martin, ed. *The Wreck of the Titanic Foretold?* Buffalo: Prometheus, 1986.

Heyer, Paul. *Titanic Legacy: Disaster as Media Event and Myth*. Westport, Conn.: Praeger, 1995.

Hoffamn, William and Jack Grimm. *Beyond Reach: The Search for the Titanic*. New York: Beaufort, 1982.

Hyslop, Donald, Alastair Forsyth, and Sheila Jemima. *Titanic Voices: Memories from the Fateful Voyage*. Sutton: Gloucestershire, England, 1994.

Kuntz, Tom, ed. *The Titanic Disaster Hearings: the Official Transcripts of the 1912 Senate Investigation*. New York: Pocket Books, 1998.

Lord, Walter. *The Night Lives On*. New York: William Morrow, 1986.

———. *A Night to Remember*. Holt, Rinehart, and Winston, 1955.

Marcus, Geoffrey. *The Maiden Voyage.* Viking, 1969.

Tyler, Sidney F. *A Rainbow of Time and of Space: Orphans of the Titanic.* Tucson: Aztec, 1981.

Villiers, Captain Alan and others. *Men, Ships, and the Sea.* Washington DC: National Geographic Society, 1973.

Wade, Wyn Craig. *The Titanic: End of a Dream.* Rawson Wade, 1979.

Winocour, Jack, ed. *The Story of the Titanic as Told by Its Survivors.* New York: Dover, 1960.

Web Sites

The Discovery Channel Online
http://www.discovery.com/

Encyclopedia Smithsonian: The *Titanic*
http://www.si.edu/resource/faq/nmah/*Titanic*.htm

Jim's *Titanic* **Site**
http://www.intercall.net/~jsadur/*Titanic*

Molly Brown House Museum
http://www.mollybrown.com

The Official *Titanic* **Movie Site**
http://www.*Titanic*movie.com

Titanic **Information Site**
http://www.netins.net/showcase/js/*Titanic*

Virginia Newspaper Project
http://www.lib.virginia.edu/cataloging/vnp/*Titanic*

Movies and Shows

A Night to Remember (1958), directed by Roy Ward Baker, starring Kenneth More

Raise the Titanic! (1980), directed by Jerry Jameson, starring Jason Robards

S.O.S. Titanic (1979), directed by William Hale, starring David Janssen and Cloris Leachman

Titanic (Nearer My God to Thee) (1953), directed by Jean Negulesco, starring Clifton Webb and Barbara Stanwick

Titanic (Broadway musical) (1997), directed by Richard Jones

Titanic (1997), directed by James Cameron, starring Leonardo DiCaprio and Kate Winslet

Titanica (1992), directed by Stephen Low, an IMAX film

The Unsinkable Molly Brown (1964), directed by Charles Walters, starring Debbie Reynolds

Index

311

I

T

About the Author

Jay Stevenson has written and coauthored numerous books, including *The Complete Idiot's Guide to Dinosaurs* (1998) with Dr. George R. McGhee, *The Complete Idiot's Guide to Philosophy* (1998), *The Dictionary of Legal Terms* (1997) with Hayden Mead, *The Essentials of Grammar* (1996) with Hayden Mead, the *Entrepreneurs, Inventors, and Discoverers* (1996) volume of the *Grolier International Biographies* series with Stephanie Girard and Robert DeLaurentis, and the volume on *Visual Artists* (1996) in the same series with Robert Coleman. He has also lectured and published articles on the 17th-century British poet and philosopher, Margaret Cavendish, Duchess of Newcastle.

Dr. Stevenson received his Ph.D. in English literature from Rutgers University where he teaches writing, literature, and cultural studies. He holds an M.A. in English from Boston College and a B.A. from Grinnell College in English and anthropology.

Sharon Rutman is cofounder of Titanic International, Inc., a leading *Titanic* society. A *Titanic* buff since she first read Walter Lord's *A Night to Remember* when she was 10 years old, Ms. Rutman lives in Queens, New York.